Teleph
E

Executive Coaching

EXECUTIVE COACHING

Exploding the Myths

Tony Chapman

Bill Best

Paul Van Casteren

First published 2003 by
PALGRAVE MACMILLAN
Houndmills, Basingstoke, Hampshire RG21 6XS and
175 Fifth Avenue, New York, N.Y. 10010
Companies and representatives throughout the world

PALGRAVE MACMILLAN is the global academic imprint of the Palgrave Macmillan division of St. Martin's Press, LLC and of Palgrave Macmillan Ltd. Macmillan® is a registered trademark in the United States, United Kingdom and other countries. Palgrave is a registered trademark in the European Union and other countries.

ISBN-13: 978–1–4039–0261–0 handback
ISBN-10: 1–4039–0261–5 handback

This book is printed on paper suitable for recycling and made from fully managed and sustained forest sources. Logging, pulping and manufacturing processes are expected to conform to the environmental regulations of the country of origin.

A catalogue record for this book is available from the British Library.

Library of Congress Cataloging-in-Publication Data

Chapman, Tony, 1951–
Executive coaching : exploding the myths / Tony Chapman, Bill Best and Paul Van Casteren.
p. cm.
Includes bibliographical references and index.
ISBN 1–4039–0261–5
1. Executives—Training of. 2. Business consultants—Handbooks, manuals, etc. I. Best, Bill. II. Van Casteren, Paul. III. Title.

HD30.4.C484 2003
658.4'07124—dc21

2002193089

Editing and origination by Aardvark Editorial, Mendham, Suffolk

10 9 8 7 6 5 4 3
12 11 10 09 08

Printed and bound in China

To our clients, wives and partners. They provided the inspiration, opportunity and sustained support for us to capture our collective learning

CONTENTS

List of Figures and Tables

Figures

Tables

PREFACE

Historical Origins

One recurring question for us, as for many other authors, was 'why write?' For some practitioners the act of writing is a delight, a medium for open expression, a marketing opportunity, a creative reflection and a therapeutic review. For some of our academic colleagues it is an absolute role requirement, without which promotion is unattainable. Excluding the last, for us it has been a little of all of the above, but mainly a considerable challenge; at times a trial rising to Herculean heights. Such effort may imply inadequate levels of competence but certainly reflects the difficulty we have found in articulating and agreeing what we believe, how we deliver development coaching, and how best to convey this to others in a way that will be engaging and stimulating. So why did we start?

Understand first of all that we are a group of networked consultants. Many have alluded to managing independent consultants as akin to 'herding cats'. So it was with this book. There is undoubtedly a need for self-expression and personal recognition behind the desire to commit to paper for us all. We freely admit it. The prospect of creation and delivery gave us all a great thrill. During early planning discussions, the authors disclosed their respective ambitions. Probably like you, we felt that we had at least 'one book's worth of experience' (if not the ubiquitous novel) inside us.

Supported by client encouragement and with such testimonials as the one below, we remain convinced that what we have to say is of contemporary value to others in developing executive coaching capabilities. In addition, many may benefit from a deeper understanding of the coaching process from the perspective of a consumer. However, we are not so self-regarding as to believe this book will have wider appeal amongst the general public. We are executive development coaches, working with business executives, assisting their development.

David Van Valkenburg, Chairman of Balfour Associates Inc., recently described his view of the value of an executive coach as:

> my second most trusted advisor – the first being my wife – for the past 20 years. As President and CEO of three USA and one UK telecommunications companies, I have greatly relied upon my executive coaches (one in the USA and Tony Chapman in the UK). They have always provided an honest appraisal of my performance, challenging my personal practice and goals, revealing to me my inner self. They needed to be great listeners, available as a reflector for my self-doubts and fears, and to assist me to very clearly communicate my vision for the business. Each executive coach provided unique assistance to me through effective evaluation of me and my executive management teams. The ultimate value of an executive coach can be demonstrated through my growth as a more effective executive as shown by positive trends in each successive executive position. (personal communication)

Our initial enthusiasm was further fired by a critical reflection on client assignments conducted over recent years. Between us we have achieved what clients acknowledged as successful executive and leadership development assignments, supported by tangible results. It seemed appropriate that in conducting a stocktake we might document what we discovered. We collectively considered the implications of writing such a book. As important as its creation was its marketing and distribution – being published and reaching our readership.

We also discerned that this was a work that could not be completed without several component contributions. As we envisaged an international focus for coaching, we needed the input of our colleagues currently active in Europe, the Middle East and the Asia Pacific region. We recognised the reality of diversity in coaching style and the concept of 'equifinality' – reaching the same coaching end point by different routes.

Bill Best and Paul Van Casteren, my co-editors here in the UK, contributed significantly to the creation of Chapters 1, 3, 4, 7 and 8 and the construction of the 'Capable coach' competency model. Ken Hedberg, President of Personnel Decision Research Institue in the US and widely experienced in coaching in Europe, presents multinational coaching issues arising from his own experiences (Chapters 10 and 11). Iain McCormick and David Crookes, both trusted colleagues during my work in Hong Kong, address coaching challenges in Asia Pacific and the Middle East respectively (Chapters 12 and 13). In Chapter 5, Ben McCausland, a seasoned leader executive himself, reviews the historical origins of executive coaching from a UK perspective. I am largely responsible for the remaining elements and for presenting the unifying themes which run throughout the book.

As coaches, we have helped many others to develop their coaching capability. Although we don't subscribe to the view that, as with most crafts, you can just tell people how to coach, we know that sharing experience can often provide a shortcut to those embarking, or already embarked, upon a comparable journey. This book is one device for sharing experience, from which others will draw conclusions, hopefully some different from our own, and examine and then develop their own practice.

Next we thought long and hard about how we would present what we had to say. We quickly rejected the 'how to handbook' formula because we regarded it as an oversimplification of the coaching process. It also didn't match our view of how others might develop most effectively using the book. We all knew of models of development and methods of planning coaching assignments from start to finish and found these guides useful on occasion, although they always became limited as soon as the assignment was underway.

The practice of executive coaching is more complex than a causal 'boxes and arrows' model can portray and we did not want to trivialise what we regard as a *craft*. We therefore determined to work with the reader as we do with our coaching partners: take real-life experience, review it critically, celebrate and learn from success and then explore options for changing future practice.

Finally, we wish you bon voyage as you embark on your personal development journey and in your future coaching practice.

TONY CHAPMAN
ECC Ltd, Bedford

How to Use This Book

As mentioned above, we didn't want to write a prescriptive 'how to' guidebook, but in coaching there is a fine line to tread between being too directive, letting others find their way, and being too passive. We want to provide a valuable resource to the reader who is interested in developing their coaching capability or understanding the process as an executive consumer or both. We have decided to share our views and experience as well as encourage the reader to question what we believe, what we have done, and to ask questions of the reader.

The first chapter presents our philosophy and beliefs with regard to coaching and sets the scene for the case studies presented later and the underlying approach we have adopted.

We subsequently present an overview of assessment practice as the key early stage in coaching. Although factually correct, this review reflects our beliefs and preferences and, again, is not intended as a prescriptive text.

In presenting executive 'coaching in action' case studies, we outline previous assignments, although personal and client sensitivities have made name changes necessary. We have followed simple guidelines in describing the case studies; presenting both success and failure to give an insight into how the coach (and the coached where appropriate) felt at different stages in the assignment. We saw this as a more personal account to engage the reader but also offer more opportunities for you, the reader, to reflect on your practice and beliefs.

There are also workbook-style questions accompanying some key chapters, designed to stimulate your thinking and development action planning. In conclusion, we have distilled the lessons we have learned from our coaching assignments into our 'Review of Best Practice'. A touchstone rather than a checklist, we believe it to be a useful stimulus in formulating or evaluating your own best coaching practice. As part of this process, you are invited to consider your next coaching development actions. Now is a perfect opportunity to move from analysis to action.

ACKNOWLEDGEMENTS

We all recognise the key role of those clients who consistently demonstrate a value for the development of staff at all levels in their organisation.

Particular thanks are due to the best executive team, from a population of around 200, with whom we have worked. It was the Rolls-Royce Executive Team (ex R.R.A.), led by John Glanville; other members were Duncan Goreham, Paul Whetton, Chris Mead, Pete Dolan, Steve Garwood, Steve Ludlum, John Caulfield and David Noble.

Every effort has been made to trace all the copyright holders but if any have been inadvertently overlooked the publishers will be pleased to make the necessary arrangements at the first opportunity.

CHAPTER 1

Introduction

Achieving the goal, getting from A to B, crossing the chasm, getting to where we want or need to be, making the most of what you can be, achieving your potential – applicable to us all, but particularly pertinent to the philosophies of those with senior leadership responsibility. These people, who are nominated executives, are typically those who command significant resources, the most important of which is, of course, the human resource, that is, you and me.

At this point, some of our readership is considering the relative value of people compared to other assets, such as natural resources, capital, technology, market and product resources. That can be seen as a tragic comment on our commercial philosophy. It shows how far our analysis of economic and business models have objectified the human race, reducing them to intervening (and sometimes interfering) variables. It's a debatable point, but if people are removed from organisations they tend not to operate effectively – even an automated warehouse needs an engineering team to maintain and rectify faults. Executives often have the nominal responsibility for setting and executing strategy. As Larry Bossidy, ex-CEO of Allied Signal, states succinctly, 'people bet on people not strategies' (Tichy and Charan 1995).

It's clear we need the right people doing the right things in organisations. Here we will concentrate on the executive population. As we have seen too often in recent times, when organisations employ the wrong people, do the wrong things or both, it can create massive and negative impact on markets, consumers and employees. Recently there has been an unprecedented catalogue of corporate scandals which has massively impacted business confidence. Between January and August 2002, share prices fell 40 per cent on both sides of the Atlantic, stimulated by the fraud and bankruptcy at energy trader Enron. Subsequently Global Crossing,

Xerox, Tyco, Worldcom, Adelphia, AOL Time Warner, QWest, Halliburton, Johnson & Johnson and Bristol Myers Squibb all reported trading difficulties, either sponsored by inaccurate reporting, fraud charges or investigations by the SEC.

It's useful to debate with those who lead organisations how they value their people. Many say employees are the corporation's key asset, the most valuable resource, often providing the competitive advantage for their business. Unfortunately, few seem to act in a manner consistent with those statements. This mismatch or disconnection, often combined with adverse media comment on the equity of executive reward packages, can lead to a cynical and negative response from the workforce.

This book is about one method for developing people, specifically executives, hence executive coaching. It is also about building coaching competency for executives, so, we hope, doubly useful.

A Unifying Philosophy

Sentiments which best capture the tone of our collective coaching practice come from Kahlil Gibran ([1926] 1987, p. 67). He reflects, in his timeless manner, our feeling about the role of the executive development coach when he speaks to his description of teaching:

> No man can reveal aught but that which already lies half asleep in the dawning of your knowledge,
>
> The Teacher who walks in the shadow of the temple, among his followers, gives not of his wisdom but rather of his faith and his lovingness,
>
> If he is indeed wise he does not bid you enter the house of his wisdom, But rather leads you to the threshold of your own mind.

Whilst we share a diverse breadth of experience of success and failure in international executive coaching, there is a unifying philosophy which brings our practice together. The values underpinning this philosophy are familiar: passion for people growth, development responsibility for potential, nurturing and exploiting scarce leadership talent. Whilst in practice this philosophy is often broadly expressed in stylistic terms, at the core of our coaching philosophy remains an enduring theme: 'The desire to create a significant and qualitative difference at work by helping to deliver human potential.'

Most contributing coaches describe their 'personal journey' leading them to executive development coaching. Our belief is that in the process of change the coach is rarely untouched by the experience of development they provide. Indeed, for many, such personal development opportunities are a powerful driver to sustain commitment to their professional coaching practice. As we will see later, those who authorise and execute programmes of change are well placed to enjoy considerable development as a result.

My Journey to Coaching

For my part, the journey to coaching craftsman continues. Early international manufacturing management experience with Unilever in the UK and Germany informed and stimulated my preference for working directly with people contributing product value rather than with inanimate objects. Only after considerable experience, coaching study, training and development did I feel equipped to take responsibility for contributing directly, as a coach, to others' development. Only with deeper organisational insight, self-knowledge and awareness about the personal implications of significant work and life transition did I feel authorised to coach others through such experiences.

Twenty years later, I find I have still more to learn than I have already learned. Having tutored and coached on several continents with over 2000 managers and leaders, it feels timely to reflect critically on our experience to date and capture what we feel are valuable, coachable themes. These themes we see as central to the successful development of executives in organisations and thereby to the successful development of business organisations.

But the route to coaching described above sounds rather too neatly prescribed. My development as a coach was more of a roller coaster of opportunism rather than a planned progress towards a desired career goal – often incoherent and only with the benefit of hindsight having any clear linkage. I know it's no different for many others, maybe for you too. Careers aren't neat sequential packages of growth and success. That's another myth – to which we make executive reference later – careers happen in hindsight and often make sense only through the discipline of writing a CV. As a result of our selection, assessment and coaching practice, we have reviewed thousands between us. My colleague Bill Best describes them as: 'often colourful works of fiction, seeking to weave a coherent storyline through an apparently random sequence of events.' As is widely reported, single lifelong careers occur less often in contemporary business.

As a coach, colleagues and clients describe my strength as commercial focus and directness. I can only concur. I experience strengths in stamina and perseverance. I know my way around executive boardrooms and appreciate the pressure of leadership in organisations. I ask challenging questions but still remain overly optimistic for clients, and too easily frustrated to have achieved mastery of the coaching craft yet, but I'm working on it.

Much of my development as a coach is the result of experience with clients, my fellow authors and of course my wife, Julia, so my heartfelt thanks go to them all for their help.

The following chapters distil a collection of coaching experiences from successful practitioners. One of the key indicators of success in coaching as in other walks of commercial life is repeat corporate client business. All the contributors to this book have at least ten years' continuous success in executive coaching consultancy.

The case studies are presented to illustrate the executive coaching assignments conducted by the authors. They are future focused, seeking to build on the experience of the past to promote a solid foundation for development coaching assignments to come and thereby help improve their chances of successful outcomes.

Whilst coaches sometimes need to refer to past patterns of behaviour and historical experience, the core of development coaching is concerned with achieving goals by doing things differently or doing different things in the future. Figure 1.1 contrasts development coaching with counselling.

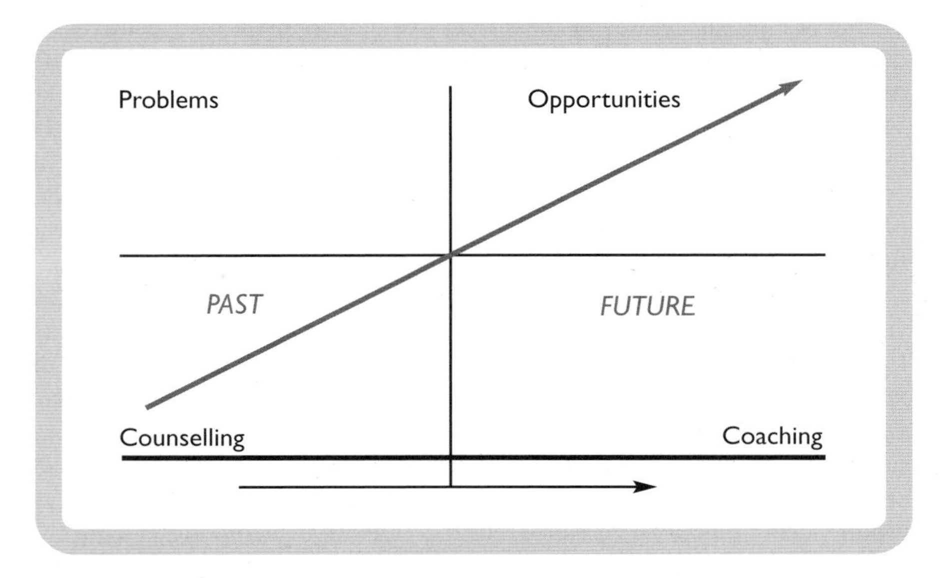

Figure 1.1 A development coaching focus

Executive Coaching Assignments: Some 'In the Box' Thinking

Executive and leadership coaching has grown and continues to grow significantly as a popular development tool. A brief foray into any search engine creates hundreds of coaching providers presenting their unique selling proposition. It's an extremely fragmented market, unregulated and characterised by small-scale providers as described in the contemporary review of executive coaching by West and Milan (2001). Indeed Berglas (2002) projects that from a base of 10,000 executive coaches in the US today, he expects there to be 50,000 in five years' time.

Large development organisations (including the 'big five' consultancies and university business schools) tend not to provide significant development coaching resource. Indeed, in bidding for a large-scale coaching assignment recently, we found ourselves able to offer more experienced senior coaching resource than several business colleges ranked in the top ten of European business schools. As suggested in a recent review of executive succession in the UK's *Financial Times* (Moerk 2002):

> Business schools provide more general development for executives. But the frequency of this approach is in direct contrast to its effectiveness. We found that HR directors rated standard business school programmes as less effective than individually tailored ones, particularly coaching. One-to-one coaching focuses on leadership skills, such as emotional intelligence and strategic orientation. The growth of coaching for senior executives shows many organisations are on the right track with individual development.

Coaching is clearly a very popular contemporary development practice. Hallstein Moerk, senior VP of Human Resources at Nokia, recently described the role of coaching in his portfolio of education and development offerings: 'We think coaching is a most powerful tool.' Highlighting one key benefit derived from coaching, he continues: 'People do better in their jobs when they have opportunities for self-reflection which coaching provides' (Moerk, quoted in *Financial Times* 2002).

An Executive Coaching Taxonomy

Table 1.1 shows the origin of coaching and the attitude of client organisations requesting coaching. These reflect the approach of a consultant coach entering a client organisation intending to coach specific executive

Table 1.1 Organisations as coaching clients

	Assistance receiving (reactive)	Assistance seeking (proactive)
Bridging the gap (demands of the past)	Change-resistant Denial/bad hire Job jeopardy In crisis	Change-oriented Overtaken by events Overpromoted Self-awareness
Extending competence (demands in the future)	Change compliant New environment New demands Wait and see/fast-follower	Change-focused Looking ahead Predicting change Staying ahead of the game

incumbents. We can classify the commissioning client organisations and/or individuals according to the development needs that are identified and one's perception of their approach to coaching.

'Bridging the gap' refers to those instances where there is an agreed level of performance that the individual is failing to meet, or at least some shortfall from a minimum acceptable performance is identified (not always by the individual). This is based on what individuals in the role have needed to do in the past and need to do now.

'Extending competence' covers those instances where current performance is acceptable, or even very good, but the need for something extra, some additional competence, is expected or predicted to grow in importance. If the need for 'extra' or new competence is 'real', and we'll explore this later, it is of course only a matter of time before not having this competency becomes a shortfall and hence shifts into 'bridging the gap'.

Given that this separation is arbitrary, the reactive/proactive split is even more so. In general terms, we see a difference between those who seek out help and those who take it up as a last resort. 'Assistance receivers' respond to circumstances and some stimulus in the environment. It might be that they've tried other routes, unsuccessfully, find they don't have sufficient expertise, or even time, or maybe are simply following what others have done without giving too much thought as to whether there might be other ways of tackling the same issue. It is literally putting yourself in others' hands – like going into receivership when you're bankrupt but, in this case, with reference to ideas or options.

The 'assistance seekers' are more proactive in looking for help that can accelerate change, in this case through enhanced learning and development. We could distinguish them from 'receivers' in that they approach obtaining assistance with a much lower level of reluctance. This is not to say they are better at doing it, as judgment may not always match motivation, that is, they may get the wrong help.

From experience, we know that organisations, divisions, departments, teams and individuals don't fit neatly into one box in all activities. For example, many technical departments, such as IT (to target an easy stereotype), are often heavily focused on extending specialist technical competence and pursue this proactively, whereas they may not address, say, the skills necessary for the effective management of people, in the same fashion.

In each of the quadrants in Table 1.1, I have used some terms to describe the likely occupants. At present, we experience a significant number of assignments in the top left-hand quadrant, although this is slowly changing. These are the emergency calls. 'We've tried everything else but if John doesn't change that's the end of the line!' These individuals may have been promoted into positions for which they do not currently possess the skill to perform effectively. Occasionally, this was known or suspected, but they have been promoted based on their potential and they were expected to develop the skills quickly. Alternatively, the job characteristics or environment may have changed significantly around a previously competent individual. In any event, the realisation is that the individual is not coping and things cannot continue as they are; similar to those individuals used as examples of ineffective leaders in Goleman's *Emotional Intelligence* (1996). Important here is the reactivity of either the individual or the commissioning client, 'problems' are generally at an advanced stage and the coach is playing the role of 'remedial paramedic'.

There are different approaches to contracting coaching from client organisations dependent upon corporate as well as national culture. In the US, clients have a more progressive approach to coaching their leadership talent. It reflects a development philosophy that is more 'you don't have to be ill to get better' than 'call in the remedial help'.

The top right-hand quadrant is again occupied by those who may have been overpromoted or left behind by changes in the demands of their environment. By contrast, they may have been identified earlier or at least the coach probably gets to them sooner. Here there is a more concerted effort to avoid derailment, and the coach hopes they have been brought in sufficiently early. This said, because of the nature of the change required to bridge a gap, a certain amount of time pressure exists.

The development needs of those in the lower half of the table differ from those above, in that here they are looking at 'extending competence' for the individual. That is, the individual's current level of performance is acceptable, in that they are probably meeting all the demands of their role, as it has been defined in the recent past. Now, either because of promotion, significant changes in the organisation or the market, new competencies are demanded. In this respect, a shortfall is being anticipated or predicted but has not yet had significant impact. If the need for the competency is real, this will become a genuine and recognisable shortfall in the near future.

Those in the bottom left-hand box are faced with a perceived need to change, although what this means and how difficult it will be to achieve may not be clear. However, being 'assistance receiving', they might be seen as changing only as the need to do so becomes more obvious, in fact as the likelihood of a shortfall becomes more concrete. More importantly, in this instance, they may pursue other methods of achieving the change in individuals, for example issuing lists of new competency requirements, promoting the need for change or running general training or orientation programmes, before bringing in a coach.

In the bottom right-hand box, there are those that might be perceived as ideal clients, both 'extending competence' and 'seeking assistance' in a proactive fashion. This combination can reduce the time pressure associated with achieving the desired change, at least in comparison with the other categories, however, those pursuing change proactively are rarely less demanding. In this group, I would include those clients who install or assign a coach in advance of individuals taking up new and more demanding posts.

So having looked at what the clients might be, let's take a look at what that might mean for the coach beginning and managing an assignment with them. Table 1.2 has the same categories as Table 1.1, but here the descriptors refer to the issues that coaches may need to be aware of in dealing with the different types.

In the top left-hand box, there is possibly the most frequent UK coaching assignment, 'job jeopardy'. It is probably most frequent because it is often the easiest to sell; 'distress purchasing' is a very successful area of retailing. Generally, by the time the coach gets involved, decisions

Table 1.2 Coaching: vendor beware!

	Assistance receiving (reactive)	**Assistance seeking (proactive)**
Bridging the gap	'Easy to sell' Strong imperative 'Last roll of the dice' May be too late	Ready for the sell Timescales tight Promises count Benchmark to aim at
Extending competency	Question the sell Not convinced yet Must convince on benefits Manage timescales	Looking to buy Quality supplier critical Needs possibly unclear Could aim too high

have already been taken about what to do and the main discussion between the client and the coach is 'how soon can you start?' Whilst this is good news for development coaches selling work, and for internal coaches trying to raise the profile of coaching as a development option, the downside is obvious. Coaching is rarely, if ever, an instant fix. Where it is, there is either a simple skill to be learnt and applied or the coach is unusually gifted – I have only experienced the former. In this box, the time and emotional pressure is likely to be high and the expectations of coaches occasionally borders on miracle working. In any dealings with clients, setting and managing expectations is always critical but, in addition, coaches need to manage their own expectations – can they actually help the individual achieve the change desired? It may be prudent to decline the assignment, but at the very least one should be absolutely clear about what might realistically be achieved in the time available.

In the top right-hand box, clients may have 'discovered' or realised the need for an individual to develop but differ from the previous example in that they are more prepared to obtain assistance for them to achieve this. With more faith in the contribution a coach can make, expectations might actually be higher. Consultant coaches will get the business if they can demonstrate, or convince others that they have, a way of facilitating the desired change. In doing this coaches obviously need to be realistic about what *can* be achieved and by when. As always, targeting where some 'quick wins' might be obtained is vital and this should be based on what is impacting most negatively on performance at the moment.

In the bottom left-hand box, the client is concerned with developing competence in an individual in a more proactive way but the decision to involve a coach is probably based on less proactive thinking. They may be following what others are doing (including using coaches), identifying a lack of in-house expertise or just finding themselves short of resources to facilitate an individual's development. The issues confronting an external consultant coach here are familiar – does it really take that long and must it cost that much? There is a need to demonstrate that one has a clear method of achieving the desired change, but first the change or development needs clarifying. This means defining what will be observed that is different from today's performance and how it will be measured – some criteria for success. Anyone with experience of developing competency frameworks for executives within organisations will appreciate the occasional tendency to generate an ideal shopping list that is too often based on 'sound bites', for example 'entrepreneurial thinking'.

In the bottom right-hand box, those that are looking to pre-empt the need for change are also pursuing ways of staying ahead of the game in bringing it about. There are some 'mature' coaching organisations that either coach internally, or appoint external coaches where appropriate, as a matter of course, and regard them as a vital component in maximising personal development.

In summary, executive coaching resembles other areas of change and the matrix presented above can be adapted and applied equally to large-scale organisational change. Clients approach change with different perspectives – meeting needs that are apparent, predicted or even created. They may have a clear notion of what is required, or not, and a realistic or overly ambitious view of how easy this might be to achieve.

Distilling research from numerous corporate examples, Kotter's (1995) 'eight steps to transforming your organisation' checklist for change demonstrates the parallels between what is required for successful organisational and personal change:

1. Establishing a sense of urgency
2. Forming a powerful guiding coalition
3. Creating a vision
4. Communicating the vision
5. Empowering others to act on the vision
6. Planning for and creating short-term wins
7. Consolidating improvements and producing still more change
8. Institutionalising new approaches.

Indeed, the checklist served as a powerful prompt in a recent executive coaching assignment. Tim, the president of an international investment business, used the eight steps as a review formula whilst acting out his personal coaching development agenda. In his case, Tim's leadership development agenda as incoming president and CEO was intrinsically linked to the development of the business. Restructuring, building and leading an emerging executive team required Tim to learn 'on the run' as he built and led a reformed organisation acting in quite uncharacteristic ways.

As Witherspoon and White observe (2001, p. 28):

> Coaching for development can be intense, analytical, and may represent more threat to some learners than coaching for skills or performance. Of all the coaching roles, coaching for development tends to involve a deeper focus on

> executive development and personal growth. As one coach has said, this [type of coaching] is easy for people who are introspective and enjoy root canals!

They identify four distinctly different roles based on a primary function of helping and teaching the client how to learn:

1. Coaching for skill acquisition (learning focused on current task)
2. Coaching for performance
3. Coaching for the 'executive's agenda'
4. Coaching for executive development (focused on the future, exploiting potential talent or moving into a new situation).

Here we will focus on item 4, but occasionally stray into the territory of 1, 2 and 3.

So why don't all organisations provide an internal development coaching resource and practice themselves? We have discovered many reasons. Most commonly, it is part of a general avoidance of assuming responsibility for people development, including executive development. Some of the most frequently mentioned reasons we heard were:

- We use experts. Business schools/external agency programmes satisfy all our management and executive development needs
- Development of our people is all outsourced as it is too expensive to employ full-time resources
- Development of our people is not a high priority for our managers or executives.
- Development of our people is not a priority
- Development of our people is not part of our key strategic business goals
- We 'buy in' talent when required, we don't 'grow our own' talent
- Investment in people development has been found not to be worthwhile historically
- Our managers/executives are not skilled in this area.

Many would concur that at the heart of development and learning in organisations is feedback. Physical systems work more effectively with feedback (for example electromechanical or electronic devices such as an engine management system is dependent on regular, timely, reliable feedback). Even learning to play a sport like golf relies upon feedback, albeit acceptable to varying degrees. So why not people development? We found the most commonly expressed reasons for not giving feedback are:

- Feedback is too difficult, we have not been trained to give it
- It exposes judgments and risks stable relationships
- It provides an unclear benefit for tangible discomfort
- Tasks with tangible benefit are more attractive/preferable
- Don't know what development feedback is or how to do it.

Most organisations operate sub-optimally, and one responsible element may be the absence of, or presence of poor, feedback. Our aim is to help to develop individuals inside their working environment. Many have experienced the impact of external agencies providing public development programmes, such as business schools who claim to offer a complete leadership development process. Unfortunately, such development progress is rarely sustainable, as the participants' environment – including immediate work group – is rarely party to the development experience. Whilst typically a useful individual networking experience, development benefit can be significantly enhanced and extended by 'in-house' development coaching back at work.

Myth: All Feedback is Developmental

One example illustrative of the power of development feedback emerged during a leadership team development programme at a Rolls-Royce subsidiary company in Derby, England. The division's MD was discussing feedback with his newly appointed Marketing Director, Richard. I was the coach in this development conversation, encouraging both to give feedback and we were in the early exchanges about current practice inside the business when the following dialogue took place.

Me: 'Do you give Richard regular feedback at work?'

MD: 'Yes, I think I do. I've given Richard quite a lot over the past 12 months since he's joined the company. We have a good relationship in that respect, I think.'

Richard to MD: 'You do give me regular feedback; but it's always of one type – positive. I don't believe there aren't areas for me to improve. It takes the edge off the positive comments and the praise too.'

Me to MD: 'Why do you think Richard sees the feedback as all positive?'

MD: 'I'll ask him in a minute, but from my side, my sense is that I try to be positive and encouraging all the time with my people. I don't want to demotivate or hurt them.'

Richard to MD: 'When you deny me the feedback for improvement (development feedback), you deny me the opportunity to improve and that hurts me.'

The MD at this point looked very thoughtful. Later, he described his personal philosophy and values to his team, which helped Richard and his peers understand why they only ever received positive feedback. All his team members requested more critical feedback and shortly afterwards the MD felt able to begin to factor in developmental feedback to his executive reviews.

Whilst executives commonly cite 'not enough time' as a good reason not to coach or develop people, it can be illuminating to explore how executives do spend their time. Time management consultancy is now a mature industry and training opportunities are legion. It is rare to find executives who will admit to having any 'free' time on their hands. It is seen as worthy to be overloaded, under constant time pressure, continuously busy, with no time for non-work activity such as vacations or family. A laudable expression of the Protestant work ethic perhaps, but it raises the questions:

- Is it inefficient/ineffective to be this busy?
- Is our executive confusing being busy with doing business?

If you have enjoyed the luxury, as we have, of 'shadowing' business leaders in a typical day's work, you will have found that, like us at work, they choose elements in their daily work routine, with sometimes up to around 30 per cent of the daily schedule being self-selected. Again, like us, they choose to devote significant periods to:

- Aspects of work they enjoy
- Aspects of work they are good at
- Aspects of work which add value, are recognised and rewarded.

Referencing Hercules' Law (Chapman 1982), 'A strength overused becomes a weakness', it can be equally applicable to enthusiasm, intelligent analysis, thoughtful introspection/reflection, strategic focus, detailed, objective decision-making and using intuition/gut-feeling in decision-making, so that overemphasising those areas of work which we prefer and where we excel risks ignoring other potentially key parts of work that are necessary.

We all agree that time, like people, is a very precious resource for organisations. It represents the opportunity to add value, exploit assets and create profit. It is, therefore, disappointing to discover how much time we spend waiting. Most of us spend a lot of time waiting. You do, we do, even highly paid senior executives do, although they can become very upset when it happens. It's part of our lives. It's the period between having decided what we want/need to do and doing it. Academics describe it sometimes as queuing or the phase between analysis and implementation, a natural place to 'dwell' when we've decided what needs to be done but have yet to do it. Have you ever stopped to work out how much time you're in this state? Don't do it now, it may constitute waiting. Unless you've attended one of the ubiquitous time management programmes, you probably haven't. Think about only the time you can control, not traffic jams or delayed flights.

Think about those times when you've decided to implement change – give up smoking, go on a diet, give more feedback, coach someone with potential, take a committing, uncharacteristic, perhaps risky or unusual step. You may be visualising what it may look like when achieved or reflecting on the plan leading to implementation. Saul Bellow (1976) describes it as being often pejoratively labelled as 'sloth, inaction, sleeping at the wheel'. In reality, it can comprise our most creative moments. They also include the moments before waking or sleeping, where many issues of the day are reflected upon and sometimes resolved. We can also label it as denial, hesitancy, avoidance, procrastination, building up courage or momentum, but it appears in the same form, *inaction*. Our belief is that coaching is about helping others move more quickly to action than other development activities.

Coaching is one useful tool in developing leaders now and for the future. It is a core competence for many successful executives – developing others has become a sustainable competitive advantage – particularly in those service organisations that have little or no other comparable asset. This book is all about executive coaching – coaching for those with senior leadership responsibility in organisations. It presents a philosophy, model and practice of coaching which has been effective for clients and professional coaching practitioners who have contributed to this book.

As already indicated, the term 'coaching' covers a wide range of applications. A helpful concept here is the 'coaching continuum' (see Figure 1.2). Different coaching styles are set out on a scale whose variation indicates the depth of relationship between coach and subject. This reaches its greatest intensity on the far left – the interpersonal or therapeutic counselling context, assumed to be outside the typical organisational setting. However, today, with the transformation of family life as a traditional and stable source of counsel, the challenge to the manager of people to adopt such a role is common and widespread. For completeness, mentoring has been placed on the far right of the figure. Although having much in common with the coach, often demanding a similar closeness of relationship, the mentor may often seek different objectives and be in less frequent contact with the participant.

This book has been written with both the consumer and the provider of the coaching service in mind. So if you're either coaching or being coached, at the executive level, then this book should enhance your understanding or inform your practice, or both. If you believe, as many of our corporate clients do, that a key element in the skills repertoire of successful executives is the development of self and their people (McCall 1998), be they direct reports or immediate team members, then building coaching skills is key to developing this strength.

McCall, as a result of extensive research conducted by the International Consortium of Executive Development, outlines the 11 dimensions

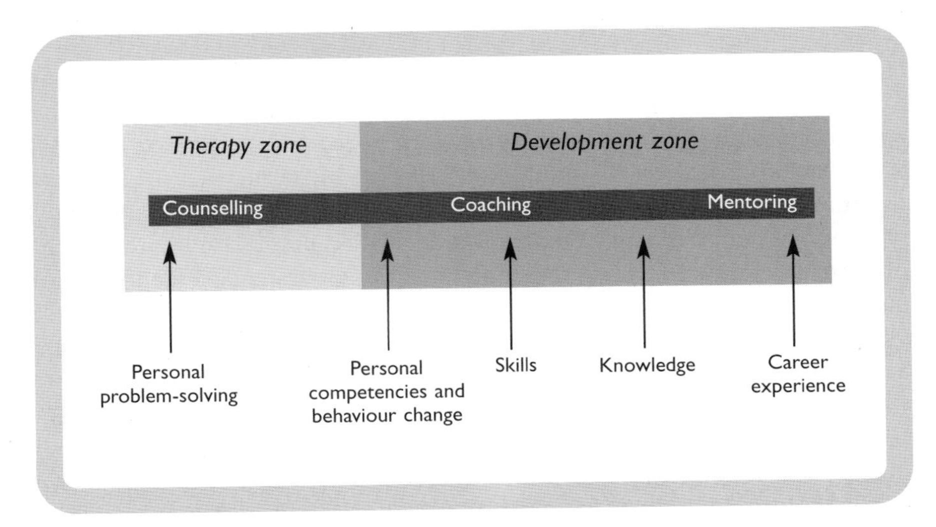

Figure 1.2 The coaching continuum

proposed as criteria for early identification of global executives. Four of the 11 refer to aspects of people development:

- Brings out the best in people
- Seeks and uses feedback
- Is open to criticism
- Learns from mistakes.

For many reasons in our postmodernist business society, we occupy a point of development maturity in the process which creates and sustains corporate life where coaching (or targeted development) is popular and appears to be able to deliver enhanced development outcomes.

Let's also outline what this book is not about. It's not about an in-depth exploration of:

- Life coaching
- Fitness and sports (individual and team) coaching
- Career coaching
- Therapeutic counselling
- Life-balance readjustment
- Family therapy/relationship development.

However, our coaching conversations often touch on all the above. For example, it is common for coaching conversations that examine the nature and quality of relationships at work to include discussion of characteristic approaches to managing relationships outside work. It is familiar for male executives, having embarked upon a coaching programme and receiving considerable feedback, to recount the responses of their partners on sharing the content of the work-related feedback. To quote one recent comment, a partner remarked: 'I have been trying to tell you that for the past 15 years with no success … why should you need a highly paid coach?'

This book is not about speculative theory, about what *might* happen. It's about what has happened and how it was achieved. Not that we eschew relevant theory or useful models, we present several that have been tried and tested in practice. Unlike some of our more academic counterparts, we present only those models that have worked in the past for real clients. R.D. Laing, in *The Politics of Experience* (1990), echoes our feelings precisely when he says 'Theory is the articulated vision of experience', likewise, for us, 'this book begins and ends with the person'. Another point of departure from our more theoretically biased colleagues is that these models are derived from experience. Having worked and debated at length with our academic peers, we can support the hypothesis that most useful models in this area are derived from leading-edge practitioners in business.

Myth: Coaching is the Contemporary Development Panacea

It is apparent from popular and academic literature that coaching has enjoyed growing corporate success and commensurate popularity over recent years. For a commentary on the executive coaching market and its growth, both West and Milan (2001) and Fitzgerald and Berger (2002) accurately capture the current market status and characteristics. Whilst it is a fashionable development activity for companies and executives, coaching is popular for many reasons, in our view some of them more worthy than others. A cursory review of hundreds of assignments suggests coaching is popular with clients because:

- It is viewed as an executive status symbol
- Targeted coaching delivers better returns on training and development (T&D) investment than the 'director's sheep dip' programme approach popular at university business schools and external public programmes
- It provides further justification for the existence of the HR department
- It is a reward or perk for the successful completion of a leadership role
- It forms part of a retention strategy, where high turnover threatens sustained business success
- It provides one element in a corporate recruitment package, potentially enhancing corporate competitive advantage where talent is a scarce resource
- 'Big hitters'/'gurus' say it is important (Jack Welch, Larry Bossidy, Jim Collins)
- It is an effective device for developing the emerging and existing leadership potential of an organisation

- It represents a potent resource for resolving performance and career development issues.

You can probably tell that we left the best two until last. Our collective belief is that effective coaching can accelerate the process of reaching the point of action described above. Whilst contemporary development models are presented and reviewed in the following pages, our approach is predominantly pragmatic. We are, in common with our clients, primarily concerned with action, getting things done, achieving plans and goals. Our book is a companion for anyone considering executive coaching from a practitioner or consumer perspective. Both will gain benefit in terms of practical insight and understanding best practice.

Myth: Executive Coaching Delivers Easily Predictable Outcomes

Maybe we've all being doing it wrong all these years? In our experience, coaching rarely follows a simple sequential process with easily predictable outcomes. It may lend itself to both a scientific approach (applying a logical, structured coaching methodology employing well-researched, reliable and valid analytical tools) as well as aspects of an artistic framework which captures a more flexible, intuitive style.

The transition development model described below is our preferred starting point for a discussion about development and change with executives. In terms of the application of an existing model or theory to a coaching assignment, the challenge for the coach is to remember to use the experience of the person to be coached to build *their* world model. As the late R.D. Laing, a radical therapist, describes eloquently (1990): 'I can never truly *give* you my experience of the world but I can begin to understand yours.'

We believe executive coaching can be usefully defined as a *craft*. The quality of workmanship created is determined by the nature of the raw material, the coach's tools and his acquired skills and talent, built through experience 'on the job'. The choice of which tool best suits which assignment is a measure of the skill of the coaching practitioner, as in any craft. So here these approaches are presented as a buffet, a kind of menu, a pick-and-mix, designed to provide some of the key ingredients for effective coaching practice. It is not intended to propose a prescription, encouraging the standardised application to every assignment. It would be rather convenient if learning and development was a 'straight-line process' logically building in sequence from A to B. It would be profoundly helpful if it followed a simple causal flow, control these variables in this manner and out pops the desired development outcome. It would confirm the validity of all those simplistic consultancy models with boxes and arrows used to impress leaders in organisations anticipating or experiencing dramatic corporate change.

Numerous stories about large-scale change programmes abound, often ending with a less than completely successful outcome. Kotter (1995) describes organisational change as probably the most challenging contemporary aspect of the executive role. Implementing change is tough and fraught with uncertainty. 'Expect the unexpected' seems to be part of the necessary built-in flexibility of any change initiative. Our experience focuses more on the personal impact of change on the executive responsible for delivery. To illustrate, we turn to the case of an executive employed by a global car manufacturer, recently promoted.

Case Study

Changing the Leader's Style

Responsible for the project leadership and delivery of a new medium-sized global car, Phil, a VP and senior leader of this US auto manufacturer in Europe, invited me to attend his project review meeting. Most of the programme was a departure from traditional practice for the project team, learning new skills as they moved through the development stages of the project. I too was in the early phase of building my executive coaching experience.

A project remit involving 'concept to customer' planning, including engineers from many different cultures all contributing to the project delivery, reflected the scope of the programme. The project was in trouble. Missing both interim budget and schedule goals, Phil's approach was to increase his control and become even more of a micro-manager of the project.

A four-hour project review ensued. It explored the most minute detail of the development process, finally alighting on one area of brake technology and the associated challenges.

Case Study cont'd

Phil took the engineering team responsible for the hold-up to task. In public, under the gaze of around 50 participating international project team members, Phil dissected the problem and challenged the responsible team to resolve the technical and organisational issues acting as a bottleneck for the entire project.

Phil was, and is, a very fast analyst, invariably arriving at a logical proposal for resolving problems before anybody else. He was known for his 'big brain' and capacity to see to the heart of an issue – first. But, as Goleman suggests (1996), substantial intellectual capability just gets you to the executive starting post.

We both came out of the meeting tired, but for different reasons. Me from listening and familiarising myself with a new business vocabulary, shorthand, mnemonics as well as process issues (power, alliances, conflicts and so on). Phil from doing most of the talking, chairing the meeting and attempting to personally resolve most of the technical and organisational problems facing the project. In short, Phil was a very hands-on leader.

He asked me straight off, 'How do you think the meeting went?' I liked his direct question. It suited my style, was why I liked it. I referred to the textbook on giving feedback for coaches. Characterised by objectivity and distance, it was an approach I rarely employed.

Myth: Giving Feedback in Practice is Reflected by Textbook Checklists

As we subsequently discussed in our lengthy debrief – almost as long as the meeting itself – I gave him my feedback based on what I felt was effective. Phil wanted to know about how effective I thought he had been in leading the process. I was comfortable to share my perspective but explained that this was based on both my observation and my interpretation of what I felt 'effective' may be.

This is commonly a point of departure from the textbooks on coaching feedback. I find that experienced executives often express a need to explore the values and experience of the coach. They want feedback,

***Case Study* cont'd**

'warts and all', unexpurgated. Even impressionistic feedback is legitimate to many executives we have coached. They want to know how they appear on first meeting.

In Phil's case, my first impressions supported his view of his emerging development agenda. He appeared in my office one evening enquiring about executive coaching. 'Hi, I'm Phil. Tell me about coaching as I'm in a new leadership role, running a new project in a new way.' He is about 2 metres tall, with a direct economical manner of expression and a booming voice. He towered over me as he stood at my desk. After a few minutes, he invited my early impressionistic feedback: 'What do you think so far?' 'Well, you have an aggressively ambitious business agenda and you present yourself in a similar manner', I suggested. 'OK. Thanks for your candour. That's what I've been told before and I need to do something about it.'

Textbook checklists concerning feedback refer to objectivity in feedback, avoiding potentially polluting the feedback with an overlay of coach values and prejudices. In Phil's case, as in others, he expected a judgment concerning his effectiveness. We later unpacked the additional learning from this exchange and explored Phil's characteristic style of giving feedback. Clearly, the arbiters of Phil's effectiveness were the project team themselves and their subsequent performance.

Coaching: Art or Science?

It is both an art and a science, because it's a craft. Coaching embraces both the unpredictability and predictability of human behaviour. Science teaches us theories and rules to learn and reduce uncertainty, to build predictability; take the experimental method, for example, it's about ensuring the same procedure or method creates the identical outcome. Most of us want to understand causality. Large numbers of people watch news broadcasts seeking to understand the root cause of an event. We like to know what we need to do to achieve the desired outcome, science can help us with either the answer to that question or propose a method to find an answer. There are numerous models and theories of human development (Hudson 1999) which have been useful in executive coaching. In terms of the application of an existing model or theory to a coaching assignment, the challenge for the coach is to remember to use the experience of the person to be coached to build *their* world model.

We have observed too many coaches attempting to 'shoehorn' an existing model into a coaching transaction when it is clearly inappropriate. Although commonly practised by academic researchers, the act of forcing the fit of errant data to an existing model is not good scientific practice.

So, in summary, it seems that a purely scientific, logical, stepwise methodology for achieving development has considerable limitations for coaching. As described in Figure 1.1, coaching focuses more upon future possibilities, less on historical problems.

Ed Schein (1996) performed a valuable service to coaching by categorising organisational cultures hierarchically (executive, engineering and processing cultures), helping to understand better the characteristic corporate challenges which face each one.

There are many useful frameworks for structuring the coaching process but the nature of each coaching assignment is unique. Given a similar personality profile and a similar coaching context, outcomes rarely appear similar. The challenge remains: no two coaching assignments are the same. Whilst we present here some *typical* or *common* coaching development issues – significant career development, new role transitions, managing cultural diversity, building and sustaining successful virtual teams, leading corporate change initiatives – each individual coaching assignment is unique and, as yet, no development process panacea exists.

Whilst we will describe practical examples of the above as well as propose our views of best coaching practice, there remains no prescription for success in these development challenges. Despite numerous attempts from contemporary organisational theorists and consultants to synthesise the diversity of corporate life into tidy packages of insight, it often has the appearance of organisational stereotyping, and can be equally useful in practice. Defence organisations, pharmaceutical companies, engineering, high-tech, sales focused, trading companies, financial services, Chinese family businesses, French-based multinationals, Middle-Eastern oil corporations all share some common characteristics, and the coach needs to understand the cultural corporate context of each one to be effective inside them.

As described in Chapter 3, there are some generic analytical tools we can apply across many coaching programmes to aid understanding of the individual executive's work environment and, whilst there may be many more similarities than differences, it is often those differences which can provide a key to enhance coaching effectiveness. Analytical tools and models designed to aid understanding of the individual *are* widely employed as are a broad range of coaching methodologies (Hudson 1999). We also apply a methodology to coaching reflected in the 'A4' approach common in most of the following chapters that contain practical coaching examples. We track milestones and review progress using conventional metrics, and we do agree success criteria prior to the commencement of coaching. So, quite a logical, rational, almost scientific approach, one might say. So where is the art in coaching? It represents the other half of the coaching craft. It's born out of experience, of both mistakes and successes. As most of us have felt, the impact of personal failure can lead to more deep learning than comparable success.

The hunch, instinct, the feeling, the imaginative insight and improvised intervention may be the most critical determinant in achieving commitment to action from a coaching partner. Our preferred coaching relationship approach is to form a partnership with the coaching participant. This is not always possible in every assignment and in every coaching session. The role of 'coach as expert' is sometimes required. Here lies danger for the inexperienced coach. The power imbalance implicit in playing the role of expert can be problematic, in that it can lead to a lack of ownership of development actions on the part of the coached.

Other artistically derived approaches such as taking a holistic rather than atomistic or compartmentalised approach to coaching, dealing with the whole person – not just focusing on skills building, the 'bolt-on behaviour' approach – demand a more creative and flexible coaching style. The coaching process, when effective, always reveals insights for both coach and coaching partner. However, revelational insights and major surprises for the coach can distract from focus on the coachee's development at a critical time. Whilst they both need to achieve a development goal, often within a prescribed timeframe, the route to its achievement is often co-determined, in close combination with the coaching partner.

Review Questions

1. Do you currently coach others? If so, how would you describe your style?
2. Do you need to? If you answered yes to this and no to the above, why don't you?

3. What is your ambition for coaching (self or others)?
4. Where are you in the matrix?
5. What do you think are your strengths and areas for development as a coach?
6. What are the business goals that will be achieved by coaching (others or being coached yourself)?
7. Describe your approach to change. How have you developed over the past five years? Had you taken a video of yourself at work, at home and in social settings five years ago, would you see any visible differences in your behaviour compared with a video taken today? If so, how did this happen? If no visible change is evident, why do you think there have been no changes?

CHAPTER 2

A Model for Development Coaching: The Transition Curve

One enduring coaching tool is the transition curve model which is used by coaches as a useful analytical device to help understand and determine several key data and plan an appropriate coaching programme. It has had wide application in our executive coaching practice over the past 20 years. It provides:

- An image to understand better the 'roller coaster of change' in work life
- An analytical device to help to identify how the coaching partner has experienced change in the past, how they have managed key career development changes in the past and typical responses to the prospect of significant change at work
- A positioning tool to determine where the coaching partner sees himself in the process today
- A mechanism that proposes which different coaching responses are most appropriate at different stages in the development process
- A practical design tool for planning executive development programmes and individual coaching processes – trying to get people to commit to their development (moving fast to stage 5 on the curve).

Just as the coach can use this as a useful design tool, so can the executive employ the same device to coach his or her own team. Thinking about where others are currently positioned can lead to a more informed coaching intervention.

In common with the executives we coach, a core competency for a successful executive coach is a fundamental understanding of the process of development and change. Almost every executive in our experience leads a change or development programme. Invariably, leading the implementation of a change programme, designed to improve the performance of the organisation, is a key element in many executive remits. The transition curve model described in Figure 2.1 below is one way of understanding the processes that people and organisations experience when significant change occurs. Coaching is one practical tool that helps individuals to achieve successful development.

Individual Transition

Behaviour change is a slow process, as Goleman (1996) notes in his book about 'emotional intelligence'. He supports coaching as

> you need a structure that is tailored to you and supports you over months ... that's why executive coaching is growing, having someone working one-to-one on a range of skills. It is a very effective method if the coach is good.

Generally, we found executives have two simple approaches to career management – we've called it the '*learn or leave*' syndrome. Most of the executives we meet are in a hurry, they're people impatient to achieve. In many roles, given adequate tenure, we find the challenge of development faces the ambitious. Changes in role, boss, remit, merger/takeover, technology/product marketing strategy may all inspire the demands of significant change, that is, the executive will need to learn new skills to be successful. For some, the level of change required can be overwhelming (see stage 1 in the curve) and lead to departure, often at stage 4 (probably the worst place to leave, as a new curve is embarked upon but at a lower level of self-confidence – having failed to adapt to the demands in the old role). For others, the challenges of development are met and development occurs successfully, moving through stages 5 and 6.

One significant difference we see in the management and executive population over the past 20 years is that it is rare to meet those who believe they achieve stage 7, namely because further change occurs which starts a new change process in train; don't forget, this is a process not a prescriptive model – you can go forwards, left to right or backwards on this model – which has been found to be a useful illustrative model of the experience of those in organisations who undergo significant change.

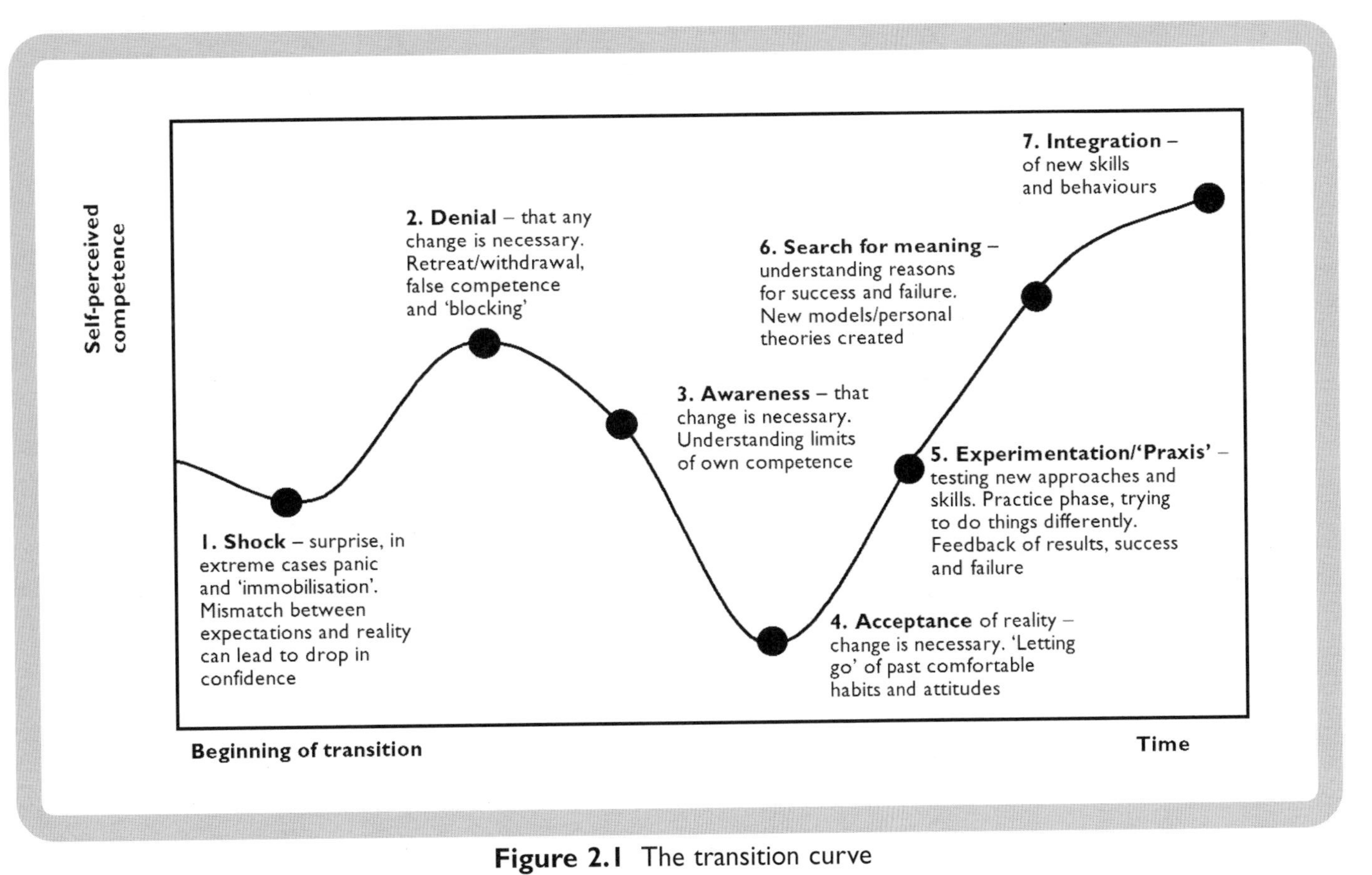

Figure 2.1 The transition curve

Source: Adapted from Adams et al. (1976)

Whilst emphasis is naturally placed on the achievement of key tangible business results, few organisations act in a way that embraces the practice of individual development in parallel with business and organisational development. Focus on the development of others is now seen to be a more legitimate part of a manager's role. Tichy and Charan (1995) described Lawrence Bossidy, CEO of Allied Signal, as 'a charismatic and persistent coach, determined to help people learn and thereby provide his company with the best-prepared employees'. At the core of this description is a belief that business goals can be more effectively achieved by helping people to learn and apply their learning at work.

Change in the business environment in the last decade has become a more rapidly fluctuating, visible and more powerful influence on our lives both at work and at home than at any time previously. Whilst the focus in management and business texts are typically on Western organisational life, drawn predominantly from experience in North America and Europe, comparable discontinuity has and is taking place elsewhere in the world, particularly in the economies of the Middle East and Asia Pacific. The development process described in this chapter has been repeatedly refined and tested over the past 20 years of experience working with business leaders and managers undergoing significant transition. Indeed it formed the basis for a leadership development process for managers in the Ford Motor Company for several years (The 'Leadership in Transition' programme). The transition model suggests one approach by which personal development may be more effectively understood and managed. The role of coaching is central in successful management of such a change process.

Many commentators have suggested that the rate of change in business is outstripping effective organisational, and therefore individual, responses. Some have said this is particularly common in the UK. Leaders over many years (Michael Edwardes – BL (1983), John Harvey Jones – ICI, Iain McAllister – Ford) are particularly critical of slow reactions to change in Europe generally and, more specifically, in UK business. Edwardes suggested that 'it [change] is pretty difficult to bring about because there is more inertia in this country than almost any I know' (quoted in Cooper and Hingley 1985). It's an interesting proposition; do some national cultures negatively (or positively) impact the ability of individuals to manage change more than others? We will explore that question more deeply in later chapters, as we examine coaching practice and outcomes in several cultures.

Linking Individual and Corporate Development

A process of development which forms part of a culture change that does not directly address individuals' existing values, attitudes and behaviour defeats the purpose for its existence. As long ago as 1987, Bruce propounded such a view. In describing the dramatic change required (and achieved) to improve customer service at British Airways, he said:

> the growth of competence is inextricably bound up with personal values ... hence the failure of programmes which have set out to influence motivation and behaviour. They ignored the issue of values.

As a result of our work with over 2000 managers and executives experiencing significant change, Table 2.1 outlines some of the most critical influences on the process of personal change. Consistent with the findings of applied research (Chapman 1982), the most negative influence appears to be individual intolerance of ambiguity and uncertainty.

All these issues are linked to what Deming (1988) describes as 'the first stage in the transformation process, which is, learning how to change'. For many, the process of personal learning and change resulting from life experiences is a natural one. Whether it is adequate for employees facing accelerating rates of business change and prescribed deadlines to achieve change is difficult to evaluate amid the complex bundle of influencing factors that are further compounded by a battery of additional personal factors. Loss of relationships, other changes in home life and personal changes (spiritual, psychological insight, change in self-image or values) all contribute to the forces which can promote personal change.

The cycle described below presents one way of viewing the process of change. The transition curve model described outlines a common cycle of experience, drawn from individuals' descriptions of their responses to a significant change. This model lies at the core of a management and organisational development philosophy that departs from assumptions about linear learning. Application of the model in practice establishes development practices such as coaching as a core organisational competence to achieve both individual and corporate development goals. The transition curve model, originated from work completed by Adams et al. (1976), has been refined and developed by the authors and repeatedly tested in the context of organisational and management development processes. Whilst over the past 15 years, more than 2000 leaders and managers from over 30 industrial and commercial organisations comprise the sample in Europe, North America and the Far East, the focus has remained linking

Table 2.1 Some common 'blocks' and 'bridges' influencing personal change at work

Blocks	Bridges
Individual factors	
Lack of ambition	Ambitious for own development
Fear of uncertainty	'Acts into' situations of uncertainty (active not passive)
Intolerance of ambiguity	Has a vision of the future
Believe no change necessary	Sees no alternative to change
Fear of failure, risk-averse	Fear of failure
Lack of confidence, low self-esteem	Confident in ability to develop
Rigid view of self and potential	Copes well with risk
Fear of personal loss of power and status	Accepts others' view of self
'Too old to learn' attitude	Sees personal benefit in future situation/ welcomes the future
Can't/won't let go of past attitudes	Curious about others'/differing views
Denial of others'/differing views	Active support and encouragement from superiors, peers, subordinates
Lack of support to implement change	Stable/supportive home life from superiors, peers or subordinates
Unstable domestic situation	
Organisational factors	
Lack of visible commitment or leadership from senior management	Clear vision, collective commitment
Organisational structures/systems remain unchanged	Visible examples of change from senior management team
Culture promotes individualism	Structures and systems reflect and support change strategy
Failure of new practice and processes	Culture promotes teamworking
Selection, recruitment and promotion criteria remain the same	Successes resulting from new practice rewarded and publicised
Little emphasis on people development or alignment with initiatives	Selection, recruitment, development and promotion criteria change and rationale published
New practice unrewarded	Emphasis on people development in alignment with initiatives

the development of the individual with corporate business goals. Endorsing such an approach, Cooper and Hingley (1985) describe the individual as 'at the forefront of the change process'. Their idea is that 'businesses won't change adequately unless people do. Through their collective commitment and willingness to overcome the inertia of the status quo'.

The seven stages below outline the experience of individuals in change. It has particular relevance for those responsible for implementing initiatives that require significant development of their peers and for direct reports. It has helped people who are either coaching others or undergoing coaching, or both.

Stage 1: Shock

Case Study

The New Director

Don, the recently promoted technical director of a multinational oil exploration and processing company, is struggling with his new role. Long experience as a highly valued technical specialist in geological survey has not equipped him adequately for the challenges of his new leadership role. After six months' tenure, his superiors in the UK and the US, as well as the local HR leadership, are concerned about his current performance, especially with building his new team comprising specialist contributors.

Early coaching conversations with Don confirm that he feels at stage 1, Shock, rapidly moving towards stage 2, Denial, as he seeks to continue his historical practice and work independently, without reference to his team, with poor delegation and communication with them generally. He treats the challenge as English people often treat foreigners when they cannot understand their English language (in London particularly) – they respond in a consistent manner, but increasing the volume with each response. Here Don puts more energy and effort into doing what he has always done – and achieved significant success historically – achieving the task individually by applying his specialist technical knowledge to the group task.

Overall, he agrees that his new role transition is progressing poorly, with a general drop in confidence after the initial euphoria with which he greeted his promotion. He shares, in common with many senior managers, the 'boardroom competency syndrome', which is often displayed by newly promoted executives and concerns the executive halo-effect (see below). This exists where a leadership figure expects that he should be competent

Case Study cont'd

in all areas of leadership, even those where he has had little or no experience or training. In this case, Don feels guilty that he is not fully competent in building and leading his team, effectively delegating tasks throughout the team, as every senior manager should be. But why should he be competent in an area where he has had no experience or training?

Our coaching challenge was to help Don to build his team leadership abilities. This is where you realise, as a coach, that everything is connected. His ability in team leadership was linked not only to his historical practice as a specialist, but also his personal profile. He evidenced a high need for task achievement, low trust in others, interpersonal insensitivity, low inclusion of others' needs (low team orientation), an introverted communication style and high levels of commitment to his personal ambition to succeed in the new role. His motivation, historically, derived from personal achievement of individual tasks.

It also became apparent, in conversation with team members, that Don had not enjoyed good relationships with several team members previously. In fact, several new direct reports had experienced very poor relationships with Don in the past. Here again, was learning for the coach. Don would only be successful with the cooperation of the team members, particularly those who had low opinions of Don's leadership and interpersonal skills. During a team-building event, it became evident that no matter what Don did, certain relationships were irreparably damaged.

Our coaching focus was to help Don to move from Shock, through Denial and onto Awareness and Acceptance. Our goal was to help Don move to stage 5 on the curve, which to some extent was achieved though his practice during team-building (albeit partially successful). Through the coaching process, Don became more aware and accepting of what development would be necessary to achieve a successful team leadership performance. He also realised the change necessary in his historical motivational profile or where he 'got his buzz' in work. His motivation needed to transition. Was he prepared to accept these changes? No, he wasn't and, furthermore, he was relieved when he was reassigned to a role that exploited his specialist knowledge as an individual contributor.

Case Study cont'd

Lessons Learned

Development through executive coaching is a two-way street. It is rarely a private affair, confined to the sanctuary of the coaching consulting room. Leadership is still a social activity and requires followership to be effective. Here, the impact on others was the critical determinant of development progress, but the 'others' (team members) were unwilling to accept Don's leadership.

Many may have the desire or motivation, but that needs to be matched by leadership potential. The challenge for organisations is to accurately assess this potential and provide opportunities for application.

Don, in consultation with his bosses, was reappointed to fulfil another senior technical specialist role elsewhere in the organisation. In terms of our coaching agenda, I felt I had failed, and, despite positive feedback, the sense of disappointment created by realisation that some relationships were terminally broken was frustrating.

As the coach, I experienced the early stages of transition in this assignment – Shock (about how things really were), Denial (I'm sure we can work through this) to subsequent Acceptance (letting go) of my original optimism. This may have been a critical learning moment for me. I had to let go, not of relationships, but of my optimistic expectation that it would be 'all right in the end'. Not this time, and for several times in the future, this was to be the real outcome. A hard realisation for me here. Sometimes early optimism or positive expectations are dashed by the dawning realisation and acceptance of reality that the coaching agenda will not be met despite heroic efforts. How to sustain optimism for the next assignment and avoid too easy cynicism was the next challenge I faced.

The difference between the expectation and reality of a new situation creates in the individual a response that is often described as surprise or shock. One of the most obvious examples is moving into a new role which is significantly different from any previously experienced, or when new demands are placed on the incumbent in an existing role. Equally demanding can be the situation where the organisation is undergoing dramatic transformation.

Often driven by implementing new techniques or processes, such initiatives can demand new and unanticipated behaviour from the individual. Whilst the response to this first stage is described as shock, it could equally be surprise or, in some extreme cases, panic. There is inevitably a degree of 'mismatch' between individuals' expectations and the reality of the new situation, and shock or surprise is common due to expectations not being met.

As can be seen from Figure 2.1, the two axes are 'Perceived competence' and 'Time'. Perceived competence refers to the individual's view of his or her competence in the new situation – how capable people feel in a new situation. Closely allied to this is personal value, confidence and self-esteem, representing individuals' feelings concerning their ability to perform in the new situation effectively. In stage 1, the individual's initial response is commonly a reduction in perceived competence. The situation may not be as it first appeared. The depth of the 'dip' seems to be dependent on the size of the mismatch between expectations and reality. So the greater the difference between expectation and reality, the more the individual may become 'immobilised' – in extreme cases unable to make plans or reason effectively, giving the appearance of being unable to take the required action. In a work setting, the vertical axis is important as individuals' feelings about how effective they can be in the new situation are linked to performance.

The case study above illustrates one individual's response to significant change. As has been reported elsewhere (Fitzgerald and Berger 2002), there are many others, each bringing their own particular characteristic strengths and development needs to the change situation. The skill of the coach is to understand, highlight and exploit, both for the mutual benefit of the coaching partner and the sponsoring organisation.

Stage 2: Denial

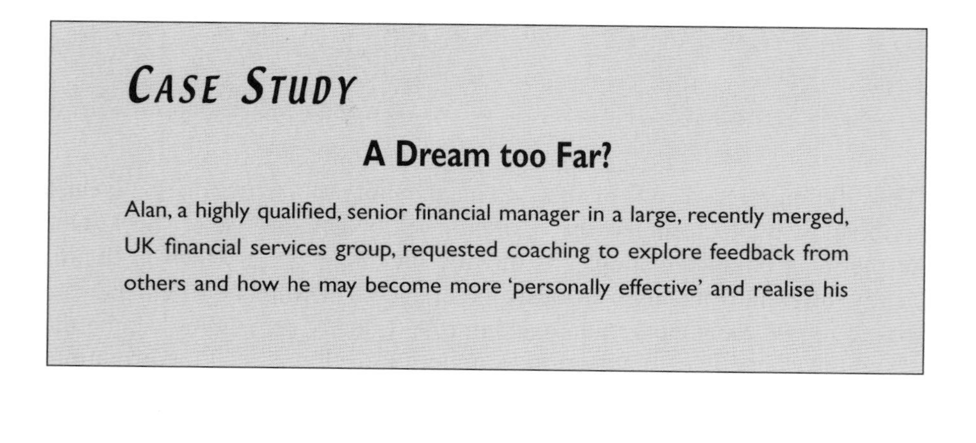

CASE STUDY

A Dream too Far?

Alan, a highly qualified, senior financial manager in a large, recently merged, UK financial services group, requested coaching to explore feedback from others and how he may become more 'personally effective' and realise his

Case Study cont'd

ambitions. He saw himself as an FD candidate in his organisation and potential CEO material for a FTSE 100 company within two to three years. However, none of his peers, direct reports or boss (or external headhunters) shared this view. The coaching assignment was subsequently redefined as one to improve leadership performance in his current role.

After initial interviews with Alan and his direct reports/peers and boss, I proposed the following coaching agenda. Distilling the feedback from interviews, the common development issues from my side were:

1. To improve effective leadership in terms of people management and communicating vision and influencing key stakeholders.
2. To develop better relationship management skills and sensitivity to others.
3. To improve team/meeting management skills – allow/manage disagreement more effectively.
4. To refine personal ambitions – test and challenge FD and CEO ambition.

Alan disagreed. He felt he wanted technical solutions to his communication skill challenge. He also saw his direct report team as not a key priority in achieving high performance in his role. More relevant for him was to improve his communication skills, to the point where he might 'win more in discussions – influence others (particularly those more senior) successfully so that my viewpoint prevails'. As coach, I suggested that he review several models of effective communication, attend a specialist communication skill development programme and identify particular opportunities to practice at work. Alan was reluctant to accept the proposal that an interpersonal skill development need required active experimentation. Having acquired every other relevant professional and academic qualification by intellectual application, here was another comparable learning opportunity.

Alan terminated our coaching relationship soon after. He felt that he was not in denial but working on another, more relevant agenda. My view remains that he was in denial of the key development challenges in his role.

Lessons learned

Movement off stage 2, away from denial, is a personal committing step – akin to abseiling, where a committing step is made – which cannot be prescribed or legislated by others (boss/colleagues/coach). It requires movement towards awareness and acceptance of necessary change, often as simple as accepting feedback from others. Subsequent action based on this feedback is predicated on:

- The existence of sufficient care about the impact of own behaviour on others (desire to act)
- The ability to act.

In hindsight, this coaching assignment was probably more concerned with a 'learning how to learn' (that is, process) development agenda than the content of what was actually learned. Referring back to comments about 'coaching as art or science', here the key development issue was probably differentiating between experiential and academic learning. Post hoc reappraisal is a wonderful thing.

On further reflection, there is learning here about co-coaching. To share, ideally with a trusted colleague, and critically challenge one's judgment/prejudice as the coach while the assignment proceeds is a valuable practice. It requires a close relationship with coaching colleagues and tests the conventional consultant's Achilles heel, that is, the existence of high quality teamwork.

A problematic issue is often the coaching assignment goals. In this case, the coaching partner preferred an alternative development agenda to that determined by his coach. As is the case with other consultancy assignments, determination of the nature of the assignment is critical. On many occasions, the original consultancy goal is redefined following preliminary study by an external, independent source. Here, the coach finds 'x' but the client wants 'y'. This is a true test of consultancy integrity, if one were required, as challenging the client analysis can conflict directly with commercial demands. One mutually satisfactory business solution was the outcome above. The organisation's overall evaluation of the assignment was that it was successful. However, it remains unsatisfactory in terms of development effectiveness in the coach's view and from the perspective of the coaching partner.

Following stage 1, the Shock stage, is the state described as Denial. Here the individual's sense of competence and feelings of ability to cope have increased. This is mainly due to the individual describing the new situation to him/herself as not significantly different from the old. Many explain their promotion by reference to their track record and believe they only need to replay their practice in their previous role to be successful. It is sometimes extremely difficult to convince an individual that he/she has been promoted not only because of their track record but also their potential. This refers to the ability to learn, adapt and develop new practices for application at some time in the future, rather than merely repeating previously successful behaviours which may not be appropriate in the new situation. Repeating the success pattern of the past does not ensure success in the future – even if all other aspects of life remain stable, which they never do!

One approach to encourage movement towards stage 3 is to remind individuals of the natural process of learning and adaptation in business life, inviting people to consider their behaviour five or ten years in the past, reflect on behavioural differences and the way that has been achieved. Stage 2 is the main 'sticking point' in the cycle. It is a place where a self-imposed block often inhibits progression through the cycle. Here individuals deny that they need to do anything differently. They deny the need to respond differently to an individual or a new business situation, even though it may require a new approach and new behaviours. Whilst drawn as a small peak in Figure 2.1, it can be rather more of a plateau for some individuals. Using an educational analogy, some students, should they deny the need to learn or develop, can block the learning process at this point by the act of denial. There is little that a coach can do to remove a self-imposed learning block. The cycle shows the individual's own sense of competence has increased. This is due to the individual denying that any change is necessary, that he or she needs to do anything differently at all, and repeating previously successful behaviours.

Stage 2 is described as a natural place to 'dwell' (Bridges 1985), where individuals collect their thoughts/energy before embarking on the next part of their change process. The way for the individual to progress from stage 2 is through personal choice. Whilst individuals can be encouraged, persuaded, cajoled or threatened, there is no guarantee that the individual will move from stage 2. Simply put, people cannot be *made* to learn or change; it requires a committing step on their behalf. Awareness at a personal level is necessary before the individual will start to move down the learning curve towards stage 3. We have found that a considerable block to development occurs when the individual refuses to accept that his/her view of self, strengths, weaknesses and potential may need substantial readjustment in the light of others' views. This may be one explanation for the existence of so-called 'organisational dinosaurs', those who never seem to accept new methods and deny the need for personal change. It is here that individuals' self-image and values are first confronted by the prospect of stage 3.

Stage 3: Awareness

Case Study

It's Now or Never: Career Crossroads Dilemma

John had been a very successful engineer and project manager in a large international aerospace engineering company. He was identified in his mid-thirties as a high potential manager with senior leadership potential. John, in agreement with his boss, felt he needed to build a 'general management perspective' in order to achieve further responsibility. As a senior engineering manager, John clearly had a preference for scientific models of leadership, applying his project management approach to all business issues. Now in his late thirties, he was identified as a candidate for executive coaching in anticipation of an executive promotion. His role at the time involved leading a large project team, working in a joint venture with external consultancies, which played to John's organisational and problem-solving skills. He wanted more. He needed to build 'general management skills', as he described them. He felt he needed to influence using other tools, taking a more strategic perspective and understanding his people better.

He was prepared for a critical review and exploration of his leadership skills repertoire. With the use of shadowing, online feedback, practical skill development and finally an opportunity to test progress – using a benchmarking 360° process – significant development was apparent over the 18 months' coaching process.

This organisation viewed high potential leadership talent as long-term investments, so 18 months was not regarded as a lengthy coaching engagement. John recognised early his career crossroads choice; a significant and common transition which confronts many successful specialists in organisational life. John was appointed deputy MD with responsibility for implementing the change strategy derived by the board. He acquired broad people responsibility, managing business improvement processes and these became his emerging strengths.

Stage 3 is the Awareness phase, where awareness of the limits of personal competence and therefore incompetence is the most important aspect. This stage is often accompanied by feelings of frustration. The individual's major cause for frustration is often confusion about how to manage the change process, for example how to become competent in areas recently recognised as deficient.

At this point, awareness may extend beyond specific areas of work to broader areas of personal strength and weakness such as competence in social and interpersonal skills. Here the process of feedback is critical. The individual appears more accessible to external news of his/her behaviour. During this period, support from colleagues in the form of feedback and encouragement can help accelerate movement towards stage 4, where positive learning takes the learner into further discomfort concerning the nature and level of personal incompetence (and thereby competence too) in the new situation.

Stage 4: Acceptance

Case Study

The Leave or Stay Dilemma

Ray took on the role of MD when he joined the organisation 9 months' previously. An atypical appointment for this large multinational, in that an internal candidate was normally appointed at this level from within. But in this instance, the business case was overwhelming. It needed new blood, a fresh direction with new ideas and approaches which would transform the traditional business practice which had brought only adequate success in the past. Senior managers felt that the business needed a revitalising initiative and Ray was part of the plan to implement a strategy for change.

Early in our first coaching conversation, Ray described openly his sense of depression and disappointment, with himself, his new boss, his work colleagues and the company. He felt that he needed to act to resolve his situation but was unclear where to start. He only knew that nobody's expectations were being met.

Case Study cont'd

Straightaway Ray saw himself at stage 4. As soon as I presented the model, he placed himself at the lowest point, 4. 'I'm there, that's me', he exclaimed loudly, unusual for such a typically quietly spoken man.

> I can feel myself there. Having slipped down that slope for the past nine months, I can truly say that is where I feel I am in my new role. What's more frustrating and annoying is that I have always managed this initial period well and have always felt more successful after this kind of entry period.

I asked him to describe further how he'd experienced his 'journey to 4' and what plans he had to move forward.

Nine months into his role, he felt disappointed, particularly with himself and his boss. He saw an overall lack of success in his new MD role, leading the financial services arm of multi-service US company. Ray welcomed an audit of his leadership abilities; although he'd never enjoyed any management or leadership training, he had managed to be relatively successful. This was a standing joke with Ray, as he was surrounded by reports who were (apparently) professionally trained through their MBA qualifications.

Ray finally met Barry, his boss, for a review meeting. Barry informed Ray about his current performance, his 'two in a box leadership model' and his philosophy comprising survival of the fittest, recounting his 'alpha ape' metaphor.

Ray remained unimpressed with Barry. But, having finally received the clarity he needed, Ray felt more able to contribute, and by using his extensive external industry network, he brought significant new business to the organisation and success to his role. However, the lessons learned had been painful for all involved. The selection process apparently relied more on hearsay and 'club' reputation than any detailed analysis of competence. The process of induction was poorly managed, with little thought given to the reaction of the organisation to an external leadership figure. Ray described the response of his colleagues and direct reports on his arrival:

> They reacted like any human body would to a virus ... they created antibodies to destroy it! I felt as though nobody wanted me there and didn't understand

CASE STUDY cont'd

(or want to explore) the vision of change I was brought in to lead. I was largely ignored, subverted or undermined during the first period of my tenure, hung out to dry. Even by those who had appointed me and now felt the initiative may have been a mistake, they wanted to keep themselves away from any muddy water that may have touched them.

By Ray's own description, he had never led a large-scale change programme before and was someone who was typically rather risk-averse himself, avoiding conflict and confrontation wherever possible. He had experienced no support from his new boss, who had appointed an internal candidate to sit with Ray as one of 'two in a box' whilst Ray found his feet. This served merely to destabilise and confuse Ray, who felt his authority had been undermined, with no clear structure to operate within.

My first response was mainly to listen. Ray wanted to unpack the past nine months and much of our first session was me asking questions and Ray unburdening himself. At stage 4, it seems that may be the most productive response of the coach. Thereafter, I gave some indication of how to move forward in development, or out of the situation (or role in the organisation), by identifying opportunities to practise new approaches.

Ray was happy to apply some conventional analytical tools to perform a leadership audit (using 360° feedback and psychometric instruments). At 53, he had never enjoyed any leadership or managerial training of development, so took the opportunity for review gratefully. An understanding of his current position (at 4), combined with the review, gave Ray the support he needed and informed his insight into his way forward into his new role.

Ray subsequently left the organisation. On reflection, did he actually move forward from 4? It's a debatable point, although from his perspective, he retired (early) on a note of success in his redefined role.

The lowest point on the curve in terms of the individual's own sense of competence is stage 4. In this region, there is an acceptance of the reality of the new situation. The new situation demands that the individual develops skills and competence in previously undiscovered or undeveloped areas. It also involves the individual in 'letting go' of attitudes and behaviours which have become comfortable, in so far as they have become familiar and habitual, albeit appropriate and effective in the old situation. This stage can also be accompanied by feelings of depression and frustration, even anger. This is often about how to move out of this uncomfortable phase.

Typical responses by individuals at stage 4 can include questions about the 'stay or go' dilemma. Working with executives who are often more transient than other members of the organisation, a common career decision is to move on to a new situation at stage 4. This can be either inside or outside the company, although an external move appears to be more common. We often hear the phrase 'I'm looking for a role where there will be a better "fit"'. This seems to illustrate three common outcomes to a career and role development challenge at this stage:

1. Leave the organisation at '4', moving away from the discomfort (can be seen as back to '2' but a more active response – find a place where my style/skill set/ambitions fit better)
2. Move to '5', seeking new opportunities for practice/experimentation – trying to do things differently – a way to progress through the learning process more effectively
3. Of course, a third response may be initiated by the organisation. That is, to remove the underperforming executive from the role and the company.

Having tracked executives post-move, we see them starting a new curve back at stage 1.

Moving on positively through stage 4 may involve the incumbent leaving the current role and accompanying situation. A positive way forward in terms of executive learning is to seek to move to stage 5. Using a sporting analogy, it is rather like developing the skills required to play a new ball game. On occasions, the ball is struck correctly and on others it is not. In learning to develop the skills required to play tennis, baseball or golf successfully, there has clearly got to be some practice and it is at stage 5 where the testing takes place. It is a period of experimentation, where individuals practise new ways of approaching problems, develop new skills and new styles of leading and managing.

Equally, it is often at this point that individuals recognise historic strengths which may have become contemporary weaknesses; whilst often a fear of letting go of past attitudes and behaviour is linked to the 'substitution anxiety', where one feels that giving up something to gain something else is too costly (rather than exploring the additional potential benefit of learning new skills).

Myth: Executive Careers are a Plannable Series of Predictable Events Leading to an Envisaged Career Goal

If we include the word 'rarely' as the fourth word in the above sentence, it begins to have more merit. In the hundreds of executive coaching assignments we have conducted, a handful of executives have claimed a planned career leading to their current role. Modesty aside, most refer to only having a career 'retrospectively'.

We have found that most participating executives agree on the link between feelings and behaviour. That is, how we feel about our work (and colleagues) materially affects our behaviour and hence performance. A supplementary question is equally revealing. Ask any group of leaders, given this generally agreed link, how many spend time/commit resources to understanding and managing the feelings of others. Without sounding like a tree-hugging session, to ignore a potential leadership tool that can affect others' behaviour and performance seems at best a missed opportunity and at worst incompetent. It's a revealing mismatch between the agreed value of a resource and the effort applied to its management.

Given the above, it is no surprise that Goleman's work (1996), has over the past few years gained so much attention in the analysis of successful executive behaviour. His central thesis supports the above. 'Emotional intelligence' – understanding and managing the more intangible part of executive life – is deemed to be a prerequisite for executive success. However, emotional intelligence (EI) is now less fashionable due to difficulties in operationalising the concepts by practising managers.

When people arrive at stage 4 on the curve, they are likely to be feeling (and maybe performing) as incompetently as they will in the entire learning process. So what happens at this stage? Put simply, 'exit' is one reaction – either voluntary or enforced. People leave the situation (organisation) or are removed from their role. A further option is to return to stage 2, a regression because, having tested the discomfort at 4, a return to the comfort of 2 is a withdrawal from the discomfort of 4. A positive way forward is to move to stage 5, experimentation.

Stage 5: Experimentation

Case Study

Breaking the Mould

Marc was a senior manufacturing manager with an automobile manufacturer in Belgium. When he commenced his coaching programme, he was about to be promoted to executive level, but senior leadership felt that further leadership development coaching would help this transition, particularly in the area of improving his flexibility and openness to new ideas. Marc agreed this may be useful. He is a very structured, organised manager. In over 20 years' company experience, he had created a rigid, formulaic approach to work. For example, to-do lists with traffic light colours: red for not done, orange started but incomplete and green for completed – transferred to the next day's diary to-do list. Marc's life was dictated by 'rules' – mainly self-imposed and self-determined. He also applied this structured regime to the management of the distinction between his work and home life.

His rule was never to discuss work with his wife or family. When he completed his coaching programme, he faced a dilemma. He wanted to share the feedback he had gained with his wife but regarded coaching as a work-related matter.

As part of our coaching action plan, the coach discussed how Marc might wish to broach this subject, initially presuming he needed a 'script' to initiate this discussion. Marc's concern was more focused on the consequences of acting differently towards his wife. A relationship that he enjoyed as stable over 20 years was now, in his view, in danger of being eroded. Interestingly, he presumed that his wife (and others at work with whom he had worked over lengthy periods) would act negatively to his attempts to be less rigid, rule-bound and structured – necessary to enable others' more creative ideas to be brought forward and free his and others' imagination to enable more creative solutions to work challenges.

Marc embarked on the agreed action plan and, on review several months later, described what was, for him, a surprisingly positive response from his work colleagues and, more importantly, his wife. Instead of fulfilling his worst fears, his wife was profoundly relieved that they could now discuss his work, thoughts, feelings, and ambitions.

Case Study cont'd

Learning: People often look to the downside, negative outcomes of change in relationships when contemplating a development initiative. If so, the coach may wish to balance the debate with presentation of the upside, positive (intended) consequences of development actions. This case also illustrated the need for continued support through practice and experimentation as well as the need for feedback of results, both successes and failures.

Key during this stage of testing and experimentation is the corporate culture. We have referred to the potential impact of national culture on personal capability to manage change. Here we consider the impact of corporate culture, often seen as a more powerful influence over individual behaviour. The Ford leadership often described to me how they could identify their people in a large crowd such as that found at an airport. Their behaviour was apparently distinctive and characteristic more of a corporate than a national culture.

The power of the Ford ideology was apparent during my work on an assignment in Hanoi in 1995. Working with professors at the National Economics University (at the time struggling to manage the transition from a planned to a market economy) who wanted to build a revenue-generating business school, we considered the curriculum infrastructure. Under question was the form of teaching material the faculty should use. Case study was agreed upon as a key resource. In considering a classic Ford Motor Company example, several members of the faculty claimed personal knowledge of the Ford business culture. One elaborated:

> I know Ford Motor Company. It has a powerful ideology and is one of the few words in English where you can add ism on the end – so we have Fordism … like Marxism and Stalinism!'

Some organisations possess a culture which promotes a fear of failure that can inhibit personal innovation and experimentation. This makes movement to stage 5 difficult. Others encourage testing and experimentation (stage 5) by empowering employees, providing new and challenging learning opportunities. The individual in this phase will typically make mistakes and have successes in attempting to become proficient in new areas of skill.

At the organisational level, stage 5 is critical. It is the stage in which organisations undergoing significant change need to introduce and practise new techniques and methods of operation. It is the period when new strategies are implemented. One characteristic that apparently contributes to success is a culture which allows the individual the 'latitude to invent'. In these organisations, managers feel they have the opportunity to practise new techniques and experiment with methods of operating their part of the business without the restraining fear of recrimination for failure. As Peters and Waterman (1982) described it, 'anti-experimentation leads to over-complexity and inflexibility'.

One example contrasting differing approaches to a 'culture of experimentation' is the Western and Japanese approach to automobile assembly. In Ford of Europe (which grew successfully on the basis of such innovations as the moving assembly line) in the 1980s, manufacturing managers described the greatest sin as stopping the line for any reason. This is in stark contrast to the Japanese approach, which has been to remedy faults, particularly quality faults, as they occur, with the famous 'five whys' approach (root cause analysis).

Case Study

Preparation for Leadership

John, a 39-year-old merchant banker, was facing a significant career opportunity. A role change taking him beyond his senior operational responsibility was on offer. His current role was a 'breeze' for him. He was well respected internally and throughout the industry as a whole, known for his integrity and his well-considered judgment. He is seen as a professionally minded man, with a care and concern for his colleagues beyond conventional banking stereotypes.

He had received consistently positive feedback about his performance in the bank for the past 11 years, which made him a successful veteran. Consistent with many other European financial institutions, the business had merged with one which provided complementary strengths, always a highly speculative proposition, but that appeared to be the formal rationale. John had prospered by this merger and found himself in pole position for promotion to fill his then current boss's role as global head of operations. This required that he lead the team of which he was currently a member.

Case Study cont'd

It was during early coaching conversations that John identified himself at stage 6 in the transition curve model for his current role but, anticipating his promotion, saw himself at 1 (Shock) on the curve again. Interestingly, his view of where he was at the time was informed by where he saw his future. John was aware that he needed to build some new skills, especially around the early initiation of ideas and judgment, inclusive debate and building trust in a team by valuing others' strengths (which were different to his). John explored many levels of self- and interpersonal analysis as well as considerable feedback. Most feedback clearly confirmed his view of the essential development issues and John commenced a programme of practice, actively demonstrating his commitment to develop the capabilities required for his upcoming role.

Here was a clear example of a coaching assignment where the participant's development was inhibited by the organisation's culture. Maybe all banks are the same, although I doubt it, having worked in three global and two large national players. Maybe I have a skewed perception, but it appeared that John's development was limited to a degree by his own practice (don't ask for feedback, keep a low profile, prefer less visible positions) but to a larger degree by the bank's culture. In short:

1. His boss did not give him direct feedback.
2. He only saw very sanitised and abridged versions of his 360° feedback.
3. His boss never coached him. In conversation, I discovered that his boss was uncomfortable with the notion of coaching John. Whilst he knew that John would never manage his new role in the same way as he did himself, he felt there were certain essential behaviours which John needed to develop.
4. The human resource development process was seen as largely ineffective – a conflict-averse, compliant and passive provider of service, generally poorly regarded in terms of value added to the business (with notable exceptions) by the business leadership.

Case Study cont'd

John is clearly an introverted leader. He had (and has) many conversations with himself about his development, ultimately initiating the whole executive coaching process in a characteristically conscientious manner. He religiously kept a development diary, noting down actions taken during the week, their outcomes and feedback collected as a result. Step by step, he moved towards developing a more inclusive and initiating style, which the new role demanded. His first step towards this successful outcome was, of course, recognition that he needed to change something. So you might say John was already on the roller coaster of his own personal development when he asked for coaching.

Stage 6: Search for Meaning

As individuals strive to learn the reasons for their success or failure during stage 5, they move towards stage 6, 'Search for meaning'. This is where there is an understanding of why certain aspects of their individual behaviour and style have been effective, and also why they have been ineffective.

Referring to a sporting analogy, it is the point when a golfer understands why the ball has been sliced or hit straight, and successful performance can be repeated. Progress through this phase can be encouraged by feedback about success and failure in practising new methods, approaches and skills.

Stage 7: Integration

We have scrutinised our coaching case examples reflecting leader's experience at this point but have found none. It may reflect contemporary business society and the rate of change in business today. No one admits to being 'on a plateau of competence', 'cruising' with no role challenges or learning agenda. Perhaps not surprisingly, it may reflect our client population which rarely includes the 'established leader'. We believe coaching clients rarely achieve this phase before another change is initiated, promoting another transition process. Here the individual takes ownership of the recently acquired behavioural 'tools' that have been successful in tackling particular tasks during stage 5 and new skills become an integrated part of the available repertoire. At this point, the individual experiences a level of competence significantly higher than the point at which the individual entered the transition at stage 1.

Development Through Coaching

Experience with many organisations in Europe, the US and the Far East suggests that for individuals undergoing a significant transition in terms of their work role, the period for an effective transition can take between 18 and 24 months. This rarely matches the most frequently mentioned period for individuals to come 'on board' in terms of their managerial performance, often said to take between six months to one year. *However, the duration of the cycle can be reduced and the learning process accelerated, by*:

1. *Understanding the process*: understanding the past and appreciating what is to come can help the individual anticipate the stages of the cycle. Whilst the specific nature of the new situation cannot be exactly anticipated, this consideration can help. At stage 1, further description of the role expectation for the incumbent can help.
2. *Providing constructive feedback*: providing feedback about the need for development is key. Here a manager may wish to embark on a coaching programme with a direct report (or peer), defining and agreeing current strengths and areas for development relevant to the new situation. Gaining clarity about personal strengths and weaknesses (increasing self-awareness) is a key enabler in the development process.
3. *Support and encouragement*: as awareness for change grows and acceptance increases, the individual can be supported and encouraged to move away from stage 4 in an effective manner towards stage 5 by having support, particularly from the individual's boss. During stage 4, it is quite likely that the individual is not only experiencing a sense of low value and personal incompetence, but it is also likely that he or she is performing relatively poorly. The danger here for the business is that the individual may leave in order to distance him/herself from discomfort, or be fired. In either case, effective progression through the individual's transition is interrupted.
4. *Opportunities for application:* providing new projects or discrete areas of work which enable the individual to apply and practise new skills is critical at stage 5, as is feedback about performance. How else does

one extend the repertoire of personal skills and breadth of style if not by personal application of new methods and evaluation of results?

Whilst it is rare to work with 'high flyers' in helping to promote their development, we have observed some common characteristics which validate the comments above concerning suggestions for accelerated development. They do not generally become blocked by denial. Quickly exploring the models of success apparent in the new situation, moving 'fast to 5' is their goal, seeking opportunities for practice and experimentation. They may appear more risky than most and express many of the characteristics of entrepreneurial behaviour.

A powerful message emerging from leaders in business organisations today is that the effective organisation is one which adapts well, one in which its people learn and develop most successfully. Managing change, understanding the transition process, provides one way of enabling individual learning and development. Experience shows that coaching can help meet the achievement of development goals. In the following chapters, a sequence of diverse coaching experiences are described. Whilst all the cases are different, a common sequence for many can be discerned, known as the A4 coaching process:

- Analysis of need
- Agreement to course of action
- Activity phase, coaching actions
- Assessment and evaluation of progress/outcomes.

Review Questions

1. Where do you think you are now on the curve (choose one position only)? Why do you feel you are there?
2. Where do others close to you place you on the curve?
3. Where are the people you are coaching appearing on the curve?
4. Where does your business appear on the curve?
5. What's your goal in terms of moving through your transition? What's your goal for progressing those you coach through their transition?
6. What's your timescale for achieving the movement you are planning?
7. What resources do you have available to you to implement your plan?

CHAPTER 3

Assessment in Coaching

He has a right to criticise who has a heart to help.
ABRAHAM LINCOLN

Assessment: The First Stage in Executive Coaching

Coaching comprises both caring criticism and development help. Assessment processes embrace both. This chapter takes an overview of the first critical step in any coaching assignment, assessment. Whether it is done informally or through more structured and overt procedures, it's hard to conceive of coaching taking place without some assessment featuring before, during and after a typical assignment. Here we look at what to expect, what options confront coaches and what might constitute best practice. Effective assessment is fundamental to successful coaching. It is typically conducted differently by coaches but aims to establish a starting point for development, both in terms of identifying a target development area and quantifying where this point may be. In addition, assessment provides the coach with insight into the individual that can be invaluable in informing the development style and content.

Why Assess?

Assessment often serves two purposes:

1. To establish the nature of the development task.

2. To provide the coach with some useful insights as to how this might best be achieved, taking into account how the relationship with the individual might best be managed.

Before we explore assessment, we need to consider the entry point to the assignment process and how this might influence the type of assessment that will be conducted, or indeed may already have taken place. In some progressive organisations, external coaching may be offered as a development opportunity in addition to any coaching that is, hopefully, taking place internally. The starting point is therefore 'take this person and coach them'. As part of this type of programme, it is becoming common practice to run individuals through a 360° appraisal process. This involves the individual completing a self-assessment questionnaire, based upon competencies, corporate values or a similar framework describing effective performance in the business. Respondents directly rate their ability to perform in these critical areas. At the same time, colleagues including the line manager, selected peers and direct reports complete the same questionnaire on the individual to produce this all-round (360°) view of the person and his/her capability. These 360° feedback processes will be discussed later, but they are undoubtedly a powerful device to use at the start of a coaching assignment. This example is one where assessment is an integral part of the coaching process, although the notion of the 360° appraisal often precedes the idea of follow-up coaching, as it is perceived to have value in its own right.

Other coaching assignments feature assessment in a rather different guise, however. In many cases, particularly when external coaches are contacted to begin assignments, assessment may have happened in a rather ad hoc fashion but is nonetheless the catalyst for inviting an external coach. Occasionally, individuals themselves may have taken stock of their situation and determined that they would benefit from coaching, either because they are particularly ambitious, or experiencing immense strain in their role, or both. They commission coaching as a development option based on their evaluation of their current status and ambition.

At other times it will be a third party commissioning coaching on an individual's behalf, sometimes after consultation with him/her, other times not. Here the 'assessment' is often presented as a diagnostic referral to begin 'treatment'; the coach is then expected to 'operate' immediately. There is an obvious need at this stage to examine and challenge any 'assessment' that has been made. Hopefully, there has been a rigorous and comprehensive evaluation of the individual's capabilities, with coaching decided upon as the best way of helping him/her to realise his/her potential. However, on other occasions something may have happened that has disturbed a senior manager and they have decided it's coaching or else! The coach has the option to work with what s/he has been told, but will undoubtedly gain more from making an independent assessment to really understand the situation.

As well as trying to quantify gaps and ensuring that the most important are explored, good assessment also provides an insight into the predisposition towards certain behaviours. Aspects such as comfort with change, ability to learn, willingness to adapt and key motivations may all be explored as they impact on the process of coaching. Without this knowledge of the individual, the coach runs the risk of applying a 'one size fits all' approach.

The above suggests that assessment really only has benefit for the coach. However, it is clear that the information made available to the coach through assessment provides a rich discussion focus for both parties. The 'gift' of seeing ourselves as others see us, perfectly illustrated by the 360° report, is sometimes one we would not wish to accept, but it is vital for addressing personal development in earnest.

It is the review of assessment findings, in whatever form, that can create a most stimulating feedback session between the coach and the coached. The data provides one level of insight into the individual, whilst the reaction and response to it can take the session, and the relationship, to another level. As part of the discussion, the individual's own view is matched directly against other sources. Agreement and discrepancy lead to an evaluation of the individual with regard to openness to feedback and ability to put him/herself in others' shoes, commonly called 'empathy'. These factors not only impact on success at work but on the way in which the assignment is to be managed and the likelihood of a successful outcome.

In summary, assess:

- To help to establish starting points and identify key areas for development
- To clarify the nature of improvements that might be pursued and the amount of movement that may be required to achieve success (however that is defined)
- To provide insight for both coach and individual with regard to personal competence and attributes as seen from different perspectives.

Assess, How?

As discussed above, assessment takes many forms (Anderson and Herriot 1997, Smith and Robertson 1993) and may not always be recognised as a formal stage in the coaching process. Here we examine some of the assessment alternatives available to the coach, and their relative strengths and weaknesses. As with most tools and techniques, individuals will have their favoured methods, and even a good tool can be used badly. Although some will consider it heresy to say, for practitioners, experience and the achievement of sound results over time generally count for more than validation figures and reliability coefficients. You will find, or may have already discovered, your own favoured approaches.

One way of looking at assessment is the route by which the information is obtained:

1. Third party reports (appraisal, interview data, ad hoc comments, 360° appraisal)
2. Self-report (self-appraisal, one-to-one interview, conversation)
3. Assessment tools (psychometric instruments, assessment exercises)
4. Direct observation.

Although ultimately any assessment relies on subjective interpretation and judgment, the methods employed in 3 are generally designed with the specific aim of increasing objectivity. In theory, they should be impacted less by personal prejudice and bias. In this sense, compared to the other options, they may be considered both more reliable and accurate, but also less 'rich'. By this I mean the methods employed in 3 focus on the target individual, generally in isolation from other parties and hence they suffer less from compounding factors that make assessment less objective. They are ideal for selection assessments where a checklist of behaviours and desired performance is used to judge suitability. In the workplace, whether we like it or not, the subjective judgments of colleagues, alongside achievement against objectives, is what counts most in assessing capability, effectiveness and promotability. We will now explore this further.

Third Party Report

The third party report is the most common source of information for coaches when starting an assignment. An individual's performance at work is constantly evaluated by other people, as most things he/she does, either through tasks or interactions, impact on someone else. These other parties are therefore a critical source of information and in some ways the most important in a work context. If you're not perceived to be effective, then you're not.

In coaching assignments where coaching is 'remedial' in some sense and has been 'recommended' for an individual, it is because impact or performance has been problematic. The coach may enter the assignment with most other parties confirmed in their belief about the individual; the assessment has been done, all the coach needs to do is get on with changing it. However, the way in which the information has been gathered, interpreted and evaluated adds a level of complexity that needs to be taken into account. It is like thinking about what hotel we might stay in when visiting another town or country. We might work from the star rating the hotel has been awarded and the description and pictures we can obtain from the owners, or we might review the comments of those who have stayed there.

The assessments made by third parties of another individual are not 'motive-free'. This is not as sinister as it might sound. There are probably more assessments made of individuals that 'give the benefit of the doubt' or 'do not want to be too harsh' as there are those that are influenced by one individual wanting to 'do another down'. Most people's experience at work will reflect the fact that negative feedback, delivered directly, I will add, can often be in short supply; at least at a time when it would be helpful.

The coach's job in working with third party reports is twofold. Firstly, s/he must evaluate any assessment made by others and decide on its veracity, accuracy and relevance, whilst at the same time acknowledging that the mere fact that a certain impression or perception has been created means that there is an issue to address. In this respect, the purpose of evaluating the assessment is really to establish if the focus of coaching should be elevating the ability to do what has been highlighted, or to elevate the profile of the individual when doing it. A good example here is the area of initiative.

Sometimes individuals are perceived as having few ideas and when they do of implementing them even less frequently. Occasionally individuals may have some ability to innovate and be able to produce examples of where they have had an impact on the business in this way; their problem is making sure people associate the ideas with them and recognise this when they are initiating them.

Secondly, it is important to gain as full a picture as possible about the individual to go beyond what might be a unidimensional profile.

Occasionally one can be left wondering how a certain individual manages to get him/herself to work in the morning with the picture that is painted, let alone function in a senior and responsible role. I'm sure other coaches ask the question 'If this individual is so bad, why is he/she still here?' The coach's job here is therefore to 'widen the lens' and get a more rounded picture of the individual. In many instances, the areas for development are in no small measure related to the consistent strengths an individual displays, and indeed may have been rewarded for in the past. Even in instances where individuals are highly regarded and coaching is viewed very positively, the first elements of performance mentioned, after a general 'doing exceptionally well', may tend to be the least positive.

So what are some of the issues associated with working with third party reports? We think they fall into three categories:

1. Relationship issues that introduce bias, positively or negatively.
2. The value set of the individual giving the report.
3. The ability of the individual to give an evaluation of behaviour and its impact on performance.

Relationship issues that introduce bias, positively or negatively

We do not have to think very long or very hard to come up with examples of where we might not be at our objective best with regard to making assessments of people. There are certain individuals who we find so engaging that their faults and weaknesses become insignificant; this is the basis on which marriage succeeds. On the other hand, even those engaged in assessment professionally find occasions when listing the strengths of a particular individual becomes an exercise in self-control and grudging 'generosity'. If it weren't for the word 'but', some assessment reports might not include any 'positives' at all.

When we read reports on individuals from their colleagues, we have to find out about their relationship to see how this might have impacted on what is being said. There will be some history between individuals, good or bad or both. There may be a sense of debt, competition and rivalry, or at other times, camaraderie that sees individuals close ranks. Sometimes there will be the question in the back of the rater's mind – 'what if it's me next?' It is therefore important to explore the length, depth and nature of the relationship to put the statements made into context.

The value set of the individual giving the report

There is often an assumption that everyone in the world sees things the same as ourselves and hence when asked to give an evaluation of a person will not only make reference to the same characteristics as we note about people, but also apply the same priorities and preferences that we do. Without labouring the point, we know this is not the case because of the different choices that individuals make in choosing their life partners and in appointing individuals to jobs that we thought should have been ours.

The questions here tend to concern where the individual is strong and weak, and why this is important. Whilst in most cases the answer to the latter question will be related to the job, in other instances it will reflect a core value of the evaluator. What's important here is not whether we as coaches agree with the value set, although often we might like to take up the debate, but that the values are identified. This is vital if individuals are to develop in ways that will be both noted and appreciated. It might be great to have all coaching partners working in a way that we find desirable but this may not help them in their own situation if the coach's values are not those adopted by others in the organisation.

The ability of the individual to give an evaluation of behaviour and its impact on performance

It is likely that anyone reading this book not only has an interest in the link between behaviour and performance, but also regards themselves as someone able to make observations about what people do and the effect this has on both the things and others around them. However, there are some who either do not have an inclination to think in this way or may not be particularly effective in performance. In some ways this is linked to what an individual's value set might be: some may stress task activity and delivery, for them, *how* this is done is largely immaterial.

It's no surprise therefore that individuals vary in the usefulness of the reports and comments they can provide. The level of detail offered will depend on that individual's comfort in talking about behaviours and their ability to do so. On the other hand, the reports given about individuals can be very good in terms of range and detail but sometimes are mere expressions of frustration. The key to getting the most from this source of data is effective questioning. As with any interview, the key is knowing what you need to know before firing off questions. It can be helpful to have a list of key skill areas, or competencies (Boyatzis 1982), in mind and these can be established by asking about the key demands of the role.

Once beyond middle management levels, moving into the first executive leadership roles in most organisations, the key skills required look fairly similar irrespective of the industry sector. Without being overly precious about similarities and differences, a core set of competencies used as an interview guide will at least create a more rounded and comprehensive profile of the individual than will an unstructured conversation. A lot of time, or at least a disproportionate amount of time, can be spent talking about deficiencies or what might be improved and developed, whilst areas of effectiveness disappear off the agenda. This can leave the coach searching for a balanced view.

Apart from avoiding the 'lop-sided' view of the individual, the other area to understand is where that individual's energy goes by preference or default. For example, it is not unusual to encounter highly successful individuals (as measured by achievement of business results) needing coaching on how to work with others more effectively at a fairly basic interpersonal level. This can result from having devoted all their energy, historically, to meeting business goals, delivering against deadlines and hitting targets in the past.

Important here is the proposition that although a behaviour change is being sought, there may not be a reward system in place to encourage the required behaviour. Also of interest is why the person's behaviour may have been 'accepted' to date but is now regarded as in need of development or change. In Daniel Goleman's book *Emotional Intelligence* (1996), there are a number of examples cited where such change is described as necessary. The main justification seems to be that the individual has climbed to a level in the organisation where they now need to influence different and more powerful corporate members.

Having examined the contribution of third parties to the assessment process, let's inspect those who provide them.

Feedback from the boss

In looking at the source of third party reports, we start with a special case and perhaps the most critical, the boss. In every coaching assignment, a key contact and source of information is the direct line manager of the individual. He or she may have instigated the coaching, either as a matter of course to accelerate development or out of concern over performance. Which of these two applies can obviously impact on the nature of the assessment provided. Typically those that are concerned about the level of performance will tend to focus on problems rather than strengths.

In either case, one 'assessment' that needs to be made at the outset of any coaching assignment is about individuals' managers. How competent are they? What are their strengths and weaknesses? What do they focus on in evaluating their direct reports? How is the individual managed? What is the relationship like? These are questions best explored in the context of actual assignments, and so I will not dwell on them here but hope readers will note how they come into play in some of the case studies that appear later in the book. Suffice to say that there is good reason why counsellors and therapists working with 'problem children' meet with the parents and often focus as much attention on them as they do on the child.

In those cases where 'problem cases' are being referred to an external coach, it may be more typical to encounter a boss whose talents, or interests, lie somewhere other than in coaching. As part of this profile, he/she may be less willing or able to articulate the difficulties that the target individual is displaying or he/she is encountering with him/her. On other occasions, the boss may be very good at pinpointing some of the issues but less inclined or able to do anything about them. In some instances, now more common with so much geographically remote reporting, bosses may know little about how their people behave and may be feeding back a summation of comments from others. In any event, it is possible that it is this assessment that underpins perceived success in the coaching process, so gaining a good understanding of what will need to be different at the end of it all is crucial.

Another factor to be taken into account is sponsorship. Typically leaders may be expected to support the individuals they have hired more than they do those they have inherited, especially when looking at issues of underperformance. In those instances where an external coach has been hired, it is important to establish the boss's role in ensuring success.

In exploring the assessment made of the individual, coaches need to know if their input is the 'last roll of the dice' or if they are working in unison with bosses to help individuals realise their potential. Again this is more a part of the coaching process (which will be illustrated and expanded in some of the case studies later) than it is an aspect of assessment, but it is during the construction of one's view of the individual that other factors will emerge.

Feedback from HR professionals

This group is included as a special case because they are often regarded as the in-house experts on all matters related to individual performance and development, and hence frequently feature in the commissioning of external coaching. The role of the HR function within the organisation has generated enough copy in its own right so is not the subject for discussion here. In terms of an input to coaching, what is important to note is that it has many roles to perform within the business with regard to advising, supporting, influencing and decision-making. The human resource role is not therefore simply the arbiter of 'objective truth', but is responsible for shaping the organisation and helping to train and develop the people within it.

In working through the assessments that those in HR can provide, it is important to understand the pressures under which they are operating and the strategic HR that exists or is being developed. In providing an assessment of a particular individual, they also have some objectives to meet and a management population to help manage. All this means that they can be an important source of information about the context within which a coaching assignment may be taking place, aware as they are of some of the 'behind the scenes' events and agendas of those involved.

We have enjoyed some invaluable conversations with individuals from within the HR function about prospective executive coaching assignments. A capable human resource professional will know how the individual is regarded within the business and give an evaluation of his/her 'stock'; in simple terms, is it moving up or down? They may have been instrumental in arranging coaching as an option once the decision had been made. It is always worth exploring how an individual is regarded more broadly and, going forward, in the light of what will be required in the future.

Feedback from peers

This group has the potential to evidence the greatest range of assessment-influencing factors of all, even when talking about the same person. Often closer to the individual in terms of working relationship and level of responsibility than other groups, they can generate some strongly held views and some of the best feedback.

It is important here to explore the nature of the relationship, past and present, and the basis upon which assessment has been made. As with other groups, the need for examples supporting expressed views is a necessity but the reasons for giving either an overall positive or overall negative assessment of the individual give some key insights into the way in which the relationship is managed. In those situations where peers are customers of the individual, the level of service attained may be expected to impact significantly on the ratings given, even on non-task specific competencies. Where individuals are unable to give everything their customers want, due to pressure on resources and competing priorities, more negative ratings can be forthcoming. It is therefore important to identify compounding factors that will influence an assessment from these quarters.

One additional point concerns the limitations that exist for this group making ratings on some competencies compared to others. Whilst they are well placed to make ratings of teamwork, communication, influencing and initiative, for example, they may have fewer quality opportunities to view individuals developing their people. Their perception of how this is done, and how that perception has been formed, is fascinating, just as it is when looking at ratings made by the boss of the individual, but may often be more about impression than observation.

Feedback from direct reports

This group again has some particular features with regard to the assessment they can provide, in that there can be a very close working relationship (in the best cases) but a somewhat restricted view of the individual in action. Direct reports get to see their manager in a range of activities but do not necessarily have the best insight into how that person works with his/her peers and own boss. This is not to say of course that the assessment is any less valid.

In addition, it is key to look at the motivations of members of this group when giving an assessment. Managers who act as 'best friends' and are perhaps tentative about stretching their team and putting them under pressure to achieve might be expected to be rated more sympathetically than the manager who is perceived as a 'slave-driver'. Whilst this is a simplistic overview – in fact individuals can be rated poorly for not giving responsibility – other incidents that have had a personal impact on members of a team need to be explored. Managers who have created opportunities for their staff and supported their development might in turn be supported against the view of their peers or own manager. Those managers who have not paid attention to developing their staff may be seen to be ineffective at all other competencies. Once again these elements are themselves vital pieces of information about what the target individual may need to address, but they can also impact on the breadth and objectivity of the assessment.

360° appraisal reports

Having examined the various groups that might provide some assessment of the individual to be coached, let's look at one assessment method that utilises input from all these in a structured fashion. The 360° report, as explained briefly earlier, is generated by the target individual, his/her boss, peers and direct reports (and in some cases other groups such as customers) each completing a questionnaire. The questionnaire, usually the same for all respondents, typically presents statements about what the individual might do within his/her job. For example 'Speaks clearly and concisely' might be one questionnaire item included to obtain a rating on 'Communication'. Respondents then rate the individual with regard to his/her effectiveness at this behaviour. This is either done as a measure of frequency or quality, for example 'Extent to which competencies are used – Not at all, Little, Some, Great, Very Great'.

Again, this is not the place for a technical discussion of the merits of alternative scales, but those interpreting 360° reports need to be aware of what they are actually measuring. Typically, individuals seem to lose track of what the words in the scale are actually saying and focus on high versus low ratings. This is a personal view, unsubstantiated by rigorous research but based on the use of different scales during the development of certain 360° instruments. This implied that respondents did not distinguish between how often they saw a behaviour and how good it was, it was just 'good' or 'bad'.

The items in the 360° questionnaire are often generated from the core competencies that the organisation feels relate to doing the job, held by the target individual, effectively. There are variations on this theme, with 360° reports addressing the application of organisational values in addition to or instead of behavioural competencies. Either way the principle remains the same.

Most commonly, 360° reports present the ratings of the individual made against the competencies (or values) down to the item level and by respondent group. The boss's score is presented just as it is, whilst peers and direct reports are presented as two group ratings to maintain confidentiality. The ratings are the result of the qualitative scale as shown above being converted to a numeric score, in this case a five-point scale where 'Not at all' would be equal to 1 and 'Very Great' would be equal to 5. Thus, easy comparison can be made between high and low scoring competencies, high and low scoring items and between the relative ratings awarded by the different respondent groups.

In addition to this wealth of 'quantitative' data, other 360° tools make use of this contact with respondent groups to collect more qualitative data in the form of their comments. These can be in response to specific questions, for example 'How might this individual be able to improve in his/her work?' or collected in an open-ended section either at the end of the questionnaire or in the course of completing it. Whilst processing of the numbered ratings is fairly straightforward, the processing and presentation of verbatim comments can be more contentious. Some practitioners believe in distilling out common themes, whilst others, the authors included, believe that verbatim comments should be just that and interfering with them only serves to dilute their value.

In the authors' experience, individuals who are likely to defend against, explain away or simply deny the perceptions of others find the numeric ratings easiest to deal with. We receive comments that certain people are 'known to be tough markers' or 'will have scored it there because of a recent project we worked on together'. Here the coach has recourse to the relative ratings attributed to different competence areas, for example 'so why is that one area scored much lower than everything else?' and must endeavour to get the individual to face what is in front of him/her, that is, 'it is their perception and hence you have an issue to deal with whether you think it valid or not'. However, with verbatim comments, the message is much less easy to duck. The challenge here is for the coach to help the individual to work with candid, heartfelt and sometimes raw and emotive comments. Reading a statement, as I once did, that 'there is no area in which John displays any competence at all' may tell us more about the rater than it does about the individual but it is feedback that needs managing rather than dismissing.

The 360° report pulls a mass of data together in one place but still requires interpretation. In some organisations, individuals are left to work through the reports on their own. This is very hard when there are tough messages contained therein and we do not hold with this approach at all. On the other hand, it can be tougher, from a development perspective, when the news is all good – all high scores and nothing below a suggested 'norm'; where do individuals go with that? Here we encounter another of the potential traps in the use of 360° reports: pass/fail scores. The use of numbers to enable comparison and ease of interpretation can lead individuals to think that they are in possession of a rigorous measurement tool and the kind of irrefutable evidence about competence that the organisation should act upon.

Often the coach will find individuals asking the obvious question 'Am I good enough?' or more likely looking for confirmation 'but these scores are good overall, aren't they?' It is natural for any of us interested in how well we perform to want to know our 'score out of 5'. Good managers get 3.8, bad managers get 2.4; there is a seductive simplicity about the output from a 360° report, it seems to offer the kind of objective, hard-to-obtain data that we all want – 'just how good am I?' A note of caution must therefore be heeded; this is a collation of perceptions, collected by getting different individuals to use, in their own way, a scale that looks objective and scientific, but it is not pure science!

However, the benefits of using a 360° report far outweigh the potential drawbacks. This is often the first opportunity that individuals have had to receive feedback that is so rich and diverse. Not only does it include the perceptions of a range of individuals with whom the individual interacts and upon whom he/she impacts, it also offers more structured and comprehensive feedback in terms of the behaviours covered than is generally available. This really does provide a more rounded picture of the individual, with potential strengths and weaknesses addressed and, most importantly, this is done in the context of what is important within the organisation.

Therefore, the coach obtains a fairly comprehensive report on what individuals are perceived as doing well and what they are perceived as doing less well. As with all feedback, the strengths often indicate why weaknesses may be perceived and this can help individuals better understand what it is like to be in others' shoes. The balance of the report is also helpful, determining priorities for development and specifying, because the behavioural examples may be quite precise, exactly what it is individuals should look to change to be more effective. Rather than be presented with general feedback, such as 'not good with people', 360° output can highlight what the individual does or does not do in interactions, for example, that is counterproductive, for example 'listens carefully to what others have to say' may be scored low. This sort of detail can help individuals when they come to formulate a development plan because the focus is much sharper and the specific actions they need to take are more clearly indicated.

Third party reports summary

At the start of this section, we outlined some factors that could impact on this source of data. These were:

1. Relationship issues that introduce bias, positively or negatively.
2. The value set of the individual giving the report.
3. The ability of the individual to give an evaluation of behaviour and its impact on performance.

Although in one sense we might wish to eradicate these factors from our measurements, they are in themselves key factors in understanding the perception others have of the individual who may be the subject of coaching. Rather than viewing them as contaminating factors, it is important to get to a deeper understanding of their strength and impact to really maximise the benefit of coaching. There is probably nothing that better illustrates the point that coaching does not take place in a 'vacuum' or a laboratory. The improvements achieved in performance by an individual may be intrinsically noted by him/her, but are only 'real' once they impact positively on others.

Self-report

We have just taken a look at the factors impacting the accuracy of third party reporting and, with a change to the first point, the same list might be seen to apply when we report on ourselves.

1. Motivations and temperament that introduce bias, positively or negatively.
2. The value set of the individual giving the report.
3. The ability of the individual to give an evaluation of behaviour and its impact on performance.

Motivations and temperament that introduce bias, positively or negatively

Whereas with third party reporting we considered what the relationship between the reporter and the subject might be like and how that would impact on what was said, here the concern is more with what will influence the nature of the report that individuals will give on themselves.

When 360° reports first came into common usage, it was more often the case that scores in self-reports would be lower than those given by other respondents. This trend has now reversed and self-scores tend to be higher. There may be many reasons underpinning this overall change, but what is clear is that despite the structure of these instruments staying pretty much the same over time, the way in which individuals choose to respond to them has altered.

We can think of individuals who fall into one of two broad camps: those who are modest and seek to underplay their capabilities, perhaps because they are self-effacing or because they do not wish to be surprised by a series of scores that make it look like they overrate themselves – possibly a way of getting one's retaliation in first. The other camp would feature those who are confident in their abilities, determined to demonstrate that they are confident in their abilities, or simply blind to the truth. They may also be right about competence but failed to provide others with enough opportunity to see it; an issue in itself worth addressing.

Another factor that may play a part in influencing self-ratings is the level of morale. In particular here we may consider individuals who are aware that they are underperforming and have begun to lose confidence – perhaps those at stage 3 on the transition curve. Experiencing some mild form of depression, individuals may underrate their performance significantly, or merely repeat feedback they have received even if at first they felt it unwarranted.

Coaches must therefore give individuals a chance to talk through how they have perceived themselves over time and in the context of the organisation. Are there factors or has there been specific input that has caused them to alter the way in which they see themselves, or report how they see themselves? In some organisations, it is seen as a reflection of a lack of confidence to admit weaknesses, whereas in others it is deemed necessary to be one's harshest critic. There is also some evidence that those who do best in organisations are those who publicly eschew weakness but identify where they are and work on it in private.

The value set of the individual giving the report

The ratings we make of others obviously say something about what we deem to be acceptable, good, important and hence of value. When dealing with third party reports, coaches are sometimes testing out the alignment of values between the relevant parties. In the case of self-report, the values are not only more explicit, they also provide important information on the likely success of the development agenda that may emerge subsequently. Anyone that expresses the view that they have little time for others and believe that task delivery and results should dominate all aspects of work is unlikely to make great strides in the field of interpersonal rapport building.

Thus, although the ratings assigned by individuals to each of the competencies and behaviours may not be influenced by what the rater values, the significance and priority they put on each rating will. This said, it is possible that those who value people skills will rate themselves higher in this area than on task-related competencies because this is where they devote most energy. Conversely, we have encountered individuals who are adept at certain competencies but consequently extremely critical of their abilities in that area, for example there are the super-structured planners who always remember and go on about, say, the lack of fine detail in their latest project plan.

The key point here is that individuals tend to prize particular competencies very differently. Thus individuals who maybe value the achievement of results above all else may rate themselves lower on competencies related to people skills, such as relationship building, but declare that this does not concern them. Here the coach knows that the first step is to get agreement about what is important and why.

The ability of the individual to give an evaluation of behaviour and its impact on performance

Just as with other raters or appraisers, the ability of individuals to self-critique varies considerably. To start with it is hard to 'observe' ourselves doing something when we are actually doing it. Additionally, we cannot report on the impact an action has on others in the same way that they can report directly how they felt; at best, we can only state intention and perceived reaction in others; unless we ask for feedback. Thus we are disadvantaged from both a vantage point and processing perspective, even if we can match the best evaluators in the world on ability.

Alongside these cognitive constraints, individuals also have their own understanding of what particular competencies entail and a benchmark for what makes for good performance on each. Individuals may expand or simplify the make-up of a competency; they may include either too many or too few behavioural indicators to define competence, or extend or diminish the scope of the competency overall. In addition, individuals will have their own view on what is poor, acceptable or exceptional performance against a competency; in this respect all competence is 'self-referenced'. Therefore, there needs to be discussion and agreement about what acceptable performance really looks like before any quantification of a potential development shift can be made.

As with all ratings and appraisals made for development purposes, the overall 'scores' on competencies are relatively less important than are the comparative ratings given to each. For example, where individuals rate themselves high on most attributes, it is interesting to see where they admit to even a little weakness. Conversely, those who report few strengths, nonetheless rarely put everything at the same low level. This said, for the coach, the discrepancy between self- and other perception is a critical starting point if such an anomaly exists. Determining which of the perceptions is correct is largely irrelevant; it is closing the gap between them that needs to form the focus of attention.

An added complication when dealing with self-report is that we work only with what the individual chooses to reveal and disclose. This is particularly true when an interview is used to obtain an understanding of the individual and rate his/her behaviour. Anyone familiar with interviewing, especially in recruitment, will testify to the difficulty one can have in establishing the truth. Interviewees can generally select the examples they will present and, if they choose, rewrite everything from the part they played in a particular situation or event to the reaction of others and the overall result achieved, depending on their capability to substantiate a departure from what really happened. If you do not have experience of interviewing, you may wish to consider interviews you have had where you may have been a little economical with the truth.

A number of studies have demonstrated the relatively poor predictive power of selection interviews with regard to identifying those who will prove successful in the future (Dougherty et al. 1994, Anderson and Herriot 1997). However, the need we seem to have to sit opposite others and assess them directly for ourselves is so compelling that, despite these findings, even business psychologist consultancies still interview potential candidates. Of course, as they will tell you, they are not the people responsible for the poor predictive validity coefficients.

Although relatively weak against other selection methods, interview quality can be increased significantly by ensuring it is appropriately structured and focused. The questions asked in the interview should be targeted at tapping into real-life examples from the individual's work experience and designed to elicit information against the competencies. There should also be a standard rating scale, used on completion of the interview, which outlines the key behaviours indicative of good performance in each of the competencies.

Having devised an interview schedule that will cover all the areas of interest, the skill of the interviewer is, of course, required to make it work. Open questions and persistent probing of examples is practically all the interviewer has at her or his disposal to develop a picture of the individual and test out the level of openness and honesty in the response (Bradley 1992, Flanagan 1954, Sackett 1984).

In conclusion, self-report plays a special part in any coaching assignment, as it is not only an initial assessment tool, but also features as the fundamental type of exchange between the coaching partners. The majority of coach and partner interaction tends to be 'interview' in style, albeit often conversational. The coach will be asking questions and the individual will be answering them, generally for his/her own benefit. However, it pays for coaches to be aware of the potential paucity of the information which they get back. In getting to the 'truth' (and by that I mean honest and open disclosure about one's own perceptions and feelings), nothing achieves more than mutual trust. However, in the absence of this, or before it can be established, persistent questioning, probing and judicious use of silence can be invaluable to the coach.

Assessment Tools

In this section, we will look at how the twin aims of assessment in coaching, that is, facilitating insight and establishing a focus for the individual, can be achieved through the use of tools that have been designed primarily for the purpose of assessment for selection. Typically used when evaluating an individual's suitability for a role or post prior to appointment, these tools are now used increasingly in development processes and coaching. In looking at these assessment tools, we will separate them into three broad categories for ease of consideration:

1. Psychometric instruments
2. Business simulation exercises
3. Role-play exercises.

Each of the three provides a slightly different dimension in assessing individual capability and orientation and we shall look at the pros and cons of each approach. This said, these differences are used to advantage by their powerful combination in the assessment or development centre process. By taking candidates through a series of exercises and activities that perhaps feature all these types of tool, it is no surprise that the predictive power of the assessment centre procedure exceeds any other assessment process.

The tools: what are they?

Before going into what each type of tool can provide, and where it may be found lacking, let's define what is meant by the categories we are using. To simplify, we define psychometric instruments as that group of tests and questionnaires that are completed by individuals, either in paper and pencil format or via a computer, both without input from others. A further subdivision that may help is to separate out 'ability tests' and 'measures of personality'.

Ability tests cover reasoning skills with varying formats focusing on numeric, verbal and abstract reasoning; examples of this type of test would be GMA-N/V/A and the AH and VA series. Critical thinking tests look at aspects of reasoning such as deduction, inference, recognition of assumptions, evaluation of arguments and interpretation. There are many available on the market, although restrictions are generally imposed in order to ensure that users have been through training on how to administer and score the tests and then interpret the results. This said, one can buy books of tests for practice purposes from high-street shops. There are also books such as *Test Your Own IQ*, which feature similar tests to those that will be discussed later.

Ability tests, sometimes referred to as aptitude tests, can be thought of as 'intelligence tests', in as much as they look to measure the ability to assimilate information, achieve understanding and solve problems. In most instances, they correlate with estimates of intelligence made empirically and performance on other tests of similar design. This is no place to get into a debate about the nature of intelligence but, as with all tests, the critical factor is choosing one that is fit for purpose. For example, testing numeric reasoning skills may not be vital where the job holder will devote their energy to generating creative designs in the fashion industry.

In our experience, unless a full-scale developmental assessment is to be conducted at the outset of a coaching assignment, this type of tool tends not to be used. When coaching is to focus on the ability to relate to others, as it so frequently does, measuring the competence of individuals to reason may not be priority; anecdotally coaches often hear, 's/he's very bright but …'. In addition, there is a resistance to putting 'intelligence' to the test once individuals have got to a certain level – 'we know s/he's bright because s/he couldn't be a vice president otherwise!'

Resistance (albeit passive) is found amongst those in the organisation as well as in individuals themselves, unless there is a feeling that the individual has a difficulty with handling complexity or keeping up with his/her peers and colleagues in debate. Apart from these occasions, there seems to be concern about finding out something 'we' don't want to know, or want to feed back, and perhaps concern that 'I' might be next.

One benefit of testing ability is that it can give insight into limited capacity, which might be placing an individual under strain or, more palatably, provide information on thinking style, a trait that might impact on how individuals deal with others. As an example, and I speak personally, some psychologists are the worst for intellectualising about how people operate, with well-reasoned models and profiling tools, reducing individuals to numbers and norms in our pursuit of 'objective' data to work with, but can simply lack empathy.

The second type of tool under the psychometric instrument banner is what might loosely be called *personality tests*, although this description is in itself a misnomer. They are not tests, in the sense that there is no pass/fail mark, that is, 'has a personality versus does not have a personality', but they are a test for 'type' of personality or the components that go to make it up. Commonly encountered instruments in this group include: 16PF, OPQ, CPI, MMPI, NEO and, perhaps a little different to these, the Myers–Briggs type indicator.

The aim of these instruments is to provide a personality profile of the individual. They do this by obtaining an individual's response to specific items in a questionnaire that have been designed rigorously (in most cases) to tap into traits such as dominance, emotionality, self-control, sociability and so on. The individual typically completes a multiple choice questionnaire where he/she is required to indicate his/her personal preference from a limited range of options, for example do you (a) like to go to parties, or (b) like to spend time alone reading?

It is from the responses to a number of such items that scores against trait dimensions are calculated and then the combination of scores from all the dimensions measured is interpreted to give a more complex overview. This profile or 'pen-portrait' attempts to describe and predict how an individual will tend to act or respond in different situations, such as when dealing with others when under pressure and so on.

This data is obviously dependent on the quality of information provided by the individual. This may be distorted because of a lack of self-insight or a desire to manipulate the output. I am still amazed by individuals, seemingly intelligent from their other test results, who will either ask the question or, more hopefully, make the observation that if they feel the right answer for them is 'A' but they instead mark 'C', the test results might in fact not be accurate for them.

Business simulations have evolved through the development of the assessment centre, where a range of activities are used in combination to evaluate the skills and potential of an individual. These are exercises that mimic aspects of working life to, in effect, put individuals into the same work environment as they will encounter in the target role and see how they tackle it. A 'model' answer is used to decide how well individuals have performed, often using competencies as a framework for describing desirable and effective behaviours.

One example of a business simulation is the 'in-basket'. Taking its name from the receptacle into which communications, requests, instructions, demands and feedback might be deposited for the occupant of a particular role (now most often 'virtual'), the exercise generally involves the following:

- An individual is given background information on a fictitious organisation, its environment and performance
- The individual is informed that he/she is to occupy a particular role in this organisation, often because some misfortune has befallen the previous incumbent (anything from leave of absence or serious illness to light aircraft crashes and kidnapping – more confirmatory evidence of what a dangerous business management can be)
- The individual is presented with a series of communications about tasks, people, finances, customers and so on, each of which presents some problem, big or small, requiring attention. Often there is a link between some of these communications indicating underlying causes or issues. The range and nature of these issues can be written to reflect the demands and challenges of the target role
- The individual writes responses to these communications indicating what he/she would do and how he/she would do it
- The written answers are scored by trained markers and/or explored in a debriefing session with an assessor.

A large number of problem issues that may face an individual entering the target role can be presented in a relatively short space of time. His or her way of dealing with these may be captured in a way that reveals matters of preference, for example 'he/she deals with technical issues but does not touch people problems', and also may give indications of style, for example 'strong control and command with direct orders issued versus a more involving, empowering approach'. Thus elements of focus, decision-making and planning directly related to the job for which he/she wishes to be considered can be evaluated. The disadvantage of this approach is that although it is superior to asking questions in interview along the lines of 'what would you do if … ?', because all issues are presented at once without signalling in some way what the candidate is to focus upon, these remain thoughts and not actions, and good intentions may not be delivered in reality, either in the way one would like or to the quality standard that would be desired. This is where the role-play exercise comes in.

In *role-play exercises*, the emphasis is on carrying out tasks and being observed doing them. They are powerful in testing out capability where interacting with others is fundamental. They basically test if someone can 'walk the talk'. Common role-play scenarios involve individuals meeting with their 'boss', a direct report or a peer or customer either in one-to-one meetings or as part of a group. Quite often these role-play exercises are used in conjunction with an in-basket and the characters are taken from this. A variation on this is the meeting individuals may have with their peers going through the same assessment process – here there is a halfway house where no 'plants' are playing a role but every participant is being themselves whilst occupying a role in a fictitious organisation. The format for these exercises tends to be:

- Provide the individual with advanced warning of a meeting that will take place soon with a named individual or individuals along with a brief as to what the meeting might be about
- Give time to prepare for the meeting (although some assessors and commissioning managers consider this to be unrealistic)
- Conduct the meeting with role player(s) and observer(s) (although some assessors look to take on both parts)
- Score the performance against competencies or a 'model answer' template.

This type of assessment is a bridge between 'contrived' assessment processes and the fourth method of assessment we shall consider later, observation in situ, where the individual is observed actually carrying out his or her job.

In role-play exercises, we enjoy the benefit of seeing someone do something at first hand rather than working from reports. The added advantage is that because we may be the person making the observations, we can be certain that the subsequent evaluation is absolutely right.

Now we will take a look at each of the evaluation methods in more depth and explore their strengths and weaknesses.

Psychometric instruments

In considering psychometric tools, let us first review ability tests. They tend to be used less often in development work of this type because the focus is often interpersonal style and orientation. They can still provide useful insight into thinking capacity and type. At an overview level, we can make some basic assumptions: those who handle complexity more easily will tend to be more successful at higher level posts. There is a weight of evidence that those rated as more intelligent are more successful at work, and the work of authors such as Elliot (1996) and Elliot and Clement (1994) builds on this model. It is reasonable to suggest that this success may be attributable to factors indirectly related to raw intelligence, such as perhaps higher level verbal skills making for engaging conversation and rapid insights, but the results indicate that if you select on intelligence alone, you increase the chances of making a better appointment than perhaps selecting measures of personality.

The debate on the nature of intelligence has occupied a lot of academic thought and generated some stimulating propositions. The work of Gardner (1983) speaks to the variety of 'intelligences' that exist, accounting for divergent as well as convergent thinking, talents in music and the arts, as well as more traditional (and businesslike) definitions of being intelligent. In a similar vein, Goleman (1996) has highlighted most successfully the need to consider 'emotional intelligence' when evaluating suitability for jobs and competence in management and leadership, as has McClelland (1973). Here we will only concern ourselves with what we might and might not be able to get from more traditional tools that examine reasoning skills (for example GMA series (Blinkhorn 1985), AH (ASE 1984) and AMT series (SHL 1999)), critical thinking (for example Watson and Glaser (1990)) and deductive reasoning (for example Raven's matrices (Raven 1995)).

First, what do these types of test indicate? As intelligence-type tests, they tell us about an individual's ability to assimilate information and make sense of it – either to solve problems or work out the right answer, demonstrate comprehension and understanding or develop a framework of understanding in order to identify trends and patterns. We can infer that those who are able to do this quickest and most accurately, and to the higher levels of complexity, will be better at handling ambiguity, at least intellectually, and therefore be more at ease than those who struggle. Note that a high score on these types of test does not mean that behaviour of this kind will be observed; we have maybe all experienced being incapable of doing something because of pressure or feelings at the time. The bright person who feels overawed by the environment may not sparkle as either he or she, or we, might wish. However, coming from the opposite direction, there is little evidence that, aside from good luck or judicious use of others, individuals who lack the raw capacity to process complex information rapidly and accurately will somehow manage this type of problem-solving effectively.

Here, we must start to go beyond test results to think about potential impact and how we might use the results when coaching. The first use we might make of the results is to check that the individual has the wherewithal to cope with the demands of the role in which he or she finds him/herself. The test results might confirm reports that the individual appears slower than colleagues in debate or easily thrown when others take her or him away from a prepared script into areas for which he or she has not prepared. Similarly, frustration for others caused by poor quality analysis or proposals of limited scope and vision may, in part, be attributable to the individual not having the highest ability to think in this way.

Similarly a 'contraindication' that has surfaced in assignments we have completed concerns the type of problem at which individuals can excel. As a simple example, one might consider problems involving the analysis of objective data versus the use of subjective data. As a general rule, deduction and the 'scientific' method tend to rely on objective thought processes: taking hard data, testing its veracity and drawing sound conclusions from a logical sequencing of what is available. This is quite different from dealing with, say, people issues, where data comes as opinion, conclusions are based on inference and decisions made by more intuitive means. Within business, there is a great need for objective-type thinking, which may be thought of as seeing things in 'black and white'. However, as Goleman and others point out, there are many shades of grey to be considered and where people are involved these are almost guaranteed. So the benefit of using tests of this type is that one may explore the ability of individuals to handle complex and subjective data and if found lacking here that may be a significant contributor to underperformance.

However, what we are looking at is performance on tests. The correlation between test performance and on-the-job competence is better than that for personality test scores and success in role playing, but still there is a gap between solving paper and pencil tests and delivering in the world of business.

As previously mentioned, there are often other factors that cause individuals to underperform. Whilst lower intelligence may restrict individuals in what they can take on with regard to problems, it does not prevent them being effective by other means. For example, making full use of others to help to resolve problems is a vital leadership competency, and preparation is to be recommended even for those smart enough to think on their feet and 'wing it'. One drawback for the development coach, and perhaps why this type of test features rarely, is that developing intelligence is probably not possible, although developing different techniques for thinking is.

As always with tests, the coach should caution against placing too much trust in the results obtained, even though the output can be seductively unequivocal. The deduction that can be drawn is that this may have an influence; what that influence is and will be is a matter for conjecture. Having established that note of caution for the use of ability tests, we will see how much more guarded we need to be when using measures of personality.

As described above, we are discussing those psychometric tools that provide personality profiles set against a range of dimensions. The aim of most psychometric instruments is to identify fundamental traits of individuals. These may be regarded as the basic building blocks underpinning how they act or the raw material they bring to any situation. Within reason, they change less as an individual grows older and so may indicate a predisposition to act in a certain way that should concern both the individual and his or her coach.

This personality profile information is usually most engaging for participants, whether they agree with it or not. A rich source of data for discussion, as it is after all about them, the response to what is contained in feedback or a report can be as revealing as the data itself. On occasion, one can see the very behaviour in dispute played out in full during a debriefing discussion. We have found personality-focused, psychometric tools to be immensely powerful in facilitating the understanding that individuals might develop about observations and perceptions reported in the workplace.

The profile that emerges for an individual not only helps the coach to make a 'post-match prediction', that is, 'it is possible that you are regarded as being distant and disinterested in people because you are personally very reserved and often prefer to spend time alone', but also assists both parties to devise the best way forward in developing an approach that will work for the individual and be seen to work by others. For example, those who show unshakable emotional stability may find it hard to work out why others are affected by seemingly (to them) harmless comments. Appreciating that there is a difference between them and others may be obvious from interactions, but seeing their own response as unusual to others, and why, can help with accepting this as a development need rather than an innate weakness in almost everyone. As a way forward, it is easy to instruct individuals to be more empathic and consider others' feelings; but it is better to focus individuals on how they phrase their statements and to purposely check out feelings with others that otherwise they may not detect or interpret. Of course, all this first requires the will to change what is happening now.

In a similar vein, the 'non-assertive' individual may justify every non-assertive interaction quite plausibly. In our experience, one of the most common reasons for avoiding conflict is given as 'political savvy'. Supposedly this is about using guile in achieving one's aims, and being smart in 'working the politics of the organisation' – a characteristic of the organisation which these individuals only serve to exacerbate. It also fails to register with these individuals that those people careless enough to be asserting their views and pushing for what they want do not seem to suffer unduly, although they are seen as heading for some sort of 'day of reckoning' when the meek shall inherit, well, all the best jobs. With these individuals, it is important that they appreciate where they sit on a measure of assertiveness, just to understand that everyone is not like them, even if they should be. More importantly though, the coach benefits from knowing what kind of demand it will place on individuals to behave in a similar way to their peers and hence what size of step might be possible to start getting there.

Encouragingly, personality questionnaires can also reveal potential or, perhaps more correctly, 'potential potential'. A profile may suggest some strengths, or at least a predisposition to act in a certain way, that are not being observed in the workplace. As one example, indicators of creativity may be present in the profile but be dormant or suppressed in the work environment. Individuals rarely argue with the 'diagnosis', as few people regard 'being creative' as a stigma, however, they may also allude to interests in creative pursuits in the past or outside work. In coaching these individuals, the coach should feel that s/he has struck a nugget of gold, some latent talent that might be given its head for the good of the individual and the business.

The chief benefit of using personality questionnaires tends to be the fact that they focus on fundamental elements of an individual's make-up; the underlying traits that will govern or guide how acquired expertise and knowledge, including what might be called 'life skills', will be applied. They get to these both relatively quickly and cheaply and generally reliably if the individual actually completes the questionnaire honestly. They cover a wide range of attributes, they allow predictions to be attempted and they help to facilitate an understanding of where an individual sits relative to others, which in turn helps him or her to understand why others are different. In addition, they engage the interest of those being coached.

So what are some of the limitations of using personality questionnaires? Test publishers spend a lot of time both maximising and then proving the validity (it measures what it says it measures) and the reliability (getting, near enough, the same result twice) of their instrument. Without getting into a possibly litigious debate about how this is demonstrated, suffice it to say the 100 per cent dead-on accurate instrument has not yet been devised. We may say that the likelihood of the profile being wrong is extremely remote, but that outside possibility of a poor profile-to-person fit would be enough for an able lawyer to raise doubts amongst a jury were the feedback of questionnaire results to be refuted by the recipient. This is not to say that 'personality questionnaire results can't be trusted', but we do find some practitioners' unswerving belief in the accuracy of their favoured instrument counterproductive for the purpose of making progress in a coaching assignment. As always, the feedback can be offered but if it's not accepted, move on. We never really know what the absolute truth is.

Like the 360° reports we spoke of earlier, where ratings of an individual's performance against competencies is provided by self, boss, peers and direct reports and then collated into one feedback document, personality questionnaires require interpretation. In the first instance, this means taking the output against the different dimensions that are referenced by the personality questionnaire and interpreting this in terms of likely observable behaviour. This can be done with varying levels of complexity and success. Many test publishers recognise this and have produced expert system software that can produce pen-portrait-type reports. Of necessity, these apply certain algorithms to detect important score combinations and generate characteristic descriptors for what is in the profile.

If we think of an instrument such as Cattell's 16PF (ASE, 1994), so called because it provides a measure on 16 personality factors, we can start to think about how complex a profile might get. When scored up, each factor has a bipolar scale with 10 points on it. This represents a normalised score, such that a normal distribution or the bell curve would cover the 10 points. The largest number of people, that is, the 'hump' of the bell curve, would be across points 4, 5, 6 and 7; the proportion then diminishes at the two ends so we see a small percentage of people scoring 1 or 10. To simplify, we might think of people scoring low, medium or high on each scale – so in effect three (not 10) possible scores.

A personal observation is that some practitioners barely go beyond declaring what is high and low on each dimension in the questionnaire results and do not delve into combinations. This results in a rather stilted commentary, when we have individuals told that they are 'about on the norm for assertiveness', without perhaps referring to aspects of sociability, optimism or emotional stability. I have also found that some computer-generated reports for certain instruments do little better than this.

The need for skilled interpretation is highlighted further when we come to the next step: making inference or transference into the workplace. The general nature of personality questionnaires is sometimes revealed by participants asking 'shall I fill it in as if I were at work, or outside work?' Already revealing how individuals view their personal make-up and their ability to draw upon or suppress certain elements at will to in some way maximise their own effectiveness, this suggests that individuals may agree with the profile for one situation but not another. However, a more common issue for those using personality questionnaires to inform the coaching process is moving from personality traits to in-work competencies.

The 360° questionnaire has the advantage of presenting competency-related items for consideration, which is not the case in many personality questionnaires. The dimensions measured are more general in their nature and hence some translation may be necessary. Without this translation, those receiving the feedback from questionnaires may quite rightly respond with 'so what?' It is noticeable that a number of test publishers are trying to address this issue, both by making the questionnaire items more work-focused and by developing work-focused report formats that look at clusters of dimensions in terms of competencies such as communication and decision-making – albeit that this tallies with your own view of 'competencies'. However, there always needs to be a bridge between personality profiling and the recognition of its impact and potential.

This brings us to another area where we might usefully compare the output of personality questionnaires with that of the 360° process. As mentioned above, personality questionnaires give indications of preference and predisposition or orientation to act in a certain way. They are not direct measures of capability and competence in the common sense of the word. The 360° appraisal declares 'your boss regards you as good at … and not good at … ', whilst, as discussed above, there are catches in how 360° questionnaires might be completed, it still carries ratings of ability. Some personality questionnaire items are aimed at asking direct questions about how individuals perceive themselves at, say, 'persuading others', but this probably moves them more towards the self-report of the 360° questionnaire than a reliable measure of capability.

The correlations between personality questionnaire results and observed behaviour are mixed. In developing personality instruments in the past, research tested out the profiles produced from questionnaires with independent ratings of personality traits by professionals. This is a bit like testing personality results against the observations recorded through a 360° appraisal completed by those supposedly expert in making these assessments. Whatever the flaws in this might be, it was an attempt to say, 'if my questionnaire profiles this individual as "assertive", would other people agree with that statement on the basis of their interactions with them?'

I raise this methodological issue for one reason: currently, some questionnaires are validated by testing the results obtained from them against the results produced by other questionnaires that they mimic. Whilst this ensures for the purchaser something akin to own brand products matching the taste or feel of an original branded product, it raises questions about rigour. If I validate my questionnaire against another with which I intend to compete in the marketplace, and achieve 95 per cent agreement – pretty good I'd say – what have I actually developed if that instrument in turn agrees with the 95 per cent level of another? My odds of getting things right seem to be reducing.

We have mentioned already that measuring intelligence can be more successful in predicting success than the use of other psychometric instruments. However, the door appears to be left open for other measures because, as Goleman (1996) shows from his studies, there are other factors that account more for success and failure than pure intelligence. The problem for us is, can we measure this other part in a way that allows us to make more accurate predictions? The good news is that people can still confound attempts to 'classify' and 'pigeonhole' them; in most instances attempts to profile the 'ideal' person for sales, typically, or other generic roles have not met with great success, although certain 'knockout' factors might be applied to reject those more likely to struggle. This said, there are many successful introverted salespeople and those in planning roles do not necessarily have to be self-organised. There may be a predisposition to act in a certain way but, thankfully for those coaching others, people can and do learn and do not simply act according to some preordained blueprint.

It is in this regard that respect for the instrument's limitations must be maintained. A number of years ago, when working on an assessment and selection course for airline personnel, I sat in wonder and bemusement as I listened to a well-respected and experienced practitioner dispense wisdom on the subject of the 16PF and its power. The audience, all seasoned professionals in their own right, were fascinated by the prospect that an instrument could profile two potential terrorist types, the 'loner leader' and the 'follower dupe', as I recall. Unfortunately, as the subject was discussed, we discovered that these were not unique profiles for terrorists – they merely held up under scrutiny for the sort of 'post-match prediction' we have discussed above, that is, once you knew something about the person you could see in the profile why they might act the way they did. I'm not sure that the added spice of 'loner leader' being 'the sort of profile you would get in some trade union leaders' did much to put any perspective on this profound declaration.

I mention this only because psychologists, as a profession, seem to wrestle to find proof that there is scientific rigour in the discipline. I know pure scientists working in the field who tend to scoff at this idea. Still, it causes some practitioners, and those coming from an arts background or with a need to pin their hopes on some third party kind of assessment, to invest too much in the power of this type of tool.

If further evidence of limitations were necessary, I would urge anyone who has completed personality questionnaires on training or team-building events to compare themselves with others in the room that 'came out the same'; Myers–Briggs lends itself to finding 'people like me' very easily. The authors of that instrument would not even start to claim that having the same type makes you some sort of clone, but it can be fascinating to examine differences just as it is to see the similarities. Further refinement of that instrument, Step 2 (Briggs and Myers 1992), illustrates why some of these differences exist even though the overall type is the same.

In conclusion, personality questionnaires provide a method of getting to underlying traits that influence the behaviour and responses of an individual. They have a framework of dimensions that can be applied to anyone, and can be used to establish how individuals compare with others through the use of standard scores and norm distributions (a way of deciding what is average for a population and how the individual compares against this). However, we all have unique personal histories. The debate continues about 'nature versus nurture' and the proportionate influence of both; however, the impact of family life, social background, education and a million other chance occurrences mean that personality is not an immutable silicon chip implanted at birth.

Business simulations

In this section, we will consider business simulation exercises such as the in-basket described earlier. As outlined, this is an exercise where individuals are told that they are managing a team, department or organisation as presented to them through background information. Generally, they are then asked to respond to a series of communications, usually delivered in one hit, and make decisions about what to do on each, if anything. This assessment tool is effective for examining an individual's approach to work-related issues such as delivering results, managing people, organising and planning, strategic thinking, decision-making and so on. In fact, a whole raft of competencies can be tested out through an in-basket simply by introducing relevant items.

One of the great features of this type of exercise is that it presents realistic situations and problems for individuals to tackle, in order to get a sample of them 'at work'. In approaching the tasks, individuals reveal aspects of their personal style and focus. Some concentrate on resolving operational problems and ensuring delivery of results, whilst others may prioritise people issues. For some, analysis may be kept to a minimum and decisions made rapidly, whereas others might instigate comprehensive research and work with others to decide upon a way forward. Some will produce detailed plans and instructions for their 'direct reports', whilst others may offer general pointers and overall direction. In some instances, individuals may even start the process of developing and growing their staff.

There is a distinct advantage here over the interview method of obtaining information about typical approach. Even for very skilled interviewers it is hard to probe examples from the work environment without astute interviewees presenting themselves in a favourable light, with their actions fully justified by the circumstances they choose to relate. The interviewer wasn't there, so they may remain unconvinced because they lack the evidence to prove their hunch.

Within the exercise, the communication style and breadth of communication and involvement of others is also demonstrated. The style may be concise and direct or more expansive and inclusive; there is often a discernible difference between those who are task-focused and those more people-oriented in the way responses or messages are phrased. This sample of work behaviour can be obtained fairly rapidly, and developed further by a debriefing session that allows the assessor to probe responses further and provides individuals with an opportunity to expand on points they may not have made clear.

This brings us to one of the potential drawbacks in how this exercise is often conducted. The reliance on the written medium can obviously create some restrictions on the quality of information. Pressed for time, individuals may skip details or make their responses terser than they would normally. In addition, the rationale behind certain actions may not be explained even though administrators of the exercise encourage this to be included. This difficulty is exacerbated when the exercise is presented in the individual's second language, often done because a standard approach is used and typically we find the official business language of an organisation is English. This is why we tend to use the debriefing session to alleviate some of these issues.

Role-play exercises

Role-play exercises are similar to business simulation exercises, as an attempt is made to mimic some aspects of working life and expose individuals to this in a way where the environment is controlled and standardised. As mentioned previously, role plays focus, primarily, on the evaluation of interpersonal skills. These include establishing rapport, building relationships, communicating clearly, influencing, assertiveness, questioning and, of course, listening. The scenarios used range from one-to-one meetings with a role player who will be the individual's boss, a peer, a direct report, a customer, or perhaps a supplier through to group meetings where more than one role player is involved.

The great thing about this type of exercise is that one can observe the individual 'in action'. In interviews, individuals may describe how they review performance with their direct reports, delivering tough feedback, handling push back, coping with emotional reactions and identifying and supporting development objectives, but in the role play we can see both if they choose to do this and if they can actually do it.

The brief given prior to role-play meetings tends to be fairly broad, indicating who individuals will meet with and some background to their position and potential issues that they might raise or one might raise with them.

Direct Observation

Like the 'fly on the wall' TV documentary or CCTV cameras scanning public places for misdemeanours, the power of direct observation of individuals in action is obvious. Nothing can compare with the kind of pure social anthropological study of behaviour for at least offering the opportunity to view the individual behaving in a relevant context.

Effective coaching is dependent on the coach and individual establishing a common understanding of events, or perceptions, and then formulating and subsequently working on an agreed development plan. This is facilitated by shared insights often resulting from assessments,

Table 3.1 A comparison of alternative assessment methods

	FOR	AGAINST
Psychometrics	■ Cover a range of capabilities ■ Provide useful discussion points ■ Give insight into what might otherwise remain hidden ■ Engage the coachee	■ Only predisposition or preference not actual ability ■ Despite high validity not 100 per cent ■ Not on-the-job competence, all inference ■ Requires integration and interpretation
Business simulations	■ Way of testing out capability at actual job demands ■ Provides useful information on the focus and priority setting of the individual	■ Dependent on the relevance of the exercise for the job role and the design quality of the exercise ■ Assumptions can be made about the rationale and motive of the individual
Role-play exercises	■ See the person in action, not just talking about what they might do ■ Direct observation	■ Do not provide information on what the person will do in the long run – just a snapshot of skills ■ Tend to focus the individual on an event and he/she reacts to this – no guarantee he/she would choose to do this in the first place

which are in turn derived from situations and events. The closer both parties get to sharing an event, the better the chance of establishing this common ground. In all the assessment methods we have looked at so far, there is an element of 'distancing': either of the coach/observer from the time of the behaviour or from the environment in which it would normally take place, or both.

In our executive coaching assignments, we typically aim to achieve a relationship of trust, because this is critical to a successful coaching relationship. This provides a framework where individuals will allow, accept or hopefully invite direct observation of them performing their everyday work. This is the point at which all the rhetoric about one's own behaviour and others' observations can be put to the test, without the ready escape route provided by some of our assessment techniques that it is 'not like real business life'. This has the potential to provide the kind of insight that all the other methods of assessment we have discussed are trying to deliver. We believe that there are some basic reasons for this:

- Individuals are more compelled to act in their 'normal' fashion when in their everyday situation than in any other environment we can create – they simply cannot help themselves
- We gain a better understanding of the working environment and the other 'actors' who contribute, elicit or encourage individuals' 'normal' behaviour
- We influence the behaviour less than in other scenarios.

Some of these points are subjective judgments, so let us explain our position. Like the assessment exercises discussed above, it would be expected that putting the individual's capability under scrutiny would have an impact on how he/she might approach a task. This is notable in the initial stages of direct observation when the individual will include the observing coach in at least some small way, acknowledging his/her presence, rather than treating him/her as a piece of the furniture. However, it is our experience that individuals actually report, 'I forgot you were there' once they get into the task in hand.

In addition, to explain away the behaviour observed in meetings, for example as a result of the presence of the coach, becomes a little difficult, unless individuals claim extreme nerves or their behaviour is significantly better than normal. We all express a sound rationale, even if formed post hoc, as to why we did things in a certain way or reacted in a particular fashion. The only other scapegoat we can find in situations that don't go as smoothly as we would like is the actions of others. Even here it is difficult for an individual to claim 'out of character' behaviour, as awareness of this needs to be addressed as much as any ineffective behaviour that is thought justifiable.

Many years ago, I led a research project examining driver behaviour. This involved devising and conducting experiments in which drivers would be observed from inside their own car, where it was always a concern that the observer would influence the approach. Occasionally, drivers would even report that they had altered their 'normal' style because of the presence of an observer. Generally, they thought they had driven more safely. This said, the variation *between* drivers rather than *within* their driving pattern was always greater and we coined the phrase 'no matter how much you think you change you always drive more like you than anyone else'. We are comfortable that this is what we see in our coaching partners, and if we don't, well maybe that's something about authenticity and consistency that they need to address.

Finally, unlike in the driver research, we have the option to follow up in work meetings with those that have participated to check out the 'normality' of what they just experienced. 'How did that meeting go?' 'How typical was that of how they usually go?' 'What was X's behaviour like today?' These are all questions that can help the coach to gauge if s/he has been treated to a stage-managed production or seen life as it really is. Of course, for the coach witnessing a good performance, even if 'out of character', it is actually good news – at least it shows that the individual can do it if he/she tries!

This said, the opportunities for observing the individual in action, even when he/she is prepared to submit themselves to this, can be limited. Firstly, there is a need to get the permission of others. Whilst the individual is putting him/herself forward for scrutiny, there are others to consider who may regard this as an invasion even if they are not the primary focus. Individuals who choose to go this route often start by volunteering their teams to be part of an observation session, primarily because they feel permission would not be refused or that they can simply impose this on others because it is about their own behaviour being put under the microscope and hence of no threat to others.

There is a paradox here: on the one hand, individuals may feel more confident about their behaviour in front of a group over which they have at least some ascribed or nominal, formal authority. On the other hand, they might risk more with this group because there is a perception that they 'should' be competent and require nothing in the way of development because of their position.

Still, there is a need to involve other participants so that most benefit can be derived from the time. This type of session is very encouraging for direct reports who have submitted comments about their boss's behaviour that they would like to see change. 'Overauthoritative', 'non-listening', 'closed minded', 'interfering' and 'aggressive' bosses can harness the support of their teams very quickly when they hold their hands up and say 'I've taken note of what you said and want to do something about it, so meet my coach'. However, the coach must also be aware of the need for support that such a bold move requires, as there are groups that will take advantage of the situation. Rather like the class that plays up because the school inspector is sitting in on the lesson and will inhibit the teacher's normal rage-filled recriminations for bad behaviour, so some direct reports can seize the opportunity to act mischievously to provoke their boss into doing something they may regret.

This brings us to another important feature of direct observation that makes it so powerful – the part other people can play in influencing behaviour. We mentioned early on the case for family therapy, not viewing the individual in isolation but acknowledging all the contributing factors. Whilst coaching Graham, the chief underwriter in a large reinsurance business, we had many discussions about his team, the problems and difficulties he had with each of them and how he dealt with these to get the most from them. His goal was to develop his leadership and people management skills. One name, Nigel, cropped up repeatedly in discussions. There were issues of him 'undermining morale through cynicism and sarcasm' and 'rarely taking responsibility despite demands for greater rewards' that were always being offered by others in the market. It wasn't until I spent some time with the whole group in a meeting in which they had the opportunity to give feedback to Graham that I realised the tolerance he had displayed to date. The tedious jibing at others' expense, not just Graham's, caused me to refocus part of the meeting, and my feedback in particular, on a more deserving case. It was at this point that I appreciated Graham's view that Nigel would never change might well be true. We had already discussed what his loss from the group might mean and strategies, primarily around the difficulty of recruiting a similarly well-placed and experienced individual, that might be pursued. However, it was Graham who moved jobs first, to a competitor, and, ironically, he returned to poach Nigel.

Assessing our own Coaching Capability

Having discussed the methods of assessment available to us to assess our coaching partners, we thought it appropriate to address here the matter of assessing ourselves as coaches. In general terms, like those wishing to practise any form of professional interpersonal analysis and development activity, we feel it is vital that coaches have a detailed understanding of their own strengths and weaknesses. This is important for the following reasons:

- As with any task, if you understand your strengths and weaknesses, effective delivery is more likely
- Understanding one's own profile of preferences, values and personal philosophy can help us to appreciate differences that exist with others

- It is inequitable to subject others to a level of assessment we would not be prepared to undergo ourselves.

We recommend that prospective coaches explore the benefit of psychometric testing and 360° feedback in order to develop their self-awareness and clarify the profile of behaviour that they are likely to display. In addition, it is vital that coaches evaluate their personal strengths and weaknesses against a set of coaching competencies in order to identify where they need to focus attention in their development as coaches.

Outlined below is the set of coaching competencies that we established as a result of a study we conducted with clients and coaches. Subsequently we applied it in workshops we held for developing independent coaches. These were used in a 360° feedback report format, completed by those who had experience of working with the individual. We then spent time co-coaching with participants on the results.

The list of competencies we present below is a framework for exploring a consultant coach's capabilities and we recommend its use for those working as external or internal executive coaches. You may use this in a 360° questionnaire format (see Appendix) with input provided by those with whom you have worked, either as colleagues or in a coaching partnership. Alternatively, you may invite your coaching partners to give you direct feedback against the criteria, providing them with a practical coaching experience. If you complete this type of assessment before reading further in the book, you may be better positioned to review your own approach against the scenarios presented to consider your responses to them.

A Competency Set for Executive Coach Consultants

The competency model outlined below was derived from a study conducted with corporate coaching clients and practising external coaching consultants. Having conducted a series of focus groups and individual interviews, the list below was established. As with all competency frameworks, it reflects the values of those who provided the behavioural examples of good practice; thus it may include behaviours you might not associate with or deem requisite for coaches and omit some that you believe are fundamental. We suggest you consider the former, and add the latter. We also welcome feedback and comments to refine the list further. The framework we developed was translated into a 360° feedback instrument and applied to participant coaches attending a series of development workshops delivered in 2001. The competencies identified were defined as follows.

Self-management

This competency is largely about personal attributes and how these are evidenced in the coaching context. Rather than describing skills in action, this competency refers to values such as integrity, openness and a commitment to self-development being put into practice. Individuals who score high on this competency are more likely to be regarded as professional and honest as they act in line with their declared values and remain true to them. They approach coaching assignments in an assured fashion without being overconfident or arrogant and present themselves as self-aware individuals, accepting and open about both their strengths and development needs.

Communication

This competency focuses on one of the most important skill areas for coaches; their ability to develop understanding through ensuring communication between them and their coaching partner is effective. In defining what it comprises, as much emphasis is placed on listening (receiving) as on presenting (transmitting), as this is key to coaches working with their client's perspective. Also included is the delivery of feedback, a fundamental element of what good coaches do, and the ability to influence the thinking of others with regard to the acceptance of coaching as a development medium. Whilst there are occasions when persuading others to a point of view might be desirable in a coaching transaction, this is seen to be less characteristic of what we have found to be good practice in coaching.

Coaching craft

This competency describes behaviour more specifically associated with the effective delivery of coaching. It highlights key skills applied during the coaching assignment that contribute to the achievement of development objectives by the coaching partner. It addresses the management of the coaching partnership, in task terms, and the ability to remain flexible in how these objectives are attained. It is this competency that, probably more than any other, describes what it takes to be an effective coach over and above the key skills that might be applied in a range of roles.

Interpersonal skills
This competency focuses on the skills that are required to build an effective relationship with all those involved in a coaching assignment. It describes the behaviours that serve to build trust and ensure that individuals are treated with respect and as individuals. It broadly encompasses the ability to empathise and recognise and manage emotions sensitively. It also comprises aspects of personal flexibility in adapting one's own behaviour to match the mood of others or the situation in which one finds them.

Coaching context
Whilst the above feedback model provides a useful insight into current coaching strengths and weaknesses, it is important to recognise that this is a 'snapshot in time' and remember that the feedback is contextual. That is, in different corporate coaching assignments, with different clients, a breadth of coaching behaviours is required.

Executive coaches often experience the need to tailor their style, approach to coaching, coaching content and practice depending on the needs of each coaching assignment. If so, they will find themselves expressing different aspects of their coaching repertoire, for example perhaps acting with one coaching partner in a more directive and initiatory manner than another.

As was evidenced in different stages in the development cycle in Chapter 2, different stages for the coaching partner in the coaching process require novel responses from the coach, rather akin to the situational leadership model (Hersey and Blanchard 1999). Like effective coaching behaviour, effective leadership behaviour in this model is determined by:

- The *nature* of the task (here the development goal(s))
- The *capability* of the person (a function of ability, potential and motivation).

For example, in the case of coaching a participant to improve people management skills, the coach needed to assess the nature of the coaching task and his ability to develop this.

On several occasions we have been invited to coach business leaders who are underperforming from the organisation's perspective. On occasion, we encountered the executive who was resistant to others' feedback – often a point where self-reliance and independence become a weakness. Part of

Case study

Feedback Denial

Patrick, the marketing VP of a large international motor manufacturer, was underperforming in his boss's eyes. There was a lack of collaboration – bordering on hostility – with other functional heads in the team, and a deterioration in some key client relationships (seeing Patrick as arrogant).

An initial coaching discussion (internally publicised as the first steps in a top team development programme) with Patrick revealed his indifference to others' views, including his boss's. His sales results indicated his function was performing well above target volumes and margins, the key indicators for success in Patrick's role.

'So, our results speak for themselves' was Patrick's opening remark. 'I am, of course, only as good as my team's performance, but they are clearly a very effective team. Whilst I can see how others in certain functions (finance, engineering) need some support in developing the team – we're in good shape here!' When invited to identify strengths and areas for improvement in others' functions, Patrick readily obliged with a considerable list. Turning to his own senior team and his own performance, he could find no areas for improvement. A worrying sign, I felt.

The next step was a 360° feedback instrument, conducted across the whole senior team, with boss, peers, direct report and some client feedback included. I returned to Patrick's office to feed back his results, which generally reinforced his boss's perspective. Patrick was very upset. I presented the feedback as gently as I could, as the discrepancy between his view and others' was clear and considerable. A few minutes of final 'rearguard defence', 'Well, that goes to show how little they know what I do!' followed by 'They're simply wrong in their perspectives!' led to a grudging acceptance that there were issues for Patrick to explore further with his team, peers and boss (as well as some customers).

the repertoire of executive behaviours that have enabled career enhancement will become disabling if taken to extremes. Potentially a cause for what is commonly described as 'career derailment' (McCall 1998), the inability to accept the validity (or accuracy) of others' feedback concerning executive behaviour is worthy of particular mention out of the above list. The case study above highlights this issue.

Negative or defensive reactions to feedback can be a considerable block to progress in coaching executive development. An entirely logical approach does not always overcome such self-imposed blocks. The validity of others' feedback is self-evident to us all when we stand back and view the transaction objectively. Other peoples' perceptions are their realities, undeniably. But in a defensive or fearful state, such objectivity sometimes eludes us all. Our role as coach is to provide the necessary support to ameliorate fear or defence but without diluting the power of the feedback – often a tricky balance for the coach to strike.

CHAPTER 4

The Role of Experiential Learning in Coaching

My journey into executive coaching has been far from typical. With no formal experience in corporate life or business school qualification, I approached the world of executive coaching from an unusual direction. However, after building and leading a small business, I discovered a passion for working with people and helping their development. After qualifying as a teacher, I established and ran an adventure holiday and hotel company which I built up over a number of years. This company was focused on providing children and adults with an exciting and fun experience outdoors – helping them, by the acquisition of the necessary skills and awareness, to enjoy and appreciate personal and group challenges in the context of outdoor activities.

Over time, I began to realise that the participants were gaining more than just skills. Through the experience, they gained psychological and emotional benefits as well. Children were gaining new confidence in themselves, teachers were becoming aware of hidden strengths in their pupils, and families often moved closer together through the shared experience. Parents learned more about their children and adults sometimes made life-changing decisions following their experience. It was apparent that the medium of the outdoors and experiential learning was a catalyst for personal development.

My appetite for development was further enhanced when in the early 1980s, through a chance meeting with a faculty tutor from a leading UK business school, I was invited to lead a series of personal and team development programmes for MBA students. Here the outdoor development experience was focused on the participant's management development rather than skill acquisition.

During the past 20 years designing and providing events, workshops and programmes for team building, individual development and leadership development, we have worked with over 150 organisations from 25 countries.

The attributes that build effective coaching relationships, direct and sensitive feedback, the ability to challenge, trust, understand and a genuine interest in development are also the necessary attributes in the world of experiential development.

My first executive coaching assignment was one I was to find profoundly challenging to my emerging executive coaching practice.

Case Study

Andrew meets Andrea on a Stroll

My relationship with Andrew, a senior manager of a large division of a global financial institution, was developed over a period of two years. It began with providing a leadership team development programme for his direct reports and a series of similar programmes for all the members of his division.

It was generally agreed that the programmes had achieved their objective: that of creating an enhanced, effective team culture within the department. Shortly afterwards I was to work with Andrew again but this time with a group of his peers and his boss. I was involved with this team in providing a four-day development event, which was focused on encouraging the participants to accelerate their own and team development. It was an intense experience that produced the desired results for the team and led to my first executive coaching assignment.

Andrew approached me shortly following this programme and asked if I would work with him as his coach to further develop his interpersonal and managerial competencies. Although I was delighted to be invited, I was also apprehensive. How could I help Andrew further his development? What did I know about running a large division in a large blue-chip company? Did I want to move into this type of demanding relationship where my lack of knowledge may become obvious and jeopardise my reputation?

To help me to alleviate some of these concerns, I explored with Andrew the reasons for choosing me as his coach. Andrew made it very

Case Study cont'd

clear that his main reasons were that he trusted me, felt I had a good appreciation of his style and its impact on the various people he came into contact with and was able to challenge him and help him develop. I felt suitably encouraged to go ahead and after agreeing aims, outcomes and the process for the assignment, we agreed on our first session, which would be outdoors. A walk in the countryside rather than a meeting in the office suited us both, as it is an environment conducive to dialogue without distraction.

It was not long before we were in an intense conversation regarding development needs and the proposed actions for practise back at work. However, there was one particular area that I felt we were not quite probing satisfactorily, an area that I had recognised Andrew was seemingly capable in some of the time but seemed reticent to adopt on a regular basis. The conversation became more intense as we probed and explored this area. Suddenly Andrew turned to me and asked if he could share something very personal with me and that the piece of information he was about to disclose may well cause me some concern.

Andrew told me that for most of his life he had felt that there was something wrong with him and that for many years now he had realised that he would rather be a woman than a man. He had been taking every opportunity to live that life. Andrew had been married for some years and had teenage children. He had never shared this information with anyone, including his closest family, and had chosen me to 'come out' .

I experienced a wave of thoughts and feelings at that moment. I was deeply moved that he was able to share this with me but concerned that I may not be able to support Andrew. I felt afraid for him, his family and others involved, and confused as to what to do and say next. Mixed with all this was a huge sense of guilt brought on by having to face up to my own prejudice.

I worked with Andrew through this major life transition over the following months as he eventually dealt with the issue of telling others, including his employer, and began the process of beginning a new life as Andrea. Andrea now has a new and very different life, is happy with herself and very successful in her new role in a new company.

I share this story with the reader to illustrate the intensity that a coaching relationship can have for some individuals and the responsibility that the coach may be offered. It highlights the need that people have to surface and share their innermost thoughts and feelings to move forward in their development – the coach, even in this case, being instrumental in that process.

The journey continues as I work with those individuals in organisations who have the responsibility, power and capability to ensure an appropriate environment for sustaining the learning and development for their people. This chapter is designed to capture some of our experiences in the field of experiential learning.

Introduction

This chapter explores the part that experiential or action learning can play in the coaching process. Throughout this book, a variety of tools and techniques to assist in the coaching process have been explored. Here we will focus on the provision of concrete experiences to support coaching interventions and the development goals of individuals and teams. In this chapter, we examine the role of experiential learning and how it can enlighten, clarify, guide and accelerate development. We show, through case study examples, how effective use of experiential learning development programmes and events can give teams and individuals opportunities to enhance their existing skills and discover new ways to improve effectiveness. Experiential learning can help to build relationships quickly and enhance personal, team and managerial skills in a practical, challenging and often enjoyable manner. It is a practical approach that helps individuals and teams to recognise the benefit of development. This is achieved by a heightened awareness gained through practice.

From our earliest days, we learn by doing. Babies and infants imitate, and experiment in learning to walk, talk and coordinate generally as they begin to acquire the requisite life skills. Children at school enhance many of their skills and behaviours through repeated practice and application. Throughout our lives we encounter many tasks which are best understood by doing. An adult example is learning to drive a car. For most of us this acquired skill set remains with us all our lives. As a tool for development, the 'learning by doing' process allows the participants to experience, feel and become more aware of the behaviours of the group and other individuals. This awareness of the impact of different behaviours on people and situations gained through activity is both compelling and memorable.

In addition, this approach to personal and team development often endures because it is not only based on the knowledge of the teacher but, even more, on the latent qualities, experiences and needs of those participating.

The consequences of decisions and actions taken during experiential exercises are often immediately apparent, providing clear evidence of performance and a shared platform for feedback, questioning and further experimentation. Although the exercises involved are not everyday executive work experiences, they are inescapably real, and replete with uncertainty as in work. The process of change, as discussed in Chapter 2, demands that leaders of organisations become proficient in managing ambiguity and uncertainty. These two aspects of change in organisations are often the most demanding capabilities to develop. Experiential learning, particularly located in the outdoors, can provide an ideal medium for such development. The following case study is an example of the effective application of experiential learning, in a situation far from the corporate context, which helped to build participants' confidence in order to address the challenge of significant personal and corporate change.

Executive Team Case Study

Crossing the Chasm – A Metaphor for Change

A large bank was facing a profound transition – flotation on the stock market. It had decided to compete with the 'big five'. As part of the necessary change, a population of potential general managers was identified for further development. We were chosen to prepare and present a series of development programmes to meet both business education and management development goals.

As a practical personal and team development component of the programme, the programme group enjoyed an experiential learning event. Based in Cumbria, in the northwest of England, a five-day programme was designed. One day-long duration exercise that the team performed was a 'chasm crossing' task. The participants' collective goal was to transfer the

Case Study cont'd

two halves of the programme membership from opposite sides of a ravine (30 metres wide and 30 metres deep) to the other by means of a transfer mechanism (ropes and pulleys) designed and constructed by the team. A day-long exercise ensued, illustrating dramatically the link between planning and implementation and the importance of effective execution.

During the indoor planning phase of the exercise, several managers expressed their anxiety about 'stepping off' one side of the ravine, suspended by a system of ropes. One individual confided in the group that he was 'petrified and probably unable to complete the exercise'. Rob, a senior IT manager, described his concern that he might let down the whole team. Clearly, as successful task completion required the whole programme membership to cross the ravine using the system, anybody unprepared to cross would jeopardise the whole project. The open expression of fear released several others to describe their various levels of anxiety. For the group, the issue of addressing some participants' fears became an important part of the initial planning phases.

As sub-teams were allocated to various technical system design tasks, Rob and several colleagues busied themselves with the suspension system by which participants would be harnessed and suspended from the rope/pulley system. They simulated the 'stepping off' experience by inviting participants to step off a chair, their bodies being supported by ropes attached to beams in the ceiling.

The planned process for crossing was simulated by Rob's team and presented to the whole team. Rob went first, stepping off the chair, suspended by the rope system. Whilst nervous, he demonstrated the critical stepping off successfully to rapturous applause from his colleagues. In hindsight, the group described the multiple benefits of this act. It addressed and overcame Rob's fear and those of some of his anxious colleagues, and also revealed the technical quality of the system. In addition, it helped to teach the value of 'modelling' during the planning phase. Rehearsing, where possible, overcoming the practical challenges to be encountered 'in the field' provided useful insight and built confidence. It also encouraged participants to visualise the whole operation in advance.

Case Study cont'd

When the system was constructed in the field, Rob crossed first, inspiring the whole team to successfully complete the entire exercise. In review, Rob led the discussion about the metaphor the chasm provided. He described the bank as entering a period of business change never previously encountered, a period of huge uncertainty. For Rob and many colleagues, this was paralleled by stepping off the chasm, trusting the system constructed by his colleagues (and tested by safety experts). It reflected the impact of excellent planning and execution, the importance of moving swiftly from analysis to action.

He also noted the similarity between the ravine profile and the transition curve, and how moving from analysis to action (experimentation), 3 to 5 on the curve, required the act of 'stepping into the unknown'. Rob's new role in the bank involved responsibility for IT-led change. He connected his learning from the experiential outdoor event to work in his closing comments on the exercise review:

> This morning we were presented with an impossible task as I saw it. This afternoon we have successfully achieved the impossible. Going back to the challenge of significant change in the bank now holds no fears for me.

Experiential learning is about providing relevant opportunities for people to learn through action. It is about setting the learners challenges, which will allow them to confront assumptions and the usual patterns of thoughts and behaviours and experiment with and develop new behaviours, skills and competencies. In the words of a recent participant:

> the experiential team building programme made me very aware of how I was perceived by others, and reinforced areas of personal development that I already knew about … It allowed me to focus closely on those areas that needed me to take action. I found it a profound experience, one that we still talk about today [eight months after the event]. Mark Wingrove, Director of Engineering, 3COM

Unlike the more passive mode required by traditional classroom or conference learning environments, participants' involvement in experiential learning is active.

Participants can use the experience to assess their needs by receiving constructive feedback on the impact of their style and behaviours and identifying areas for improvement based on performance. They can practise new competencies and personal styles and this time receive immediate feedback on the impact of the new styles and the way they are used. Teams can surface and practise with visible demonstrations of the behaviours they believe should be present if they are to mature to become an effective team.

Following experiential learning, participants are often much more aware of their strengths and weaknesses, the team dynamic and how it changes and how others see them and are better equipped to give and receive feedback ensuring sustained learning. Like most potentially useful tools, it is the manner of its application that determines the quality of outcome.

Pre-experiential Learning: Aims, Objectives and Key Outcomes

Experiential learning can simultaneously engage the head and touch the heart in a way that other training interventions cannot, but it can be difficult for people to transfer learning to the workplace or measure the results. Clarity of aims and outcomes for delegates and providers of courses is crucial in ensuring that this happens.

In the case of personal development, individuals can be encouraged to share their perceived areas of strength and development as well as their own perception of their personal style. This information, which is derived from many different sources (such as feedback from boss or peers, the result of a 360° intervention, some other form of assessment or previous relationships), can be shared with other participants as soon as possible to improve the alignment of others' perception with that of our own. Encouraging individuals to share this personal knowledge with others quickly establishes a common agreement on mutual trust and confidentiality and begins the process of developing the group into a support and challenge unit for the individuals. However, it is difficult to prescribe levels of openness and disclosure. Generally, the greater the investment in sharing self-perception as well as willingness to receive feedback for self and give feedback to others, the more an individual will receive in terms of development benefit.

It is often useful to provide participants with some probing and thought-provoking questions in advance of the experience so that they come prepared and with an understanding of the development process. Preparatory questions may include the following:

- What strengths do you bring to a team?
- What do you need most from other team members?
- How would you describe your personal working style?
- What changes would you make to this style if you could?

Further exploration can be encouraged by inviting participants to consider their style by reflection on the questions below:

- How do you demonstrate your commitment to the job to other people?
- How important is it to your job that you are well organised?
- How good are you at seeing the other person's point of view?
- How do you handle conflict?
- How do you convince others of your point of view?
- How well do you manage yourself, your energy and the pressures of your job?
- How well do you deal with information and solve problems?
- How well do you make decisions?
- How do your work colleagues describe your style?

Challenging individuals to explore their style and its impact on others is crucial in ensuring a quality learning experience for them.

Building the Senior Team

Team building and off-site development workshops for executives have become commonplace in organisations today. For many clients, organising senior managers to meet off-site to achieve a collective goal unconnected with business tasks is a significant achievement in itself.

In order to ensure the correct design for team building, an understanding of the way groups develop is valuable. There has been much research conducted into the processes that occur within groups. One of the conclusions, as defined by B.W. Tuckman (1965), is that any group or team as it develops towards an effective, productive and healthy team will pass through various stages (see Figure 5.1). Each of these stages and the relevant individual behaviours are predictable and apparent. A knowledge of these stages and the relevant behaviours can assist greatly in ensuring a clear understanding of the needs of the team. By understanding this, one can ask the right questions to discover at what stage the team is and what needs to be done to progress its development.

The four stages of development as defined by Tuckman (1965) are:

1. Forming
2. Storming
3. Norming
4. Performing.

Each of these stages is unique and is characterised by its own set of distinctive behaviours and issues for the team and the leader. Most people experienced in the field of team building or leading teams will subscribe to this theory. In order for a team to become a performing team, working effectively together and creating an environment which encourages loyalty

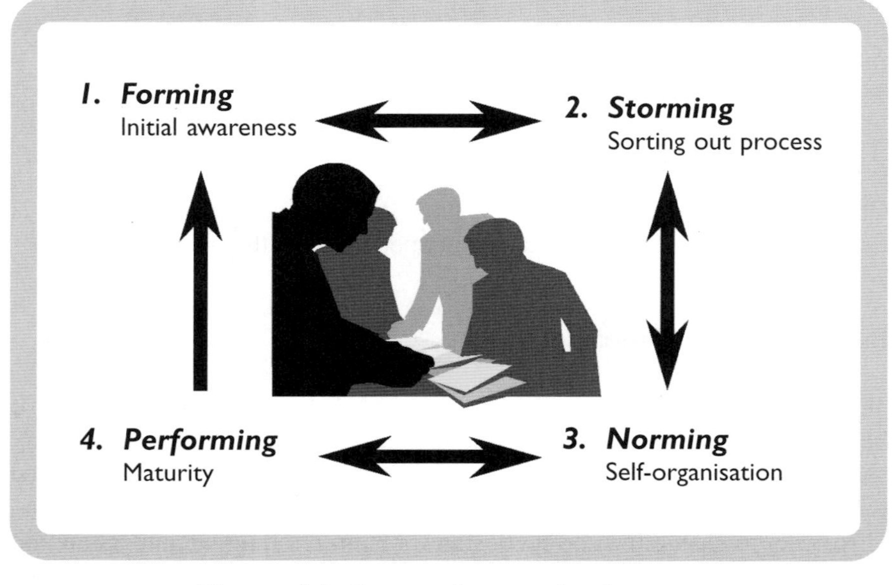

Figure 4.1 Stages of group development
Source: Tuckman 1965

and quality interpersonal relationships, they need to travel the journey through the other stages.

If we equate this model to one of personal life growth and development, we see that

Forming = childhood
Storming = adolescence
Norming = early adulthood
Performing = maturity.

These stages are necessary steps without shortcuts. Moving from childhood to maturity without the experience and learning of adolescence and early adulthood would not be realistic. Understanding the relevant behaviours, issues and needs of each stage greatly assists in the planning and design of a suitable intervention with a team.

In parallel with one-to-one coaching, identifying the starting point of those to be coached is key. In the case of teams, agreeing at which stage in the cycle of development the team finds itself is a useful starting point for any development activity.

Moving the Team through the Stages

CASE STUDY

Paul was the team leader of a management team brought together to lead a new, large and complicated project team. The project team's task was to ensure the whole company, a major independent clearing house, was compliant and able to deal with the potential problems brought on by the arrival of the millennium and address any potential challenges of Y2K.

Some years earlier, Paul had been a member of another senior team and as part of their team and personal development went on an outdoor development programme. This previous team had worked well together over a period of time, had various team-building sessions and, at the time of the outdoor event, were behaving in a way which indicated they were maturing as a team. The event was designed to allow the delegates to get to know each other at a level not easy to achieve during the normal working

Case Study cont'd

situation. The event helped the team to build strong relationships with each other and create an environment within the team, which was conducive to trust and openness. They learnt how to co-coach each other and became very comfortable and accepting of each other's individuality. They had four days of intense experiences and reviews and returned to work with a shared memorable, uplifting and enjoyable learning experience. This they utilised at work and went on to be a very effective team, which all the members were sad to leave.

Paul still remembered this team with fondness and now wanted to replicate that experience with his new team. It soon became obvious by questioning Paul and other team members that this team, although having been working together for some time, was demonstrating behaviours that were indicative of being at an earlier stage of the development towards a mature team. Questions such as those below soon showed that the members of the team were in various stages of forming and storming.

What is the purpose of this team? Why does this group of people have to work as a team? What do they have to achieve, why and in what time-frame? Are the team members aware of roles and responsibilities? Does the team know the answer to these questions? How long has the team been together? How long will they remain a team? What is the make-up of the team? How well is the team working together at present and what are the key areas for improvement? Are there any interpersonal areas of concern within the team and how does the team deal with them?

There was little or no common understanding of the primary purpose of the team, people were being polite for fear of upsetting each other and this in turn led to simple ideas and little creativity. Due to the atmosphere in the team, little or no disclosure on a personal level was going on and feedback was used very crudely, if at all. Individuals were expressing strong views, challenging others, not listening and exhibiting high levels of reacting and defending situations. There was little team identity and some of the members, due to the prevalent behaviours, were easier with working on their own or in preferred cliques and found many reasons to avoid team meetings.

Case Study cont'd

Having assessed the above through questioning Paul and other team members, it became obvious that what was required was not the intensity of the outdoor programme that Paul had been on earlier, but a more focused, less physically and emotionally stretching event concentrating on surfacing, exploring and agreeing a set of team behaviours to accelerate the team to maturity and practice in the processes for effective teamwork.

After discussions with Paul and other members of the team, it was decided to design a process which would allow the members to gain clarity on the purpose of the team, be confident in their role in the execution of that purpose and share their own experiences of teamworking. In addition, they needed to agree on a set of appropriate behaviours enabling the team and individuals to develop further.

In order to do this, a three-day, residential, 'near-doors' workshop was designed including indoor and near-doors exercises allowing the team and individuals to focus on and practise the agreed behaviours. The near-doors option provided the time and opportunities for the team to discuss its issues and ways forward.

Following the event, the teamworking improved immediately and considerably, with more collaboration evident. A clear sense of team identity emerged. There was an improved active participation by all and a willingness to work with each other, not only on the work projects but also on each other's development plans.

In order to ensure that the right provision can be made, it is most valuable to talk to as many 'stakeholders' as possible prior to any intervention. As has been mentioned in an earlier chapter, there are often multiple sponsors of development assignments. Collecting information from as many of these sources as possible is beneficial. The leader of a team will see the situation and issues for their team from their eyes and the team members may perceive these differently. In order to ensure the provision of an appropriate experience for a team, it is necessary to gain information from multiple sources. By talking to team members, the designer of the learning experience gains a first-hand account of how effective the team sees itself, the key issues for the team or individuals, how they perceive their leadership, what the workplace is like and what they think needs to be surfaced during their action learning event.

The provider of the experiential learning experience should also strive to discover as much as possible regarding the structure of the organisation, its culture and core business processes. Once the design of the event has been shaped by the information gained and agreed on with the sponsors, it is then important to ensure that delegates of the programme are clear about programme goals, process and potential outcomes. A careful balance must be struck between reducing uncertainty (a necessary ingredient in a change management programme) and providing adequate clarity to help participants to understand the rationale for the event.

The Experiential Learning Event

Whatever the preferred medium chosen, the duration of the event or the specific aims and objectives, there are some key elements of best practice. In our opinion these are:

- An understanding of the way people learn
- The effective learning environment
- The quality of facilitation
- Building an implementable action plan.

An Understanding of the Way People Learn from Experience

The key element of experiential learning is the review of performance. The learning comes from taking the time to examine mistakes and gaining reassurance from successes. All experiential learning, if it is to be a learning experience rather than a pleasant distraction from the norm, is based on the learning cycle.

The learning cycle, based on the work by Kolb et al. (1971), provides us with a model for experiential learning which starts with the experience and includes stages of reflection, discussion, analysis and evaluation of the experience. It shows us that we do not learn from experiences unless we take the time to understand what went well or not – why and how the experience could have been enhanced by different behaviours and actions, exploring the impact on the way we do things and planning for improvement. This learning cycle links reflection with action in order to enhance

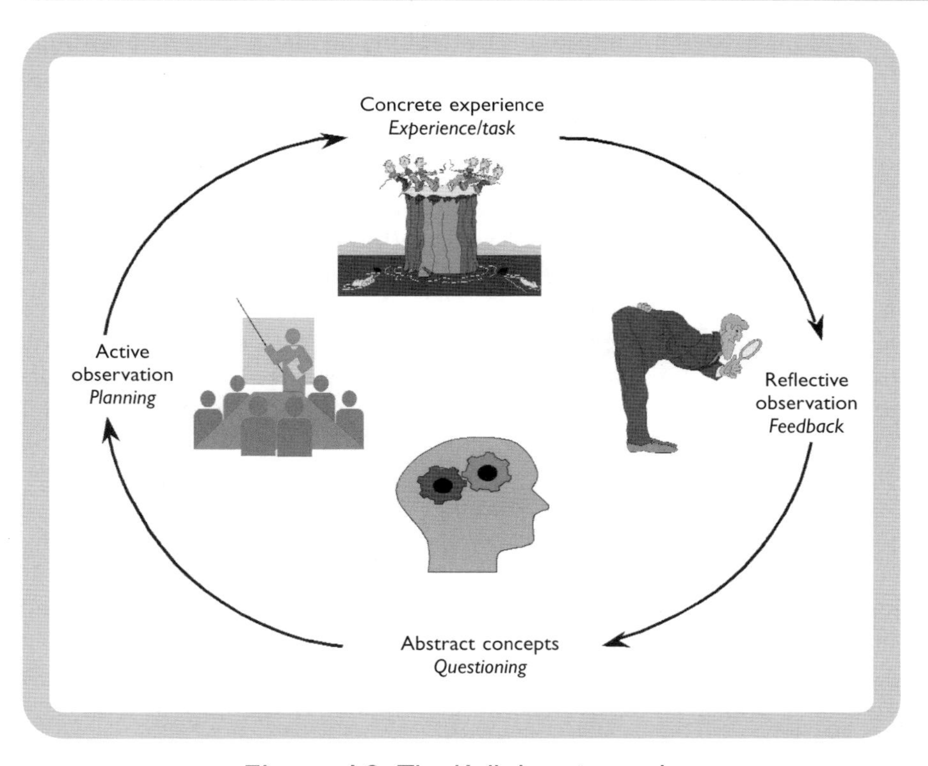

Figure 4.2 The Kolb learning cycle

Adapted from Kolb et al. 1971 for experiential learning programmes

learning from experience. Each stage in the learning cycle is now discussed in turn.

Stage 1: Concrete experience/action – here an individual or team is set a task to plan and complete. This task should be designed to provide the relevant learning opportunity. For example, if it is a team in the early stages of development, a task which highlights the necessary processes and behaviours for a team at this stage should be used. This task should be one which requires a collective understanding of the objectives, planning, role allocation including leadership, the team's capability through an awareness of team members' strengths and areas for improvement, and should be challenging for the team to complete.

Stage 2: Reflective observation/review – the most important part of the process from a learning perspective. This is the stage of the process where the participants in the exercise are encouraged to share their perceptions of the experience or task from a team perspective: What did we do well and what do we need to improve? Reflecting on the experience through feedback leads to making sense of that experience in a new way, leading to deeper understanding.

Stage 3: Abstract concepts/knowledge and understanding – this stage allows the participants to explore and understand further the result of behaviours and processes used in the experience, and to question ways that they, collectively or individually, could perform better in similar situations in the future. After reflection, the participants need to be able to make sense of the learning in their own way, to be very clear on how the learning can be used effectively in the future and what that will mean with regard to changed behaviour and attitudes. This stage allows the learners to form or reform their understanding of a situation and their impact on it as a result of the experience. It is comparable to stage 6 in the transition curve, 'search for meaning'.

Stage 4: Active observation/planning – having reflected on performance feedback, the participants may now consider their personal and leadership style and its impact. They commonly build more confidence in their strengths and become more aware of their areas for development and improvement. They form new ideas and new ways of seeing themselves in similar situations. This stage is where participants begin to hypothesise about how things could be done differently and their ability to produce a better outcome by behaving differently.

The cycle is complete when the participants implement their plan. For any experiential learning process to be effective, those involved need to regularly revisit the learning cycle.

People learn differently and to assist their learning an understanding of these differences is important. They start at different points in the cycle. Some have a preference when it comes to problem-solving of just doing it, being very hands-on and needing to engage immediately with the task. These people approach the cycle from the top as shown: do, review, learn and redo. Others would prefer to approach a task or problem to be solved by understanding more about the situation, stepping back and asking questions such as why? and what? They prefer to consider the options, make a plan for action, act, review, replan and do again.

There are those who need to move to action quickly and those that prefer a more considered approach. Experience has shown that both need each other when solving problems in teams or groups. There are benefits and constraints to both approaches. For participants to be made aware of this early on in experiential learning accelerates their understanding of the way people learn.

Effective Learning Environment

Experiential learning is about action – achieving tasks and then critically reviewing performance and exploring routes for improvement. At work, the primary focus for many, especially executives, is task achievement. A vital element of the learning cycle that all effective experiential learning depends on is the review of performance. The review process itself is key to stimulating the curiosity of participants and is dependent upon giving and receiving constructive feedback. The quality of any experiential learning intervention is dependent on the quality of the feedback shared between the participants. As described earlier, a valuable skill for coaches is the ability to give and receive feedback. Whilst a coach will always deviate from the textbook approach to feedback, the checklist below is a useful place to start:

1. *It is descriptive rather than evaluative* – describing one's own reaction leaves the individual free to use it or not, as appropriate. Avoiding evaluative language reduces the need for the other individual to react defensively.
2. *It is specific rather than general* – to be told that one is 'domineering' will probably not be as useful as to be told: 'Just now, when we were deciding the issue, you did not listen to what others said. I felt forced to accept your arguments or face attack from you.'
3. *It takes into account the needs of both the receiver and the giver of feedback* – feedback can be destructive when it serves only our needs and fails to consider the needs of the person on the receiving end.
4. *It is directed towards behaviour that the receiver can control* – frustration is increased when a person is reminded of some shortcoming over which she or he has no control.
5. *It is solicited rather than imposed* – feedback is most useful when the receiver has formulated the kind of question that the observer can answer.
6. *It is well timed* – in general, feedback is most useful at the earliest opportunity after the given behaviour (depending, of course, on the person's readiness to hear it, on support available from others and so on).

7. *It is checked to ensure clear communication* – one way of doing this is to have the receiver try to rephrase the feedback to see if it corresponds to what the sender was trying to convey.
8. *When feedback is given in a group, both giver and receiver have an opportunity to check with others in the group on the accuracy of the feedback* – is this one's person impression or an impression shared by others?

These eight characteristics of helpful feedback are taken from an unpublished handout from the NTL Institute for Applied Behavioural Sciences. See also Boyatzis and Kolb (1969) and Kolb et al. (1971) for research comparing the impact of different kinds of feedback.

Feedback, then, is a way of giving help; it is a development support process for people who want to learn how well their behaviour matches their intentions and their goals and it is crucial in ensuring learning from the process. Giving and receiving feedback is never easy or comfortable for most people, especially those with little or no experience of using it before. For some, it is more fearful than most adventurous activities that they may encounter on an outdoor event. The environment for effective learning supports safe practice opportunities, encourages openness, builds trust and mutual respect between participants and between them and the facilitator(s), and, by encouraging openness, is 'feedback-rich'.

Setting the scene, ensuring a clear understanding of the process, clarifying the parameters and agreeing with the participants on the relevant ground rules at the very start of the process is essential for the provision of a quality experiential learning experience. This stage of the proceedings should involve participants fully, canvassing their expectations for the process and desired outcomes for themselves and others.

The Quality of Facilitation

Probably the key component in ensuring successful exploitation of experiential learning and development is the quality of facilitation used to review performance. Facilitation is about managing the feedback review process and stimulating feedback. The journey towards self-awareness, personal and team development is never an easy or comfortable one.

Expert facilitation or 'team coaching' is key in the early stages of an experiential event. Setting the standards, modelling the feedback skills and leading a feedback and review process all set the stage for subsequent participant practice. As participants become more aware of the skills, competencies and processes modelled by an experienced facilitator, they usually become ambitious to practise them themselves and they can be encouraged to practise in order to integrate them into their own skill set. Most organisations today encourage teamworking, empowerment, cooperation and lifelong learning and development in order to ensure a developing workforce able and willing to accept change. The art of good facilitation is part of a necessary competency set in the contemporary business world.

What is the role of the facilitator?

The primary role of the facilitator is to enable the group to be able to maximise their learning from the experience through the process of review and feedback; to encourage individuals to become committed to decisions and actions thereby encouraging ownership.

The facilitator can encourage individuals to relax, immerse themselves in the event and enjoy self-disclosure in a non-threatening environment. This sharing of important facts and feelings by individuals through the process, seen by some as risky, of both giving and receiving feedback needs careful and sensitive monitoring and management. Participants may feel vulnerable in disclosure of areas for development and the role of the facilitator is to be vigilant and encouraging, so that the event is conducted in a supportive and positive rather than a divisive and negative atmosphere.

The facilitator needs to have a number of specific qualities in that he/she must be able to:

- *Help* in the process of learning by the active encouragement of discussion and actions leading to changes in behaviour
- *Create* a constructive learning environment quickly with the group
- *Work* to develop trust and acceptance of views, ideas and suggestions

- *Encourage* disclosure of both facts and feelings – the latter being more powerful but carrying some risk
- *Demonstrate* his/her nature as a caring critic who, nevertheless, is free from preconceptions
- *Focus* attention upon, and not be deflected from, agreed goals and objectives.

From the above, it is apparent that different skills are required at different phases in facilitation. Generally, the basic skills and behaviours necessary for effective facilitation are:

- *Sensitivity* – the capacity to put yourself in the other person's position, to create a relationship of trust
- *Good active listening skills* – listening for meaning beyond the literal, thereby being effective as an observer of others' behaviour
- *The ability to give and receive critical, constructive feedback honestly and directly* – the ability to enter difficult areas without using complex or inappropriate jargon and language
- *Commitment* – to sustain energy and enthusiasm when things go wrong. Supporting and motivating skills
- *The ability to analyse and interpret feedback* – the capacity to design and agree development action steps with participants. Constantly seeking the practice of new behaviours and encouraging further discussion regarding the facts and feelings of this new behaviour
- *Ability to build rapport* – to put other people at ease by adopting a friendly, supportive and helpful manner
- *Risk taking* – the willingness to take personal risks in exploring the group's behaviour, in developing self-awareness within the delegates and by asking those awkward questions that the group clearly do not want to ask of themselves
- *Responsibility* – the facilitator must be aware of, and take responsibility for, the powerful role that he or she has during the learning process. The facilitator must be constantly vigilant so as not to

undermine the confidence and belief that the group should have in him/her

- *Understanding* – quick to understand and interpret the dynamics of the group and control and steer it in order to achieve the desired outcomes
- *Knowledge* – acquire a broad understanding of the company context (its business processes, structure, systems, internal politics) and the demands of the participants' current role
- *Objectivity* – to be able to maintain objectivity and purpose in the face of cynicism and intransigence, but to do so without risking alienation.

To ensure a meaningful, enjoyable and thought-provoking experience, any good experiential learning session should include exercises, tasks or activities which have been carefully designed to make them stimulating but sufficiently analogous to work situations as to lay bare both individual and team processes.

Often, much time is spent in trying to design tasks that recreate situations similar to those occurring at work: competition versus collaboration, team dynamics and team processes, motivation, trust and communication to mention but a few. In many cases, more effort goes into providing the stimulus than the facilitation of the experience and the learning derived from it. As a colleague of mine, who had spent many years working in this field and has been an ongoing mentor and guide for me for many years, once said:

> Don't get too worried about the detail of exercises. Place a group of people in an open space, give them a ball of string and ask them to do something with it. A good facilitator will be able to observe the behaviours and assist the group and individuals with learning from the experience.

To ensure a meaningful, enjoyable, interesting and memorable experience, it is important that the challenges presented to the participants are enjoyable, challenging, achievable and provocative. Creating an atmosphere through the exercises that are provided in a non-work environment allows work-related feedback, which can enable teams and individuals to link their personal and private lives into the corporate context. This in turn helps people to transfer and implement their learning more effectively. Choosing exercises and tasks that engage the heart as well as the mind ensures a deeper and more meaningful understanding of the learning. The element that brings all these together to provide a worthwhile and constructive learning experience is the quality of the facilitation and the feedback stimulated by that role.

In Chapter 2, we explored the role of coaching during the various stages of the transition curve; experiential learning, supported by quality facilitation and feedback, is an effective tool for assisting and accelerating this journey.

Development Action Planning

For any learning experience to have any meaningful and valuable outcome, it is necessary to be able to identify and agree the key learning points, be clear of the changes necessary for improvement, understand how to transfer the learning back to the workplace and be able to sustain the learning over a period of time by the measurement of successes and failures. This first part of the process is referred to as the 'development action plan'.

Action planning is a vital part of the experiential learning process and one that allows individuals or teams the time and means to turn the thoughts and feelings generated over the course of the intervention into workable objectives. People have an opportunity to picture how the learning and changes required for improvement can be utilised back in the workplace. The action planning allows participants to clarify the key points and set up a plan for achieving them. The participants need to identify the actions and behavioural changes required to ensure that the learning and development is sustainable. They need to explore the potential obstructions and become aware of the implications of doing things differently in order to assess the viability and effect of their intentions.

Independent of the process of formulation, in order to ensure successful implementation and sustainability of learning, the following guidelines may be considered. A good plan should be:

- *Specific* – what exactly is going to be changed, done differently or implemented? In what circumstances, with whom and when?
- *Measurable* – how will it be apparent that progress is being made, and what will change as a result of moving forward in this area? How will it be quantified or measured? How will they know when they are successful?

- *Achievable* – is the change described achievable? If this is doubtful, what is likely to get in the way and what can be done to improve the chances of success?
- *Relevant* – how is the change going to fit in with the overall culture and direction of the organisation? Will it be accepted and recognised?
- *Time-related* – how long will it take for the plan to be successfully achieved? How often will progress towards this end be monitored? When should the measures of success described be used to review progress?
- *Supported* – where and from who is support available to achieve this? What information will they require? What is the nature of this support? How will the support be maintained over the duration of the plan?

Post-experiential Learning

Development is a journey not a destination

In talking to past participants of experiential learning, one of the most common complaints heard is that of post-event disappointment – disappointment in their own attempts at making their action plan real, disappointment in the reaction of others back in the workplace, disappointment in the lack of meaningful follow-up or confusion over what to do next. It is important when deciding whether to use experiential learning as a tool to consider the whole process. The impact of re-entry, as many refer to the return to work after an effective session, must be considered throughout the process and be a planned part of it. Questions such as:

- If participants are to return with a desire to behave differently, what mechanisms/resources are needed to support such changes?
- What are the implications of people's changed behaviours upon existing systems and processes within the organisation?
- What areas need to change to support and enable the application of initiatives determined during the process?
- How do we create the right environment for change and how do we lead/coach our people in the future?

Doing things differently is challenging. Very few of us will be competent or comfortable with using new behaviours for the first time. Individuals may be committed to a well-thought-out action plan, but the execution of those good intentions is much harder. Back at the workplace, opportunities need to be created for people to challenge assumptions and experiment with improved ways of working. Like learning any new sport or skill, such as golf or drawing, we need to practise to improve performance. The active searching out and provision of practice opportunities will help to ensure that the process does not become a pleasant but distant memory.

The learning cycle is as pertinent in the post-event phase as it is during it. Participants must be encouraged to adopt the procedure of regularly reviewing their performance, exploring what went well and why and what could have been improved and how, celebrating successes and learning from heroic failures.

Action Learning in Context

Experiential learning is a versatile tool, which can be utilised in variety of learning and development mediums. In considering whether experiential learning takes place indoors, outdoors or 'near doors', there are many practical factors to acknowledge. The size of the group will influence greatly the choice of experiential tasks and environments. In attempting to create the right environment to encourage quality feedback, large groups inevitably need to be broken down into smaller units and this requires more facilitators and space.

Consideration needs to be given to what processes the organisation has in place for supporting post-programme development initiatives. Will there be ongoing support for teams and individuals back at the workplace? Are the managers within the organisation willing and competent to provide coaching? How well does the organisation understand and subscribe to the development initiative?

The Indoors

Experiential learning can enhance any training and development session. At the simplest level, the use of tasks, games and creative activities can enliven any passive learning environment, providing opportunities for delegates to act out and role play the lessons taught. For example, a session designed to enable a team to discuss the relevant behaviours and processes required to enhance their teamworking can be enriched by the provision of some practice opportunities. The process of accelerating a group into a performing team is primarily about getting the members to surface, explore, agree and adopt the necessary behaviours and processes required to ensure effective teamworking. Providing exercises that enable the team or sub-teams to undertake and review performance against their agreed criteria for effective teamwork will generally assist in this process.

An important part of the coaching process is action. This stage allows participants to try new ways of working that are consistent with the agreed development goals. This provision of practice and development opportunities is vital if learners are to progress from an awareness of the need for change to integrating the new practices into their personal repertoire. There are a variety of experiential learning possibilities at work. The coachee and other sponsors should be encouraged to identify suitable practice possibilities such as assignments, work-based projects, roles and relationships, which will stretch the coachee and encourage use of new skills.

Another effective experiential tool for development within organisations is the action learning project (ALP). This is a management development tool, which has been used very successfully in many organisations (GE, Boeing, Ford). Action learning projects work by providing a team with a current, relevant and important business issue. The issue needs to be addressed in the short term with measurable outcomes and completed in parallel with existing work roles. The project teams are typically cross-functional, multidisciplinary and non-expert in the area of the issue.

Action learning projects are used to promote change in organisations. They benefit the participants by providing those necessary opportunities for the practice of new skills and behaviours and the learning from the delivery and implementation of the project outcomes. Individuals learn from each other by working on real problems and reflecting on their experiences and performance. They also gain from the experience of working in other areas that would not normally be available to them. A good example of how a business can benefit is illustrated in the following case.

To complement the learning and development stimulated by a development programme, a group of managers from a large multinational manufacturing company were presented with an action learning project. The task was to try and solve a problem which one of the plants was having with a paint process used on one of their products. This problem had been around for many years and much research and academic study had been put into it, with no successful outcome. The ALP team solved the problem in six months, saving the company an estimated $2.5 million. The senior manager acting as sponsor for this project was delighted that this group of non-specialists had managed to find 'a window of creativity' and come up with a viable solution.

Outdoors

Outdoor development can employ such traditional outdoor activities as rock climbing, abseiling, gorge crossing, raft building, orienteering, kayaking and mountaineering. These activities can be used as distinct individual or team exercises to focus on specific skills such as motivation, communication and trust, or combined to create longer exercises to focus on commitment, teamworking, leadership and followership. The outdoors is a challenging environment for the office-based executive. It has often been described as a powerful medium for personal development:

> I felt that by putting us in 'real life' situations as opposed to classroom simulations, concepts such as direction, leadership, decision making and just plain listening became much more easily understood.
>
> *Cranfield Executive MBA student*

For many, learning needs to be interesting and engaging in order to have a memorable and sustainable impact. To ensure clarity and integration of learning back to work, the experiential events should be designed to include the following five stages:

1. Task briefing/information input
2. Planning/design and problem-solving phase
3. Task/activity performance

4. Review of task and process. Feedback to individuals concerning their behaviour
5. Evaluation of outcomes.

The 'Near Doors'

This experiential learning medium is one that uses shorter cycle exercises, either in isolation or combined for a longer experience. The exercises and tasks used are designed to focus on specific skills and competencies such as teamworking, leadership, assessing potential or as a catalyst for a group to surface and agree on the necessary behaviours to ensure they perform as an effective team at work. The term 'near doors' comes from the fact that these team dynamic exercises are usually run in or around a hotel, conference centre or even at the place of work.

The possible range of these exercises is as broad as the imagination of the designer. They are usually short and are particularly useful in not only exploring behaviours but also the processes required for effective teamwork, such as planning, team roles, clarity of objectives, communications and so on. Because of the nature of the tasks, the environment and materials, it is easy to ensure that suitable tasks are designed to challenge teams and individuals in specific ways.

The 'near-doors' development experience is well proven in testing and evaluating team performance and leading to the formulation of team and personal action plans. New teams often use these types of events in order to formulate a team charter, that is, a collectively agreed, acceptable way of doing things together, which will enhance working practices. The 'near-doors' option is less threatening to some delegates and is easy to maintain focus on the issues pertinent to a team's needs at work. It requires less time than the outdoors and does not require the necessary specialist equipment, services and safety cover that the outdoors requires.

The example below illustrates how the outdoors and the 'near doors' can be effectively combined to produce a remarkable learning experience. The combination allows the delegates to further develop their team and personal skills in a challenging and empathic environment. The intensity of the shared experience can act as a powerful bonding agent for the team and often creates sustainable support and challenge groups for ongoing personal development.

'Near-doors' exercises provide opportunities for the participants to focus on particular issues, skills, processes or behaviours. They are usually short, easy to control and manage and provide well-tried and tested situations to which most of the delegates can relate.

The outdoor activities, if managed well, can provide the stimulus required to encourage participants to think and consider aspects of their behaviour they may not normally be encouraged to explore.

The experiential learning process shown here was a model which was used for three years working with many different teams from a large, international manufacturing company producing networking equipment and supplies. It was first used with the senior team to improve their teamworking and stimulate a culture of feedback within the organisation. A similar model was then used to cascade the experience throughout the management population in the company. This process helped to establish a common teamworking culture throughout the business and an environment for ongoing development.

These experiential learning opportunities ensured that every individual in the company who participated in the events had a shared experience with regards to location, activities and process and could return to work and share this with others who could then empathise with their experience and support their development goals.

Case Study

Use of Learning Logs and Home Teams

Day 1

The events were usually five days' duration. A member of the senior management team, who would emphasise the relevance of this process to the success of the business strategy, opened the events. Many of the delegates were from a very technical background and often arrived at the event with a great deal of scepticism. One such senior manager, opening an event, who himself had arrived on an earlier course with similar feelings of cynicism and had a positive learning experience, explained the potential outcomes of the course:

> Our organisation has grown as a result on our hard skills, our engineering abilities. Now the culture needs to change as we have grown so quickly. The hard

CASE STUDY cont'd

> skills are the technical skills and the soft skills are the way we work together and interact with each other. I have learned that for us the hard skills are easy and the soft skills are hard. We need to focus on that challenge now.
>
> *(Steve Carter, VP Engineering, 3Com)*

The learning process was designed to help the individual participants build an enduring personal development action plan. Based on the idea that we can all get better by doing some things differently, a 'learning log' was prepared by each delegate to help them build their development action plan.

A useful development tool for delegates, the log helped to create a:

- Strong personal commitment to the achievement of self-defined goals
- Clear and attractive vision of the future
- Process that supported and maintained the development initiatives taken post-programme (such processes would include resources and support from key individuals at work).

The learning logs comprised three sections: *section 1* allowed the delegates to record information derived from the various sessions during the module. In addition, it provided a place to capture feedback from other people, both at work and during the module. *Section 2* takes the information from section 1 and invites the delegate to interpret its meaning and importance. The outcome was an identification of personal strengths and development needs. *Section 3* provided a process for determining the actions, processes, resources and the timetable necessary to achieve their defined development goals. Figure 4.3 illustrates the development planning process. Each delegate was also part of a small group of no more than five that would be their co-coaching team. Time was allocated during the programme for these teams to get together with the purpose of providing a small group environment for support and challenge during the event. These teams often built close relationships and many continued well beyond the conclusion of the programme.

CASE STUDY cont'd

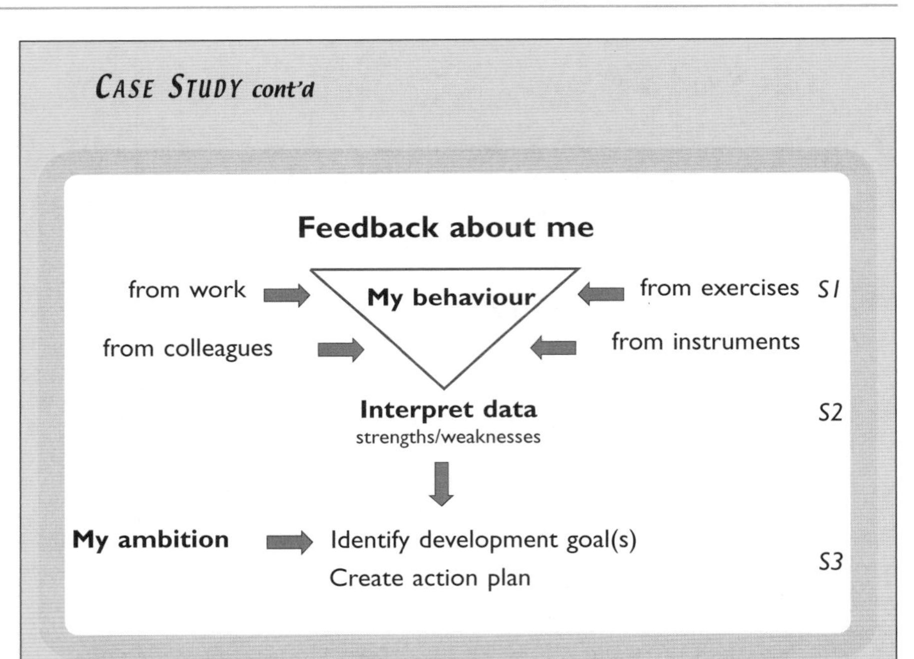

Figure 4.3 Development planning process: PDP log

Source: © ECC 1996

Having been issued with their learning logs and gathered in their home teams, a short icebreaker exercise was used to allow the delegates to work together and discuss and agree on the ground rules for their team meetings. This was followed by a session, usually at this stage observed and facilitated by an experienced facilitator, where individuals shared their findings and feelings from the Myers–Briggs type indicator and began the process of surfacing their development needs.

Day 2

The second day usually began with a detailed explanation and exploration of the transition curve (see Chapter 2). Delegates were encouraged to consider their position with regard to their development on the curve and the perceived personal and organisational blocks and bridges to moving on. The rest of the day the group was presented with a task which would require them to work very well together to successfully

Case Study cont'd

achieve a complicated project set them. The project involved creativity, marketing, design, production of a finished product and delivery to a tight timescale – the sort of project most people encounter regularly at work.

This first full day was based and operated in and around the hotel and its grounds. The delegates were provided with a variety of 'near-doors' tasks and exercises giving everyone the opportunity to work in different teams and get feedback on their personal and team skills and areas for improvement. The exercises were short and focused to allow the delegates ample opportunities to practise different competencies such as leadership, communication, planning, motivation and many more. As best practice dictates, quality reviews were an integral part of the process and the delegates soon got proficient in using feedback constructively to fast-track the learning for each other.

This day presented the delegates with opportunities for exploring their knowledge of teams and what makes teams work more effectively together, their competence in leading and managing teams and their personal strengths and areas for development. The day helped to encourage a feedback-rich, coaching culture, enabling the delegates to further their developmental learning. The final part of the day was allocated to home team time, usually by now being self-facilitated.

Day 3

This day consisted of a whole day of challenging outdoor exercise. The exercise we used was a gorge crossing. This required the delegates, after a thorough briefing on equipment, constraints and safety issues, to plan, design and build their own Tyrolean Traverse enabling all members of the team to cross the gorge. A Tyrolean Traverse is a set-up of ropes by which people can be pulled across a wide open space, approximately 45 metres across and 24 metres down – quite a task to undertake and achieve and requiring involvement and motivation by all.

The emphasis of this day was to provide further safe practice of team and personal development plans. The nature of the task and its environ-

CASE STUDY cont'd

ment recreates many of the more profound situations and tensions encountered during the working day. Issues of motivation, risk taking, openness, trust and challenge are in plentiful supply during this day. The day generally encouraged delegates to raise their game and explore further in order to understand the impact of their personal style upon individuals' and the team's effectiveness.

Once the task had been completed, successfully or not, there would be a full team review back at the hotel. This review would inevitably be a long and deep exploration of each individual's performance and the impact of their personal style. The quality of feedback now was generally very high and this review was often a turning point for people. Home team time was again allocated prior to dinner and the enjoyment of tales of brave and bold daring deeds.

Day 4

By now most of the delegates would have received a substantial amount of data about themselves from instruments used, feedback from colleagues and staff, and learning from the various exercises and experiences. The emphasis of this day was to allow the delegates the time and opportunity to clarify and finalise their personal development plan. The day would begin with a period of personal reflection, some quality time for the delegates to spend on their own, focusing on their personal development plan. A time to find some quiet space, fill in the relevant sections of the learning log, reflect on the experiences and feedback received and try to begin building a sustainable and achievable action plan. This was time for the delegates to consider areas that might require further clarification and who they may wish to speak to in more detail during the day.

To enable these conversations to happen, but to provide a relaxed and easy environment to have them in after the personal reflection, the delegates were taken on a walk. This part of the process was referred to as the 'walk and talk'. A route was chosen, dependent on weather conditions, that was pleasant but not too stretching, the emphasis being on quality conversations. It usually lasted a couple of hours and provided lots of

Case Study cont'd

opportunities for people to catch up with others who they may desire some feedback from, therefore adding more data for them.

This walk ended up at a quiet local area which was ideal for setting up a climbing and abseiling session for those who wanted to partake. There was no pressure on individuals by the staff, or indeed their peers, to participate but everyone was involved in some way because they were taught and encouraged to belay each other. A fine simile for the trust now built up in the group and the support that individuals gave to each other in the process of development.

Back at the hotel, the home teams reassembled for the last time on the course to ensure that each individual had a clear and achievable action plan. This was followed by a plenary opportunity for individuals to declare their plan and seek final clarification and feedback on it.

Day 5

The final day up to lunchtime was for the team as a whole to discuss and plan actions and activities that could be instigated back at the workplace which would have a positive influence on the culture. There were some very creative and positive projects started back at the workplace due to these sessions. Many actions that helped sustain the development work undertaken for a long time and help towards creating a culture in the workplace that would encourage and support personal and team learning and development.

Sometimes all that a team or group of individuals need is some focused discussion time to raise the issues affecting them. A more developed team will not need to spend too long on processes or even in agreeing behaviours, as they will already have covered that in an early stage but they will need to spend more time in dealing with interpersonal interactions and how to improve them. They will need to spend more time exploring with their colleagues the impact of their styles on each other, improving the quality of constructive feedback and building stronger personal relationships within the team.

This chapter has been written to illustrate how experiential learning forms a necessary role in the process of developmental coaching, to explore the contemporary best practices and give some examples of effective use.

Readers may be personally involved in the process of leadership development, whether internally or externally to an organisation. This always involves some risk, the risk implicit in doing things differently or doing different things. Moving out of our comfort zone and into the unknown is a risk but is required if development is to be successful. The following lines reflect our sentiments about the risk implicit in development.

> To laugh is to risk being a fool, to cry is to risk appearing sentimental
> To reach out to another is to risk involvement, to show feeling is to risk sharing yourself
> To present your ideas before others is to risk their loss
> To love is to risk being loved in return, to live is to risk dying
> To hope is to risk despair, to try is to risk failure
> But risks must be taken because the greatest hazard in life is to risk nothing
> Those who risk nothing – do nothing, receive nothing and have nothing
> They may avoid some pain and sorrow
> But they cannot learn, feel, change, grow or love
> Chained by their uncertainties they are slaves
> They have forfeited their freedom.
>
> *ANON.*

Experiential learning can provide an environment which encourages and supports individuals and teams in taking the necessary risks.

CHAPTER 5

From Corporate Leader to Coach: A UK Perspective on Executive Coaching

My Journey into Executive Coaching

My perspective on coaching comes from having previously been managing director of a national building society in the UK. As a coach, this experience brought me advantages and disadvantages. Among the latter was the fact that senior managers must carry in their toolkit the ability to command and control. It is a necessary tool, but one that can lend itself to overuse, and overuse and second nature make dangerous bedfellows.

To a coach, command and control is about as much use as a fire hose for watering a seedbed. This is because the decision whether or not to take any action as a result of coaching has to remain with the client. That, of course, should not prevent the coach from challenging the client, fiercely if necessary, provided the client retains ownership of the outcome. In my coaching apprenticeship, when clients asked me for advice on how something should be done, I was only too eager to leap into the fray and tell them what to do. I suspect that in those early days I must either have bred regrettable dependency or, worse still, have caused hard-won contracts to fade away as previously grateful clients grew tired of receiving ready-wrapped answers.

I had yet to learn that the role of the coach is rarely if ever to provide solutions to clients' problems. To do so may provide solutions to the problems of the day, but it is unlikely to draw out from within the client new ways of dealing with problems in general. A good coach will leave behind not tidy solutions but rather the joy of discovering the route to the answers.

There is, however, one strong advantage in coming to executive coaching from senior management: namely first-hand experience of what it is, and what it feels like, to be in the role of senior management. One of the UK's most respected psychiatrists, Dr Matt Muijen, himself a strong believer in the value of executive coaching, pointed out that, despite appearances to the contrary, everyone of whatever rank or level of ability has feelings of insecurity and needs 'confirmation that I'm OK'. That confirmation can come across with greater impact if given by someone who not only truly understands the issues, but can also draw on similar personal experience in addressing them.

With me, however, this advantage was always going to be jeopardised while I persisted in assuming that coaching was the same as instructing. Like many of those whom I have been privileged to coach, even when awareness dawned, I was reluctant to let go of what I regarded as my past achievements. The change in me was triggered by a lucky chance. I was invited to coach a person who, although herself a respected coach, had run into a minor crisis. For this assignment, my listening skills, at that time never more than beta plus, had not only to be raised to at least alpha levels but also had to be kept there throughout. When we had completed the session, she thanked me and told me it was the best she had ever had and that I was a natural coach. Whether knowingly or not, she was the catalyst that made me aware of my responsibility to develop this gift, if such it is.

In regard to self-awareness, a prerequisite to self-coaching, I was at the stage of conscious incompetence. Quite quickly, though, I found I was able to reach up into the realms of conscious competence, and before long could even detect retrospectively signs of unconscious competence. I even learned how to respect such advances and cherish them, as opposed to denying them for fear of being led inexorably into the trap of self-satisfaction. The journey appears to be more in the nature of a spiral than a cycle. As we gain in both competence and confidence, fresh fields open up before us inviting exploration. The spiral is neither smooth nor evenly paced; discovery can seem to take a long time in coming and can then pop up when least expected.

Energy as an Indicator

Energy levels, whether they apply to individuals or groups, tell us much about how we are performing. Teams that are working well tend to experience high energy levels, even when physically tired or short of sleep. When coaching teams, I encourage them to keep track of their energy levels precisely because they are such an effective means of gauging performance. If levels fall below what the team considers acceptable, it is a reliable sign that something is blocking progress. It could be, for example, a hidden agenda, or a proposal that is being pushed through in the face of unspoken disapproval, or even something as simple as a general drifting into irrelevance. Although the cause may not be immediately apparent, the symptom is plain for all to see or feel. Then any member of the team can interject by asking what has happened to the group's energy. Good teams who enjoy high levels of mutual respect and trust do not resent this and are usually quick to identify the answer.

I once lost a job through naively sticking my neck out on what I regarded as a point of principle. The experience caused my feelings to swing spectacularly. The highs arose from my pride and exhilaration at having managed to mess up and sustain sufficient courage (so I told myself) to maintain what I considered to be right. These were sometimes accompanied by short periods of very high energy caused by nothing more remarkable than raw anger. The lows, I discovered, stemmed from my resentment and humiliation. It was only some months later, when I became consciously aware of the lowering effect of these negative feelings, that I accepted I had been a perfect fool to choose to embark on battles in an environment where the values were at odds with my own. In effect, I had begun a process of self-coaching that enabled me to recover my self-esteem and, more importantly, my effectiveness. Although not a recommended route to self-knowledge, the experience was for me one of the most valuable in my life – it gave me time and opportunity to reflect on my strengths and weaknesses in ways that I had not previously even considered.

Executive Coaching – The Historical Legacy

In the final years of the twentieth century, the reputation of executive coaching underwent a surprising transformation. The ever-increasing pace of change and the pressures of globalisation eventually persuaded leaders to recognise that leadership and management are not activities that lend themselves to the application of a mechanistic set of rules. It was then that coaches, previously somewhat bracketed with consultants or counsellors and psychotherapists, began to acquire an altogether different status. A decade or so ago, coaching, other than in sport, was generally regarded as an optional extra, applicable mainly to remedy performance problems. Today, we are beginning to acknowledge that there is a limit to increasing performance just by working harder and longer, and even the most committed executive command and control practitioners are beginning to question their philosophy. Competent coaches have an opportunity to play a crucial role in the emergence and practical application of this new thinking.

In the meantime, Gallwey (1974) and Whitmore (1992) had demonstrated that effective coaching has very little to do with telling people what to do. Rather, it is concerned with helping people to discover for themselves what to do, how to do it, and what might be blocking them. There is nothing particularly new about this activity. The ancient Romans were perfectly well aware that education was not a matter of cramming information into pupils, but rather of drawing it out. The word 'education' itself stems from the Latin word *educo*, meaning 'I draw forth'. It contrasts sharply with inculcation, a word frequently found in training manuals, which derives from the Latin verb meaning to grind under the heel. Before the Romans, we find Socrates had developed a method of education now known as Socratic dialogue, or dialectic, whereby he drew forth pre-existing knowledge from his students by pursuing a series of questions and then examining the implications of their answers.

The idea that we come into the world with talents already within us and ready to be drawn out does not seem too surprising when we witness the performances of child prodigies. In the corporate context, executive coaches are required to act as delivery agents for the emergence of talent, as well as addressing blockages imposed over the years by such varied sources as upbringing, culture, tradition and 'emotional wiring'. In order to assist in the release of talent, coaches may need to create an environment in which unlearning is possible. For example, we have had to unlearn the notion that workforces consist of 'hands' (the inference being that brains are superfluous), which need only to be told what to do to achieve results, as opposed to why it should be done.

Latent Talent

Competent coaching, whether by external professionals or leaders in organisations, is an effective device for releasing latent talent and enterprise. If we look back to the second half of the eighteenth century and the first half of the nineteenth, we see a huge wave of creative talent in the Industrial Revolution. It was not the aristocrats or the landed gentry – people who were then regarded as the natural leaders of society – who fuelled the revolution, even though there were exceptions like the Dukes of Bridgewater, who were pioneers in the development of the canal system in England. In general, the landed classes did their utmost to cut themselves off from trade and business enterprise. The talent and enterprise that were needed to fuel such a massive change came from the British middle classes.

By 1880, the outpouring of British industrial talent declined relative to that of other major manufacturing countries like the USA and Germany. In Britain, the emphasis previously placed on enterprise had shifted towards control. The reason seems to have been largely sociological. Too often the heirs of successful entrepreneurs wished to accord themselves the ultimate social distinction, that is, to gain membership into the landed gentry. This led them to renounce their origins and also, if possible, to obscure them altogether. Thus, great enterprises were left in the hands of managers rather than leaders, whose job it was to ensure that nothing changed. Not surprisingly, innovation declined. To make matters worse, while enterprise and innovation were being neglected in Britain, they were being warmly welcomed in the USA. The seeds of what was to become known as the 'brain drain' were being sown.

For most of the twentieth century in the UK, management practice remained static. Protected markets in the colonies meant not only that there was little to stimulate innovation, but also the very fact of protection reinforced the need for control. Coaches were not only unnecessary, they weren't even considered. In the early 1980s, after the damage to quality, caused by the 'disposable' culture of the 1960s, had become apparent, the need for quality was recognised anew. There was much talk of the importance of excellence. This produced a surge of management energy, but without anyone appearing to know precisely why, or how to harness it. Energy was raised still higher when Peters and Austin (1986) proclaimed a 'passion for excellence'. But something was still missing. Neither tinkering with structures, nor talking about innovation or corporate re-engineering was going to help. To recapture innovation, quality, durability and value for money we had to find ways of using the latent talents in people to very much better effect.

Today we can at least glimpse the possibility of releasing another outpouring of talent, in which good coaches could and should have an exciting, fulfilling and vital role. It is as if the art of coaching, like the visual arts six centuries previously, is beginning to emerge from a protracted Dark Age. Coaches today have an opportunity to become like trusted navigators whose role is to help steer clients through the complex routes to achieving their destinations.

Self-coaching

When I started coaching professionally 12 years ago, I was given a piece of invaluable advice, namely that if I was going to be of any use I had first to learn to coach myself. Although I like to think that I have made personal progress towards this goal, I have to confess that my immediate reaction on being invited to contribute to this book was caution. But soon a persistent sixth sense suggested that my caution was not congruent with certain lessons that clients and I had unravelled together. It reminded me that I had spent great swathes of time attempting to help others to accept far greater challenges because I sensed that they were capable of meeting them. In short, was I starting to occupy a comfort zone of my own making? So I accepted.

The next question, which should of course have occurred earlier, was what to include? Every day I was becoming more conscious of the enormous responsibility of being an executive coach, especially at this time when organisations as a whole are starting to recognise coaching as a powerful ingredient in developing that rare commodity, effective leadership talent. So I determined that this would be my theme.

If self-coaching enables us to increase our self-awareness, it may also help us to spot traits in clients that we have noted in ourselves. This in turn may enable us to open up lines of questioning without making the client feel defensive or ill at ease. The coach, by referring to his or her own experiences, has an opportunity to help to develop an environment of mutual trust and empathy in which behaviour can be freely discussed. It is not unusual for clients to confide in a professional coach by revealing fears and anxieties that they would not dream of discussing with others, even their nearest and dearest.

Coaching as a Key Ingredient in Leadership

The inexorable increase in competition, which in turn produces demands for ever-higher productivity, has meant that innovation and leadership are increasingly highly valued in those organisations where competition is most keenly felt. More and more companies have specifically identified innovation and leadership as being among their core values. Today we regard coaching as an important ingredient of leadership. If we are right about this and coaching is not just another executive development fad, then it seems that coaching in one form or another will be required not just for people at the top, but for everyone involved in keeping up with, or ahead of, the competition. We also hear more today about learning organisations, that is to say, organisations in which learning is prized. The link between education, awareness and coaching has been referred to earlier in this chapter.

Leadership, innovation and learning are not likely to become embedded in organisations simply because a chairman or chief executive has decreed that they should be. Publishing values like these in annual reports, or posting them up on factory or office walls will do little when it comes to effecting radical change. Other agents are needed, among them the coaching of champions. Whether this is undertaken by leaders as part of their day-to-day responsibilities or by independent third parties who have no axes to grind and nothing to lose will depend on circumstances.

Getting Stuck

The pressures begin at the outset of our careers when we are concerned for the greater part with technical issues, and scarcely at all with management or leadership. But as time goes on, our technical experience grows, leading to promotion, after which we find ourselves increasingly involved with managerial responsibilities. For many, it can be a considerable wrench to leave the safe haven of a sound technical reputation and embark upon a leadership role, replete with office politics, hidden agendas and perhaps even questionable ethics. Add to this the sheer relentless pressure of competition, increasingly rapid change and globalisation and it is small wonder that we retreat into short-term thinking. It is in this environment that coaching can be particularly useful.

Myth: Executives and Leadership Figures Have Limitless Energy to Commit to Work

During my time as a coach, I have come across numerous cases of senior people whose reserves of physical and mental energy are no longer equal to the tasks and expectations being placed upon them. Although almost invariably in their inner hearts they are aware of being stuck, they are in denial. They have reached a grim plateau where work, instead of exciting them as it once did, has become a wearisome grind. They are sometimes too fatigued to be able even to summon the energy to find a way out and in order to avoid thinking of the consequences of having to make changes, they seek to escape by working even longer hours. Not only is family life adversely affected, or even destroyed, so are the lives of those at work who depend on the victim's performance. Where there is no time for mental refreshment or ease, sooner or later the result will be 'dis-ease'.

Given such circumstances, one might expect signs of a consequential and irresistible desire to delegate, but this does not seem to be happening. Executives can become so fearful of the consequences of being 'found out' if they let anybody onto their 'turf', that they cling onto it, sometimes with amazing tenacity. The thought that they could move onwards and upwards by letting go and coaching other people to take the strain leaves them unmoved. 'I'd like to do it but I simply cannot afford the time' is a response well known to professional coaches. Usually those unwilling to allocate time for coaching are in reality also unwilling to trust themselves to try it. They are so weighed down that they lack the necessary energy, and hence the will. Moreover, not having themselves received experience in coaching, they fear it may prove their undoing by exposing their weaknesses. They have not learned to accept that each of us is a bundle of strengths and weaknesses.

They hope to convince themselves that there is no particular need to do anything about the weaknesses because, as far as they are concerned, they are securely hidden behind a protective screen of their own making. They delude themselves, of course. For the coach, though, the opportunity to help such people to find their ways out of binds like these can be immensely rewarding, leading to long-term benefits for the client.

Leadership, Power and Coaching

Leadership is a quality that defies precise and universal definition. The more we strive to capture it in words, the more we seem to diminish it.

Robert Greenleaf (1998), who wrote beautifully on the subject of servant leadership, said, 'The only true test of leadership is that someone follows voluntarily.' James Kouzes and Barry Posner (1995) suggest that leadership is 'a reciprocal relationship between those who choose to lead and those who decide to follow'. What appeals to me about this theory is that it accords initiative to each side of the transaction. A useful question for coaches to ask can be 'what are the factors that made you choose to lead', or just as important 'to decide to follow?' The response may be 'money', but it is hardly a complete answer. It is more like a response to a stimulus than a decision.

Deciding to follow has a dynamism about it that is lacking when we merely fall in behind the leader, and it is that dynamism that can bring about self-esteem and enjoyment, both in those who choose to lead and those who decide to follow. In other words, being at the head of a group of people who follow only because they have no choice cannot really be described as leadership. It seems then that in order to lead we require more than given authority. We need natural authority, a quality that can be helped to come to light with the aid of coaching.

Natural authority has much in common with natural power, which is a subject that in this politically correct world people can be reluctant to discuss. Yet without discussion, there is unlikely to be a shared understanding of what power does and does not mean. The person who chooses to lead is only endowed with real power, as opposed to given authority, by the followers' decision to follow. Authority that is given does not confer real power; rather it defines the extent to which we may use real power. If this seems improbable, consider what happens when a powerless person is placed in authority. The result is a functionary or apparatchik, whose life is spent blocking initiatives through slavish adherence to a rule book. Reliance on a rule book may help in justifying decisions, but it is hardly a manifestation of real authority. It may help people who are experiencing the consequences of their first promotion, that is, being elevated above their peers with whom they were until recently on completely equal terms. But if we are to become leaders, we cannot rely indefinitely on rule books. Sooner or later our inner qualities of leadership will have to emerge.

In the nineteenth century, Lord Acton declared, 'all power corrupts and absolute power corrupts absolutely'. This famous aphorism seems to have led to the belief that all power must necessarily corrupt. In other words, we are so feeble that we cannot be expected to resist its charms. But if that is true, how can we lead, given that true leadership is an exercise in appropriate and effective use of power? It follows that the higher we rise in organisations, the more power we will need. But how do we find it? The answer, strange as it may seem, is by giving it away, in other words, by delegating. Here the reader may claim that delegation has little to do with coaching. This is not a treatise on delegation, but it may help to draw some connections by stating five principles of delegation and showing how they tie up with coaching.

First, we need to avoid delegating to groups because only individuals can be held accountable. Accepting the full weight of accountability gives the individual concerned the moral authority to take decisions. This is because it is with that person that the proverbial buck must stop. Coaching at any level can deepen understanding of the bruises resulting from stopped bucks. It can also hasten the healing of the bruises, which usually begins with acceptance of the blow. Surely it is better to face up to the reality of failure than to claim immunity under the protocol of a no-blame culture. The latter has a rightful place in protecting people from being humiliated, demeaned or bullied by others, but not in absolving leaders from the consequences of mistakes. People are generally quite happy to accept the trappings of seniority but balk at the pain of failure. Yet if a person is to become a real leader, it is almost inevitable that at some point he or she will experience serious failure. When this happens, it can help to remember the example of Mary Pickford, the American film star, who broke the monopoly of the Hollywood studio barons by forming United Artists. She said, 'this thing we call failure is not the falling down; it is staying down'.

Second, when delegating, make certain that the objective and the standards of performance required are clearly understood. The present climate of rapid change has shown us that unwieldy hierarchies are insufficiently adaptable or responsive to enable us to compete with the best. The result has been flatter structures. These in turn have called on us to accept challenges outside the normal span of our experience. Clarity of purpose is therefore particularly important because the risk of misunderstanding is that much greater. Acceptance of a position for which we are ill equipped may well expose us to the risk of being bruised. But so-called safe careers also involve us in risk; namely that of ossifying in the safety of a comfort zone. For a time, such safety may seem attractive, but when retirement looms and the time comes to review what we have made of our potential, those who have risked little will have little to show, except regret at not having used their latent talents when there were still opportunities to do so. Coaching can help us to find capabilities within ourselves that were previously beyond our awareness, the development of which can bring both surprise and enormous satisfaction.

Third, unless asked, it is not really educational either to tell the person to whom a task is delegated how to accomplish it, or to smother the person with support. It may be that the person to whom a task has been delegated will discover a better way of accomplishing it, and even if it takes more time to let the discovery come to light, the extra time is probably well spent

Fourth, it is important when delegating to build in a review process. Not to do so smacks of abdication rather than delegation. It is at these reviews that the leader has an opportunity to coach – an opportunity that the leader would be well advised to take, since although the task may have been delegated, responsibility for its completion has not.

Fifth, point out pitfalls or flag up danger signals. This is not the same as telling the delegatee how to do the job. On the other hand, it gives plenty of scope for coaching, unless of course the delegatee is already fully familiar with the dangers, in which case pointing them out will be an unnecessary irritant.

Underlying these five principles is the idea, disturbing though it may be to ego-trippers, that great leaders are not remembered so much for what they do as for what their people do. The leader's job is largely concerned with creating an environment in which their people flourish, and it would surely be difficult to exclude coaching from such an environment.

Coaching at any level, but particularly at senior levels, is likely at some point to touch on the subject of moral integrity. This is perhaps where there is the strongest temptation to sweep issues under the carpet, but good coaches, through the use of appropriate questions, should be able to draw the key issues out. This is more than likely to lead into discussion about the spiritual side of leadership – an issue in respect of which we may feel some diffidence, for fear, perhaps, of being regarded as some sort of new-age crank or religious weirdo. But as Jonathan Sacks (2000), the Chief Rabbi, has pointed out, spirituality and religion, although connected, are not the same, any more than are love and marriage.

Field Marshall Bill Slim (1956), the tough and rugged leader of the now famous 'Forgotten Army' in Burma in World War II, said of morale that if it is to endure it must have certain foundations. 'These foundations', he said, 'are spiritual, intellectual and material, and that is the order of their importance: spiritual first, because only a spiritual foundation can stand real strain.' Not only did Slim understand a great deal about real strain, he was about as far from a new-age weirdo as it is possible to be.

The spiritual side of leadership has much to do with inspiring those who have decided to follow. It also includes helping people to have a right sense of self-esteem. Surprising though it may seem, once trust has been established and facades have been lifted, coaches frequently find, even at the top, quite low levels of self-esteem. This is of concern because, as the Dalai Lama said in his book *Modern World, Ancient Wisdom* (Gyatso 1999): 'Lack of a proper recognition of one's own value is always harmful, and can lead to a state of mental, emotional and spiritual paralysis.' Note the words *always harmful*. Presumably if he meant sometimes, or occasionally, harmful, he would have said so. Perhaps it is in this area that coaches can do their most valuable work. If we do not or cannot esteem ourselves, what right have we to choose to lead? And what sort of signal do we send to those who may be in the act of deciding whether or not to follow? The self-esteem that good coaches draw out from their clients has nothing whatsoever to do with the clients' self-glorification, but rather with the crucially important business of knowing themselves.

Blockages and Self-protection

It is hard enough for leaders lacking an adequate level of self-esteem to recover from the knocks that are perennially dealt out to them. Still harder is the concept that we all have potential beyond – and possibly far beyond – our own estimation of ourselves. I frequently coach executives, often in their mid-forties, who struggle valiantly but unsuccessfully to keep on top of their roles simply because their lack of self-esteem leads them to conclude, wrongly, that they are incapable of finding the necessary talent within themselves. By normal standards, these people still have up to twenty years 'at work'. They almost certainly possess the wherewithal not only to rise even higher during this period, but also at the same time be more in control of their lives. Instead they are fixated, sometimes alarmingly so, on just keeping going and avoiding making mistakes.

We may be beginning to learn that learning itself involves making mistakes, but try telling that to someone who is motivated primarily by preserving what they believe to be an unblemished reputation, or who genuinely fears that reputations are made of such fragile stuff that they will shatter at the slightest shock. To such people the inexorable pace of change can be the stuff of nightmares. If coaching is suggested to them, they may well resist for fear that the nightmare will turn into reality. Moreover, unless they work in an environment where coaching is generally accepted as an effective means of improving performance, they may assume that their weaknesses have been noticed and that coaching is being imposed upon them as a last resort.

People imprisoned in such mindsets may pay lip service to launching initiatives to increase performance, but will resist them in their hearts and minds. One of the great bonuses of being a coach is accompanying such people to the point where they realise not only that they can break free, but in sharing in their enjoyment as they do it.

Hardened Attitudes

Enjoyment of executive work is not universally encouraged. Indeed there are those who suspect that enjoyment means we are not working hard enough, or that it will lead to frivolity, which in its turn could indicate lack of commitment. A friend, who although relatively young, was so widely experienced and good at his job that he was offered the post of president of the multibillion dollar organisation for which he worked. Before the final decision was made, however, it was discovered that he was in the habit of leaving his office no later than six o'clock in the evening. This so alarmed the interviewers that they imposed a condition, namely that he would have to undertake in writing to place his work at the very top of his priorities. He refused and, in doing so, lost his job, acquiring instead a temporary reputation for frivolity. In time, though, he found a much richer life elsewhere, while the former employers were left to rue the fact that their hardened attitudes had cost them the loss of a brilliant man.

Coaching can be very helpful in preventing us from hardening our attitudes. In the example above, it subsequently became clear that the attitude of the board concerned had hardened beyond the point of being able to accept that 'working smarter' might have advantages compared with working longer. Attitudes can be seen as the way we arrive at decisions we take about the way life is, or ought to be. If we are unwise enough to place those decisions beyond review, the chances are that our hardened attitudes will render us unable to adapt in a changing world.

Egos

To achieve executive status is discussed elsewhere in this book, in terms of formal competencies required to succeed. My experience tells me that this achievement may require the sort of determination that is frequently accompanied by a large ego. Protecting large egos can be a serious matter to those possessing them, and any shocks to their defences can result in worse shocks elsewhere, particularly if the egocentric executive has built up an entourage of sycophants. In such environments, it can take a brave person to point out the egocentric executive's needs for development. A good external executive coach, however, may succeed in making the required breakthrough while risking no more than the loss of an assignment.

Hard Streak

Nothing in this chapter is meant to imply that coaching is all silk and softness. The coach must be able to challenge, which means having a hard streak. It is more than likely that at some point, when attempting to move from the symptoms of a problem to the actual cause, a client will shy away from the issue or try to sweep it under the carpet. For the coach to acquiesce in such evasion will not help the client and may exacerbate existing weaknesses. For example, sooner or later senior people can be undermined or let down painfully by those in whom they have placed trust, or to whom they have delegated authority. In such circumstances, the coach may validly express sympathy with the wounded client, but if responsibility for the failure lies with that client, the coach must not join in pretending that it is otherwise. Part of the job of the coach is to ensure, as far as possible, that despite the discomfort the client understands and accepts fully his or her share of the responsibility. To do so successfully is to help to develop true strength, and thence true leadership.

Letting Go: Exiting an Assignment

Letting go can be painful. As executive coaches, we may need to help clients to discern when to let go of a particular challenge, but we ourselves also need to know when to let go of a client. The Duke of Wellington, when asked what was the most difficult thing about being a general in battle, replied 'knowing when to retreat and daring to do it'.

Rather than allowing the relationship with a client to drift inconclusively to an end, it is better to sum up the situation as fairly and candidly as possible and sign off. Sometimes, if this is done appropriately, that is to say, without attributing blame, the act of signing off may help the client to see the issues where all else failed. I have a one-time client who has since become a friend. For him making the break was a milestone experience. He had been using coaching as a personal support, a prop. Only with the removal of the support did it occur to him that he alone was responsible for his own future.

When dealing with closure, timing is of the essence: too soon and both sides will be left with a feeling of incompleteness, whereas leaving it too long can result in the relationship fading away with neither side having actively brought it to a conclusion. Coaching is often about helping clients to let go of things impeding their progress. It is not unknown for the list to include the coach. Letting go of clients is an essential part of our job, so it is as well to do it in a planned and effective manner.

The Future

Recognition of the advantages of coaching may be growing, but if we pause and reflect on how the world of work could be if coaching were to become common practice, we would have to admit that the craft (for such it is) is only in its infancy. Today many people are only vaguely aware of the potential talent waiting to be unlocked at work. Others who have seen the benefits of coaching find themselves regretting that they had not been introduced to it earlier. I recently coached a man at the pinnacle of his profession. He had achieved the sort of respect that would delight most people. His only regret was that he had not been given the opportunity to be coached twenty years earlier. In his case, the omission, as he termed it, was largely compensated for by the willingness with which he 'subjected' himself to what he had assumed would be an ordeal. On discovering that it was not, he encouraged his colleagues to follow his example. The result was a striking, yet predictable, improvement in teamwork.

One day, those who come after us may look back at the beginning of the twenty-first century and wonder why we took so long to come to terms with what to them will be patently obvious. As a result of our insatiable desire to find out more about how we and in particular our leaders in executive roles work, our successors will be better equipped to grapple with the scope of human potential and how to use it to increase performance and personal fulfilment.

Coaching in the future is unlikely to become easier, nor will the corporate challenges facing our clients will be any less daunting than those confronting them now. But by that time coaching could well be as universal and acceptable as other forms of education and development are today, thus providing our successors not only with the means of continuing to cope, but also of gaining enormous satisfaction from doing so.

Review Questions

1. As a coach, do you find yourself providing routes to the solutions to problems, or solutions to the problems themselves?
2. At which level are your coaching skills:
   - unconscious incompetence?
   - conscious incompetence?
   - conscious competence?
   - unconscious competence?
3. When did you last consider whether you have anything to 'unlearn', and with what result?
4. Why do your people follow you?
5. Have you thought carefully about what made you choose to lead?
6. How much of your leadership stems from natural authority and how much from given authority?

CHAPTER 6

Executive Coaching in Action: 'Life's a Project, Isn't It?'

Introduction

Two of the most common executive development issues we have found during our coaching work are:

1. Building self-confidence in a new role.
2. Developing people management skills, particularly the aspects of 'emotional intelligence' (Goleman 1996) mentioned previously.

The case study below reflects the transition from project manager to general manager. It captures many development themes typical of the personal growth required when a manager from almost any functional specialism (engineering, sales, finance, operations) faces the challenge of acquiring the broader skill set characteristic of a general management role. John faced just such a challenge when we first met.

Background

John was nominated as a high potential manager, identified by Rolls-Royce as a manager with much more to offer. He had already established himself as a very effective engineering project manager and at 38 was leading a £100 million project responsible for integrating several project teams from different organisations. Martin, John's boss, felt John needed further development to exploit his general management potential.

A coaching assignment was discussed with his proposed coach and a meeting arranged to test compatibility.

Chemistry, Compatability and Coaching Agenda

The first meeting was an interesting test for both myself, as the prospective coach, and John. A clear agenda for the meeting comprised the issue of compatibility and coaching rationale. John was clear about his ability as a project manager but less convinced of a need for coaching. Despite his respect for Martin, his boss, John had reservations about his need to change. John explained his thinking at the time:

> I was a successful project manager and convinced that being a general business manager was just applying project management skills in a new context. Martin said I needed to resolve some behavioural issues about my style. I apparently displayed a 'command and control' style at meetings which was seen as ineffective. I began to realise even then that I couldn't be an expert in every aspect of the project. That strategy ran out very quickly.

John's strengths were apparent. He had a track record for decisive action, was very output focused and took responsibility willingly. He was someone who challenged the status quo, and consistently maintained focus on the task. He is an energetic Scotsman with a passion for delivery and that rare commodity, integrity. He strove to maintain a consistency between what he said he believed in and his actions.

Six months after completion of our coaching together which spanned two years, meeting for a total of ten sessions, John reflected:

> I may have been in denial when we first met. I denied I needed to develop but I soon became curious about how I may improve my skills.

So he did – curious at an intellectual level. John was a very intelligent engineering manager, his capability to process complex data quickly and process an elegant analysis was a key strength for him. However, he saw the world of work digitally, decisions were made in binary form, yes or no, on or off, black or white. Only much later in the assignment did John recognise he could arrive at a judgment which was maybe grey instead of black or white. Looking back, he elaborated on this issue:

I found it was OK to occupy a position of 0.5 instead of 0 or 1, and that it doesn't have to be a transient position en route to one or the other.

John moved through this first period of denial quickly and into an inquisitive exploration of his current effectiveness. We conducted a series of meetings which covered John's current performance. His 360° feedback report confirmed Martin's feedback, peers and direct reports supporting a need to develop John's people management skills more broadly.

Myth: High Flyers Move Through Organisations Quickly Because They Don't Allow Their Mistakes to Catch up with Them

All our evidence suggests they don't. Rather like John, faced with a new situation, they move quickly through Denial (see Chapter 2) into Awareness, thereby giving themselves the opportunity to move to practise much faster than many others. A common characteristic of high flyers, those who move quickly through organisations, acquiring responsibility as they go, seems to be an ability to move 'fast to 5' in transition terms. Recent support for this suggestion comes from Bennis and Thomas (2002). Bennis and Thomas propose that an 'adaptive capacity' is a key ingredient for successful leaders. Moving to stage 5 quickly can only enhance the rate of adaption. Interestingly, they also include integrity, another of John's strengths, in the recipe for effective leadership.

John began to accept that his historical hands-on approach was becoming obsolete. In our first meeting, John was curious if I had anything new to offer him. He conducted what he described as a test of my ability to help him develop, which involved an exploration of my historical experience as a manager and latterly as an executive coach, my key relevant coaching achievements and failures and, probably more importantly, my personal philosophy on business management, leadership and my personal values.

Shadowing a Leader in Action

Apparently, I passed the test, and so did John. Our initial approach was tentative but I wanted to see John in action. He invited me to shadow several key meetings he ran and I reviewed his behaviour with him subsequently. His mastery of a command and control style was evident. He micro-managed every encounter, leaving little opportunity for his project team to use their initiative or latent talents. John needed to take more of an overview of project progress, become more strategic. This, I argued, would allow his people to apply more of their talents, him to manage the important not urgent issues, and reduce the likelihood of his burn-out – which appeared imminent judging by his stress levels at the time.

The benefits for John were clear to him after this early phase. He agreed to commit to the coaching programme we designed together. This comprised a sequence of practical actions with his team. This quickly grew to embrace the following elements:

- Extending his leadership style to allow his growth to general management, taking a more strategic perspective and allowing his team the opportunity to exploit their talent
- Understanding others better, particularly the impact of his behaviour and what drives other people's behaviour
- Building John's interpersonal skills – giving feedback, demonstrating sensitivity to others' needs
- Review of career development options.

Feedback on Coaching Style

The above coaching agenda evolved and expanded as we moved further into the assignment. In John's words:

> A career review was long overdue. But in a relatively short time with coaching I accepted that there was more than one way of managing projects and people. Your challenging me as the coach was quite helpful actually. Never threatening, sometimes inquisitorial, sometimes as leading a tutorial, but I saw my potential was blocked … by me! I could maybe have continued this style in another company but I wanted to stay with the best, Rolls-Royce. My ambition was to stay in the business and progress, I have a commitment to my own growth. So at that time I had an internal challenge too.

John was clearly committed to change. He began to implement the actions we'd agreed in our coaching sessions and began to receive encouraging feedback that he was becoming more effective with his people. His role changed too. He was appointed to lead an important change project, and physically moved to a large facility in the south. John reported:

> I was only offered this 'leading change' role as I was seen to have grown, become broader in my leadership style. It involved masses of communication and felt like herding cats. Before I had only been a sheepdog with sheep.

As we moved through our coaching sessions which were predominantly a mixture of one-to-one and team meetings, it became apparent that John was confronting his historical models of leadership. Implicit here was a critical review of his values in action which was occasionally an uncomfortable process. John's next step, he felt, was now to lead a bigger part of the business, with wider responsibility. He found a suitable leadership role inside Rolls-Royce. Today he is the business development director for Rolls-Royce Diesels, an Anglo-Norwegian organisation in significant transition. His responsibilities span a broad spectrum, from strategic planning to implementing change programmes in new cultures. It's a business turnaround role that provides an opportunity to exploit John's historical strengths as well as offering significant development opportunity. He maintains a programme to sustain and extend his development achievement. Occasional coach meetings, regular feedback from team and boss, support from nearer co-workers who understand John's development goals all help to sustain his developments, he reports.

Development Outcomes

The outcomes from this coaching assignment were to build general management and leadership capability and skills. As John explained at the coaching closure meeting:

> You can't be too precise when setting development goals as they evolve so much; if you adopted that prescriptive style it wouldn't have worked with me. It's an iterative process, if you had proposed a prescriptive process – do this in this way over this timeframe and out pops success – I'd have rejected it and walked away with no development, it wouldn't have happened, the outcomes would have been fake.

After a formal review with his boss, John declared that not only did he experience success but the organisation felt that way too. The investment had been justified. He described the independence of the coach, style of coaching and the establishment of trust between us as key criteria for success:

> With the money I could have gone to Harvard for their intensive leadership programme, saved all that time and moved quickly through the development agenda. That wouldn't have worked with the size of my change. It takes time to build a different view of me as a general manager or leader.

Coach's Postscript

In my experience, John is the coaching candidate most committed to his own development that I have ever coached. Despite setbacks during the two-year process, he always kept his focus on his development goal. He has certainly found his personal 'leadership voice' which is based upon his strong set of principles about how people should be treated at work. Fortunately, at present he finds himself in an organisation which recognises and rewards those principles in action. Long may that be sustained.

Lessons Learned

The most prominent learning from this case is how necessary it is to adapt coaching style to changing circumstances. The process overall conformed to an emerging model of coaching style. Called the contextual coaching model (see Figure 6.1), it represents an adaption from the situational leadership model proposed by Hersey and Blanchard (1998). The model describes how a prospective coach may determine an appropriate entry point and style of coaching depending upon the potential of the coaching participant and the nature of the development goal (here the coaching task).

In John's case above, he appeared somewhat unwilling at first as we commenced our coaching conversations, applying a 'coaching test' to his coach and fully exploring the nature of my expertise. From my side as coach, I began our coaching in quadrant 4, the coach as expert, then moved quickly to 3, as teacher/tutor applying rationality and logic to underpin the need to develop. We moved swiftly to quadrant 2 as trust and closeness of relationship was built and John became more confident and successful in his development actions. Now, we enjoy a more distant mentor relationship, with infrequent contact and intimacy. John demonstrated his capability and desire to take responsibility for his own development, supporting the appropriate shift to quadrant 1.

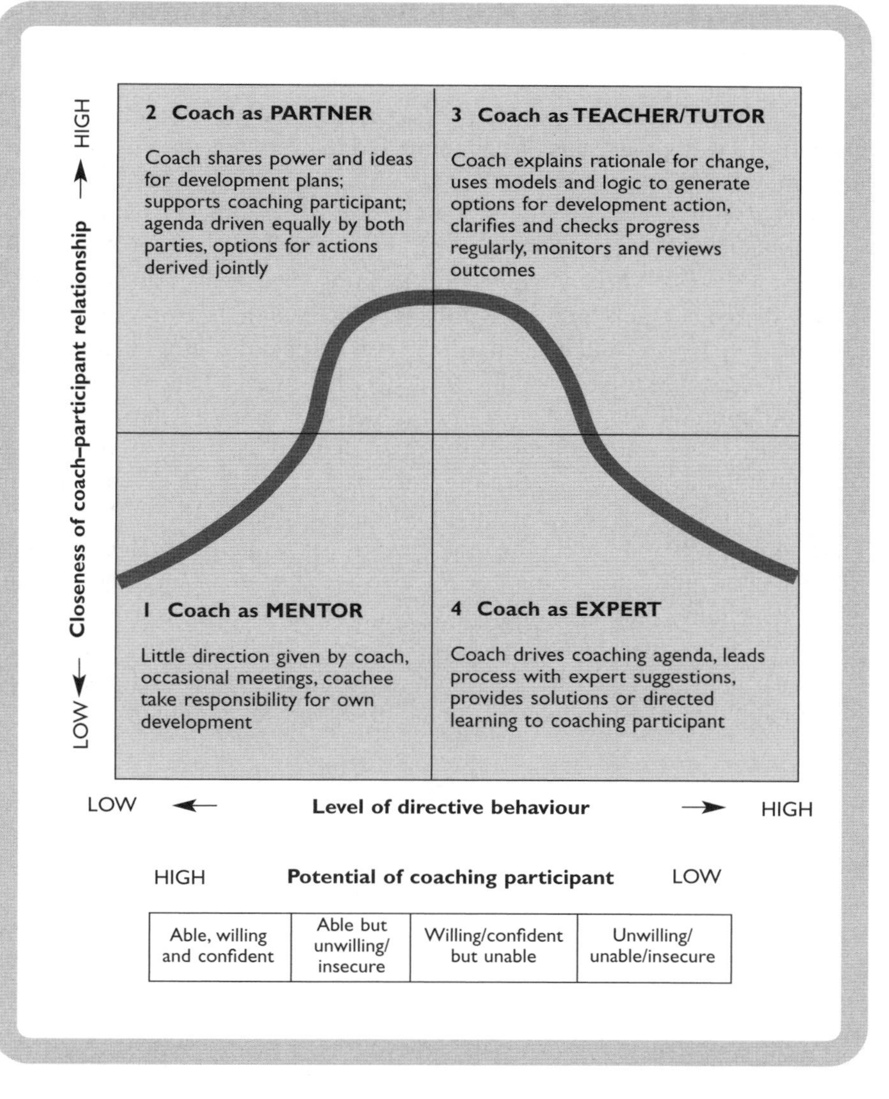

Figure 6.1 Matching coaching style to context: the four basic coaching styles

Adapted from Hersey and Blanchard 1998

The Contextual Coaching Model: Matching Coaching Style to Context

As we have remarked upon above, over the last decade the world of executive development has turned more and more to coaching as a primary tool in developing executive leadership capability. However, most connected with coaching practice would agree that there is no one best style, effective in every situation with every coaching partner. Successful coaches are those who are capable of adapting their behaviour to meet the unique demands of each coaching assignment. Adapted from original ideas presented by Hersey and Blanchard, the contextual coaching model (Figure 6.1) helps coaches to analyse the demands of their coaching situations.

Based upon the required amount of directive coaching behaviour necessary to drive the achievement of the task (defined by the agreed development goals), the level of relationship the coach creates and given a specific level of 'potential' of the coaching participant (that is, the willingness to learn and ability to develop), a certain style is identified. Expert, teacher/tutor, partner and mentor refer to the various roles a coach may adopt depending on these three variables. The task of the coach is to help the coaching partner develop in ways agreed in the coaching agenda. The style that the coach will adopt varies in different phases of the coaching assignment and is dependent on the nature of the development task.

Chapter 7

Executive Coaching in Action: Legal Eagle to People Leader

A Personal Journey into Coaching

Working as a chartered psychologist, originally much in assessment, I often found myself presenting feedback from the psychometric tests and analytical instruments, completed as part of assessment procedures, to corporate candidates, both successful and unsuccessful. On occasion, they would look to me for advice: How might they improve? What alternative behaviours might they adopt? How should they address what was 'wrong'? It was as if my acquiring some academic qualifications, reading a few books and being deeply introspective was sufficient to provide me with the necessary insight to help. I was intrigued by the notion that perhaps I did have some suggestions to offer and should help them to find a way forward, but often I was engaged by the different ways people dealt with the feedback. At that time, having seen the benefits individuals could derive from assessment data, I wondered how this source of data on performance could be channelled more specifically for development. Our development centres were born and our role as coaches established.

I am not naturally a directive individual when dealing with others. This brings its own challenges in many areas, but in coaching it has prevented me from being overly prescriptive. I enjoyed outlining my observations and the possible implications of what I saw for other work scenarios and working with executives to create action steps they felt able to apply. Seeing the benefit from a changed approach was a reward in itself. This approach I wrestled with on occasions, when individuals looked to me for 'answers'. It took a few sessions of generating countless alternative approaches, only to have my client reject them, to convince me that they really had to work harder, with my help, in finding the way forward that was right for them.

During coaching sessions, I began to appreciate my 'fit' with certain individual types and not with others. I could encourage quieter individuals to push out their boundaries a little and get those engaged in deep thought to think about how others might respond, emotionally, to what they did. I didn't take to those I considered brash and overly aggressive because that didn't match my style or value set. As I write, I'm still working on my approach to this issue.

It's no surprise that outstanding leaders are now acknowledged to be excellent coaches – although we coaches may also like to think that the formula works the other way round too. As a coach, helping individuals to discover and release potential by holding back from prescribing, managing and directing them, whilst challenging and supporting them, is the craft I have begun to develop and am committed to sustain.

Introduction to Case Study

This is the case of a British executive working in a US multinational who has been promoted to lead the legal department in one of the corporation's regions. Some members of the leadership team, of which he was a member, had begun to express dissatisfaction with his performance and these perceptions were precipitating calls for his replacement. It was aspects of his leadership behaviour rather than his technical ability that were causing concern and he was now in a role where the latter could not compensate for the former.

Case Background

I had been working for about two years with the European region of this large US multinational. One day I was called by the HR Director, Christine, who wanted to talk about coaching options for the head of the legal department, Greg. She explained that he was now in a very vulnerable position; 'the wolves are at the door', she declared, and he needed to change his approach to stay in the company. This was because he had failed to gain, or had lost, I wasn't sure at the time, the confidence of both the regional president and a number of influential senior colleagues; not necessarily because of technical capability or delivery, but basically because of the way he conducted himself in meetings with them and his lack of meaningful contribution. A classic case of 'job jeopardy'; the call for 'a knight in shining armour', a search and rescue mission – how could any self-respecting and egotistical coach turn it down?

I met with Christine and she told me she had given Greg feedback on several occasions about how others experienced his behaviour and had discussed the possibility of coaching for him. He didn't reject the notion, but was a little mystified about why this would be necessary. Christine outlined a little of what she and others had observed, how this had been perceived and the current position as she saw it. A lack of forceful projection in an environment where decisive talk and action were highly prized qualities, even if not always the best way of approaching things, had meant that Greg was viewed as 'ineffective'. The appropriate decisive action was therefore deemed to be 'replacement'. As Christine talked, it became apparent that she had taken on his case because she liked him as an individual. Although she recognised many of his faults, she appreciated that, despite how he was perceived, he had always succeeded in delivering in a very demanding environment and would be difficult to replace. A task that would, after all, fall to her.

Greg had over ten years' experience in the business, hard to find in the legal world, and was still relatively new in his leadership position, having occupied it for less than 12 months. She had, metaphorically, put the 'halting hand' up to this senior group and told them to 'back off' until he had been given an opportunity to develop. There was something of a contradiction here for me, in the way in which she perceived this senior group as very effective people managers on their own patch, as that was 'their business', and how they sought to deal with an underperforming colleague. Never mind, the 'audience', the 'critics', had been identified, I was to meet with the 'actor' who needed to start impressing them.

A Self-review from the Coach

The preliminary discussion with Christine had been enough for me to develop some feeling for Greg. This was entirely about self-perception. As an introvert myself, I had been criticised for not impressing a group of extroverts. From my side, I thought they should have taken the trouble to listen to a more quiet individual instead of just grabbing airtime. An interesting moment for me to reflect. What had I done about that feedback – apart from resent it? I had to admit that although I had made efforts to increase my input and impact, I still felt hurt about the feedback that came my way – 'wish we'd heard more from you' or 'you were very quiet' – when others might also have been informed about the impact of their behaviour on me. This is feedback I have delivered in groups but generally reactively and occasionally emotionally.

Anyway, enough about me, or is it? This is typical, I think, of the coach's dilemma at times: how do you go about coaching others to perform in an environment that you may consider, in even some small way, dysfunctional? Perhaps I could put it that part of the attraction of coaching can be to help others to succeed in ways that you don't. This may be living your life vicariously through others but that for me is part of being an effective coach; the alternative is to push others to be you. Irrespective of what my thoughts were about me, the important thing now was that I was to meet Greg and, as discussed with Christine, discuss what we might do and how he felt about working with me.

Meeting Greg for the First Time

Christine took me along to a meeting room where Greg joined us later and, after introductions, left us to talk. A short man with horn-rimmed glasses, Greg appeared rather nervous and I did most of the talking to break the ice. I made my assumptions about background from dress and speech, but felt compelled to address the reason why we were there rather than spending much time on testing these out.

This seemed to work quite well, as Greg became more engaged, sat forward and increased eye contact. Greg was unclear, still, about why he had been singled out for special and, I guessed, unwelcome treatment, and was wary of what I was all about. I explained what I thought my role was – helping others to be as effective in their work as they wished to be – and that he was my primary concern. I might need to explain this, as when I see it in black and white it sounds somewhat disloyal to the commissioning party in the organisation. However, I am clear that as coach I must focus on the individual first *within the context of the organisation.* I believe that following this path I will ultimately benefit the organisation as long as I keep its needs in the forefront of discussion with the individual.

Ultimately, for me, if the individual doesn't want to change in the way the organisation wants them to they are better off parting company. We talked about the feedback Greg had received and he only expressed his lack of clarity about what Christine had said to him. He sensed hostility from members of the senior team, but saw this as how they treated many people. I attempted a rerun of the feedback, describing what I had been told had been observed (it was alright to use this third party feedback, I thought, as I understood it had already been given) and asked Greg what he felt. He greeted this with some disbelief, as if hearing details that had been hidden from him. Christine assured me later that this had not been the case, but, in some ways, what did it matter? It may have reflected unwillingness to accept feedback on his part, or ineffective delivery of feedback by others; what was clear was that he was now targeted for coaching.

Despite reservations about the need to enter into the process, nonetheless Greg was concerned about what was going on and possibly felt I was an ally in what I sensed had become a less happy environment for him. I explained a bit about how we might work together: obtain some (more) feedback about his performance, review recent events and what had happened and take a look at current work issues and discuss how he intended to handle them. However, before we did any of this, I explained that Greg must decide if he could work with me as his coach. He said he could, but sensing Greg was not the sort of person to openly 'reject' another, I encouraged him to go away, think about it and inform Christine about his decision. This was appropriate, as it was from her budget that my fee would come.

Assessment and Agreement

With a positive response, received through Christine, I then met with Greg for our first half-day session. At this session, I wanted to go over our original conversation again to gather any thoughts Greg had had since. We talked about the meetings to which Christine had referred and I asked Greg about how he thought they had gone and how he believed he might have been perceived. In reviewing these events, Greg accepted that he would not impact on the group in the same way as others, but also regarded this as rather unfair, given the nature of what he had to present. He saw the sort of information he had to share as 'hardly the sort of thing you can stand up and wave your arms around at'.

This seems to me to be a common response to feedback from individuals. By taking an extreme view of what is being asked, it may seem reasonable to them to then declare this null and void. It sometimes feels a bit like being in a parent–child relationship to me, with the coaching partner petulantly stating 'Oh, so you want me to …' and me countering with 'I'm not saying that, what I'm saying is …'. This tack seems favourite when suggesting individuals might look to get closer to, say, their direct reports; I have frequently had individuals meet this with 'well you can't go round being best friends with everybody' or 'so you think we ought to start meeting up outside work'.

So, in response to Greg's 'observation', I decided to give him my feedback about how he came across to me. I explained that in discussions we'd had so far he was relatively quiet when speaking, hesitated even when on a subject he knew well and paused for thought at times in a way that indicated he was thinking about something but not sharing this. From my point of view, I said, I could understand how he had been perceived as unsure and hence not completely in command of his area of responsibility. For me, and it seemed to Greg, this not only clarified why he was seen in the way he was, but also gave some clues about what he might look to do differently.

As part of that session, I also gave Greg a Myers–Briggs type indicator (Myers and Briggs 1998) and 16PF (ASE 1994) to complete. Whilst I had planned to use these anyway to help me gain some insight as to what Greg was all about, I also found in our discussion that he had a number of 'problems' with those he managed and his view of 'how people should behave' was, I thought, fairly rigid and pretty optimistic, even if I agreed with many of his sentiments. He had a difficult group; Christine confirmed that there were a few 'prima donnas' amongst the lawyers, and Greg had had minimal experience of managing others before being given this key leadership role.

To his credit, he had tried to tackle some of the issues in the team, funding a team event using an outside consultant. For Greg, the event was an unmitigated disaster. He had not sought advice from HR or in-house development specialists and was not prepared for what happened. Whilst he had expected, or hoped for, a number of 'home truths' to be told to some of his 'problem people', what was facilitated was open season on Greg! Forced to receive a torrent of criticism, which he felt came from every direction, Greg emerged emotionally battered and regretful. He felt that the criticism was unjust and regarded practically everyone in the group as 'disloyal'. In this first session, we talked a lot about his group and they started to assume greater importance in our subsequent discussions. Whilst the initial brief had been focused on changing senior management perceptions or evaluations, the 'hot topics' concerning Greg were quite different.

The issue of presentation and impact, without dismissing it, but here cutting a long story short, looked to be relatively easy to tackle. There were only infrequent meetings where Greg needed to present within the senior group and sharpening his approach to these was a matter of good preparation, something he did on content but not on style, and rehearsal. We addressed the matter of what you do when you're not presenting and the importance of active involvement even on those subjects where you are 'non-expert'. Together we identified practical actions Greg could take in the next meeting to raise his profile and convince others of his competence, which, Christine thought, was being hidden.

My own feeling was that the people management side of Greg's role was not only taxing but also undermining his confidence within it. If he could resolve some of the people issues or, more importantly, develop his ability to tackle these more effectively, he would truly fill the role. The evidence for me that this was the case was Greg's own speculation about moving back to a non-managing role where he would again focus on 'technical' work rather than leadership. Again rhetorical questions like 'why did I take this on?' had to be answered, and I asked Greg directly if he wanted the role and why and if he didn't, what did he want to do instead? He had ideas about what he might do instead but, when explored, these were not what he wanted right now. Right now he wanted to succeed in this role. I asked if this was 'simply' a matter of pride that might prevent him moving on if he really did not like what he was doing. He convinced me that it was important to him to succeed in the role and we refocused our attention on how this might be achieved.

At the end of our second session, we reviewed the output from the psychometric questionnaires. The picture emerged of someone who was quite introverted, no surprise by now, I'm sure, personally reserved, assertive in a generally reactive fashion, conscientious and detail-oriented and task-focused. As mentioned in Chapter 3 on assessment, one of the great benefits of using psychometric questionnaires is not only gaining insight but also giving individuals an appreciation of the range of personality types that exist out there; all those people who are 'not like me'. I find people's abandonment, if we get that far, of the 'but of course I do that, everyone does' view of behaviour quite elevating. The psychometrics offer the opportunity to say 'the people sitting over here on this dimension or of this type don't!' Getting individuals to think about those they know who might display different characteristics then brings the profiles to life and also seems to remove some elements of 'blame' that have been attributed up to that point.

I found Greg identifying with the profile that emerged for him, which is comforting if not necessary, but, more importantly, it provided a framework for talking about the people in his group. In addition to trying to classify who might be like what, an exercise of fairly limited value, together, although I admit to leading, we started to speculate on motives for behaviour other than those Greg suspected. The transformation of a 'self-centred, emotional time bomb' into an 'ambitious achiever lacking influencing skills' started to alter Greg's view of others and how he might deal with them.

Action

We had reviewed a number of conversations, well, clashes, that Greg had been through with particular individuals. He found highly emotionally charged tirades an affront rather than an expression of frustration, as this was simply not the way he conducted himself. As a result, he would react indignantly and counter the arguments presented with facts and evidence – great in a court of law, not much use in dissipating anger. We discussed why certain individuals were more problematic than others and how he might be able to work with them more effectively. At the same time, we explored why those who he found 'no problem', typically individuals who were quite like him in one way or another, should not be left to self-manage or be assumed to be other 'Gregs'.

I guess at this stage, rather neatly, Greg really started to develop his own coaching skills. Up to this point, he had been required to give good advice rapidly and resolve problems that others brought to him. In this expert role, he needed to focus on the information he was given, think about what it meant and give a response. Now he was being asked not only to deal with a host of issues that he may not have encountered before, but also to approach them by attending to subjective and occasionally emotionally laden content, enquiring about feelings rather than practicalities, and to do all this by stepping back to help others find the right path when ordinarily he would determine this.

As part of Greg's developing approach, we discussed the benefits of addressing 'process' as well as content in meetings with others. By this I meant highlighting to others not only what was going on at the time, for example 'clearly you're feeling very angry about the recent allocation of that project', but also disclosing his own feelings about what was happening. A sound British education and upbringing had ensured that Greg did his best to keep how he felt under wraps, but there was always 'leakage' that could not be controlled fully. This move to express some internal dialogue, for example 'the more you shout at me the less likely I am to help you with the problem', was queried by Greg as it suggested being 'out of control'. We needed to work on the model of manager/leader as 'android', untouched by criticism and comments, other people's anger or their upset. Again, we had some talk of matching or even escalating the emotional outbursts brought by others, but we managed to draw back to a position where Greg would merely tell others when he was finding it hard to listen and be supportive because of the way in which messages were being delivered.

These kind of meetings were all too frequent for Greg and so I suggested we also talk about how to be more proactive, both in addressing issues with others and in tackling the tricky subject of how certain individuals tended to approach him. An important part of this was actually catching others doing things right. It was easy to constantly view Maria as the self-appointed 'union official' bringing complaints on behalf of her colleagues, but there were occasions when Greg had to admit that she raised valid points, with suggestions for change that he might implement. Therefore Greg had a target of praising these ideas when they were raised, in whatever way, and, more importantly, her approach when she raised issues in a way that encouraged discussion and gained Greg's support without the need to harangue him.

As a backdrop to the work of this group, they were under tremendous pressure to deliver against tight deadlines and frequently hampered by late inclusion by partners in the business whom they serviced. One aspect of this was that Greg took on a lot of work and really supported members of his team directly when they became 'snowed under'. However, he could also see that this took him away from coaching his team. In the recent past, this had seemed like a bonus; he couldn't have contact because he was so busy, and individuals might be less likely to complain about this because they might have need to call on his assistance in the future.

Again, this is a familiar trap for executives to fall into. There may occasionally be a need for those in more technical functions to get involved in actual work issues, they may possess knowledge and experience, or an overview, that can speed the resolution of problems for those they manage. However, the dilemma is always how much time to spend tackling issues directly and how much to spend coaching others to tackle these themselves. Ideally, leaders would coach and not do, but the world of work is rarely if ever ideal, even in this respect. Again, individuals can go for the extreme definition of coaching on tasks to justify not allocating any time to this activity. Unless there is 'ample' time, often defined as 'no deadline', and mistakes can be rectified without any cost, coaching is sometimes viewed as 'not possible'. Of course, this limits coaching opportunities to a minimum and overlooks involving others on parts if not all of a task, reviewing work that has been completed by the coach/leader and providing insight into how matters were tackled.

In Greg's world, part of the frustrations of others was occasional lack of opportunity to take on new tasks. He was in the happy position of having very able individuals hungry to take on new challenges and develop their skills. However, there were others who were not facing up to the reality that the type of work they did and enjoyed was coming to an end and would no longer feature significantly in the work of the department. This provided a perfect opportunity for Greg to be proactive in considering the career development of some of his people. One individual, Peter, specialised in drafting a particular kind of contract for trading agreements. The business was actually declining in this area, such that it would no longer generate enough work for a full-time role. Peter's approach had pretty much been denial; he expected Greg to find this kind of work from somewhere.

This was a great coaching experience for me, as it was closest to what I think pure, non-directive coaching is all about. I hadn't the slightest idea what the work was about, what opportunities there might be for transfer of skills, or the likelihood of any route Greg that might choose being effective. We discussed what options were open to Greg in raising the issue with Peter. I could ask questions about how Greg might raise the issue with Peter, what reactions he might expect and what he might do to manage these effectively. However, I became aware of how much more open my questions were when asking about possibilities for tackling the actual work should Peter decide his future lay elsewhere, a distinct possibility.

A useful lesson from all this for me was that those leading areas of the business actually know what they're doing! Whilst I thought I knew a bit about how people behave and could ask questions of my coaching partner to get him to consider possibilities he might otherwise not have contemplated, here he was sailing through a potential problem of losing what I thought was a key member of his staff without batting an eyelid. I realised that I had started to think of Greg as needing coaching input on every subject and, worse still, I had started to think about what the right answer would be in this situation.

Another 'take away', which I guess I knew from my own experience of managing people, was that although as coaches we focus attention on development, sometimes you just have to admit that some individuals don't want to change and will part company from the organisation. This is what happened with Peter. He wasn't interested in learning other kinds of work and had a job opportunity in mind, which the discussion with Greg then encouraged him to take. Greg and I had explored the various routes the discussion might take and the conversation with Peter, as reported by Greg, appeared to go well. However, on completion, I realised that I had not worked through fully with Greg what he might then do should Peter choose to resign. This became apparent in a telephone conversation with Greg, which we had between face-to-face meetings. There was unrest in the camp and this had been caused by Peter's account of his discussion with Greg. Reported back as the equivalent of a cold-hearted dispensation with Peter's services, I wasn't able to tell whether this was because Greg had been 'heavy-handed' in accepting Peter's decision to 'move on' or whether Peter had been what one might call 'mischief making'.

We discussed what Greg might do. He wanted to speak to Peter and get him to go round those he'd talked to and explain the position more 'accurately'. A quick check with Greg on the likelihood of this happening happily put this idea to bed. However, Greg still wanted to speak with Peter and I supported his willingness to tackle something which, three months earlier, he would have ignored. In deciding how best to make the approach, Greg was keen to disclose his feelings of disappointment and some anger towards Peter. Having got Greg to this point, I didn't want to discourage him but felt uneasy about how this would work. I have to admit to suggesting to Greg that he temper these expressions as 'concerns' over what might have been said, as, after all, everything coming his way was either second or third hand. This seemed to be the point that needed clarification: what message had Peter taken away from their meeting and why?

Greg felt that whatever Peter felt it was unprofessional of him to then set about telling colleagues that he had been treated poorly. I asked Greg what he really felt about Peter's departure. He regretted it but was not going to mourn the loss excessively. I asked him not only if it was feasible Peter had got that impression, but also what the impact might be on those remaining, if they believed that if they chose to leave tomorrow they would not be missed? By chance, we had generated another good example of how the people perspective in business decisions must always be a key factor to consider. For my part, it was a reminder to always ask 'and what about the effect on the others?'

During this first six months of coaching with Greg, we tended to meet every six to eight weeks and speak on the phone in between. In this time, a number of others in the team departed. This was not planned actively, as far as I could tell, but was undoubtedly convenient as it was the key 'troublemakers' who left. My information from Christine (HR VP) was that these were regarded as quite positive moves, as they were the individuals who caused her and others difficulties, as well as Greg. It struck me that this seemed to be the same syndrome as for many teachers who look back on their first days in teaching and with hindsight realise that they did in fact have their worst-ever class when they were new, inexperienced and least well equipped to cope.

More encouragingly, Maria, who at one stage was regarded by Greg as public enemy number one, had started to develop into a key player in the group. Harnessing her enthusiasm instead of blunting it, Greg had supported some of her initiatives and given her responsibility for organising work processes and practices about which she had complained. This triggered the continuance of a conversation we had had previously about developing a successor. Greg had earmarked the most senior lawyer in the department as 'most likely', although he doubted some of Trevor's aptitude for, and indeed interest in, the role when pushed. This 'nomination', not supported through any targeted development, was made on the basis of seniority and to a large extent Trevor's support of Greg at difficult times – for example he had 'put the knife in' the fewest number of times at the team event.

It became apparent that Greg had some potential prejudice to overcome and certainly some history to put into perspective. A challenge for me was not to make recommendations based on what seemed obvious to me. Maria was the only individual I had heard about (in all my time coaching Greg, I never worked with him and his team directly) who had demonstrated any inclination to take the lead, albeit that she had upset colleagues on occasion by virtue of her style. Her development, self-driven, had addressed leadership skills and she had made changes to her style and approach that had certainly improved her relationship with Greg. However, Greg felt she lacked experience and would not be able to command the respect of others in the team; the 'wounds' from the team event had obviously healed by this stage.

I had to respect Greg's judgment on experience, although I questioned his view that the leader of the group had to have the broadest expertise, but had more doubts about the judgment on her ability to gain respect. We discussed how a potential successor might be identified and, not atypically, Greg's view was that there was no real likely candidate in the group other than Trevor. My question was 'if Trevor is the most likely successor, in the event that you are run over by the proverbial bus, does he want it and how is he being developed?' I knew the answer to the questions, but it started Greg thinking about what he might need to do.

In fact, events overtook us. Trevor announced that he was taking another role outside the organisation, as the volume of his specialised type of work was diminishing. This explained why Greg accepted the announcement so matter of factly, when I had believed that Trevor was vital to the functioning of the department – how had I missed that one? At the same time, members of the group, well, Maria, were asking questions about how one became a senior lawyer. The title had traditionally been bestowed, it seemed, in recognition of time served and all senior lawyers were in their late forties or fifties. My question for Greg was how could individuals achieve the status, if it were to be retained, apart from living a few more years within the business? In a business that rewarded results and contribution, it seemed to me this should play some part alongside demonstrated competence. In the discussion that followed, Greg decided that the title should in fact be dropped, with a 'grandfather' rule applying to those using the title at present. However, this did not answer Maria's question about how one might progress within the department. Initially, Greg regarded these questions as evidence of Maria slipping back into 'old habits', although he could not this time fault the way in which she posed them. I put it to Greg that it was in fact reasonable for anyone ambitious in a business to ask their manager what was required to progress and expect some sort of considered response. Greg set to thinking about how individuals added value in the department, and this exercise actually highlighted the contribution Maria had made already. This did not lead to her becoming Greg's nominated successor but it did contribute to his continuing shift in thinking.

Exit

My face-to-face meetings with Greg ended after about 14 months, with the time between them extending at the end. We agreed an end point with a 'call-back' option should difficult issues arise; Greg has not exercised that option and even though in telephone discussions he usually greets me with 'odd that you should call at this time because …', he tends to explain the issue and what he is going to do about it in a way that would have been quite alien to him in the past.

With regard to the initial brief, within three months of our first meeting he was actually praised by Christine and, indirectly, by other members of the senior team, previously his greatest detractors, for his presentation and input at meetings. On another happy note, Greg organised a three-day meeting of his people from all over Europe and had a very successful time. He took advice from a number of parties about how to organise this, involved his group fully in planning and setting it up and did without an external facilitator – a bold move after his previous experience.

From my point of view, the assignment was a success. When I first met Greg, his tenure was in doubt; he improved his performance and that threat disappeared. He is reported as being far more effective both as a contributor in the senior team and in leading his group. More personally, I asked Greg for feedback about how I'd been as his coach. On the plus side he said he'd appreciated having someone offering a different perspective on people issues in a way that 'wouldn't have occurred to me before'. He also valued being listened to and supported in finding alternative approaches that were still 'his way'. On the negative side, I was surprised to hear him say that at times it had 'seemed like I was elsewhere'. I can't deny that during the time I spend with individuals other things do creep into my mind and occasionally pressing problems that I'm facing will break my concentration. Greg insisted that it hadn't had a harmful effect, but it made me think about how many times I may have dissuaded him from going into more detail because he thought I was bored or disinterested. I can't now underestimate the need to be open about where my mind is and to take breaks when the concentration starts to slip.

Review Questions

1. What were your thoughts at the outset of this assignment?
2. How would you have focused discussion and action planning?
3. What would you have done the same and why?
4. What would you have done differently and why?
5. When would you have terminated the coaching relationship? Why? How?

CHAPTER 8

Executive Coaching in Action: Out of Favour or Out of her League?

Introduction

This is the case of a British executive in a UK multinational. The business had grown significantly since she first joined, and this success was attributed largely to the entrepreneurial CEO, with whom she had worked very closely. The CEO was succeeded by a very different individual who came from a well-established, structured US multinational high-tech firm. Our meetings were prompted by the new CEO as he built relationships with his new leadership team. However, it was these relationships that emerged as the critical focus during the ensuring coaching sessions.

Change at the Top

An acquisitive electronics and control systems company appointed a new CEO who had worked previously for a large semi-conductor manufacturer, advanced in their approach to people development. Valuing his experience of development centres, he decided to institute a similar process of assessment for development in this organisation. He decided to have the entire top team assessed, on an individual basis, with the report reviewed with the person by the consultant responsible for the assessment and himself. This was my first contact with Colin, the new CEO, who had worked previously with the consultancy firm where I was a coach.

A series of assessments, six for those in post plus two new appointees, were conducted. These included in-basket exercises, role-play exercises, aptitude and psychometric tests, all discussed in Chapter 3. The reviews proceeded with Colin identifying and agreeing key areas for development with the individuals and I worked more closely with two of the group to help them to firm up their particular development plans and proposed actions.

One of these was Lynda, the group treasurer. Lynda had been with the organisation 11 years, longer than all but one of the top team, who happened to be her boss. She had built a strong relationship with him, Les, the finance director, and with the previous CEO, Don, a powerful, charismatic and dynamic individual, by all accounts, who had grown the company significantly in an entrepreneurial fashion until his retirement. Colin, the CEO, was brought in to take the organisation through the next phase of development which was deemed to require more discipline and structure than had previously been in place. The previous CEO had known every area of the business quite intimately and regularly intervened to guide and direct as he saw necessary. However, the organisation was now a size where this was completely impractical.

Colin was 'stock-taking' in all areas and the people were a key part of that focus. In discussion, he gave his own assessment of the top team and in general he thought he had a group that could continue to move the business forward and achieve the results the stock market demanded. His areas of doubt lay with those who had been in the business some time and grown in status but not necessarily, in his view, in competence with the business. Lynda was one of these people.

Lynda and Colin had talked about Lynda's role and her expectations and it seemed that there was something of a mismatch. Lynda envisaged a continuation of the close triumvirate relationship she had experienced between herself, Les and Don the former CEO, as they had worked together on a number of acquisitions. Colin saw this changing because the volume of the work would increase and, as it soon turned out, he would employ a specialist in that area. In addition, he didn't see Lynda as someone with whom he could work that closely. He was concerned to be more inclusive of the leaders of the key business areas and, at a personal level, valued Lynda's contribution but had reservations about her personal style and ability to work well with the rest of the team.

This perception had developed because of Lynda's reactions in meetings and some exchanges that had taken place during an off-site team-building event that Colin had organised a few months after he had joined the company; by this time he had been there four months. He, and others, found Lynda quite brusque and blunt at times, putting in critical comments in an aggressive fashion and putting others down through off-the-cuff remarks that were delivered as 'throwaway' statements at the end of tasks or when others had finished making their points. These were seen as unhelpful at best, disruptive and hurtful at worst.

Colin was concerned for this type of behaviour to stop. He thought Lynda had a place in the organisation and a significant contribution to make. Lynda had delivered consistently to high standards, had a lot of historic knowledge about the organisation and had displayed great loyalty to the business, often putting its interests before her personal life. Colin had benefited from coaching, and indeed attributed his rise to CEO in part to coaching he had received and his willingness to work with a coach to develop his capabilities; he believed Lynda could benefit similarly.

First Meeting with Lynda

When we met, Lynda admitted that she viewed Colin's suggestion of working with a coach as disappointing. When we talked about why Colin might have suggested it and what Lynda felt about the way in which she was perceived, she focused on how the situation had changed since Colin's arrival, the issues she had with certain members of the team and the problems she foresaw. From my point of view, Lynda's appraisal of the situation started to sound as though everything was everybody else's fault and, in a 'defensively arrogant' way, everyone was wrong except her.

One factor that came into play in this first discussion was sex. This was predominantly an engineering business run out of the UK. The mix of the management team was far from diverse: they were, with the exception of Lynda, male, white and in their early forties to mid-fifties. Lynda was the only woman in the top level of management; to find other female managers you went to technical disciplines such as finance or legal. So, Lynda referred to them as the 'boys' club'. They were grouped together in this way because they would drink together, and she might not join them, stay up late when she might go to bed, talk about sport, share jokes that, although she didn't say were obscene, were classed as very male humour-oriented and, as with the away-day, approach tasks in a 'macho way'. Lynda described this as competitive, trying to do better than one another and valuing 'winning'.

I admit my initial reaction was just to say, 'Grow up!' Here was someone occupying a senior post in a growing organisation who seemed to be overlooking some of the harsh realities of life, and not just corporate life at that. Times change, people change and what Lynda had enjoyed up to now might not continue, but it didn't mean that whatever was happening now was wrong just because she didn't like it. In fact, there were those who had said that the old situation was not right at all. But the possibility of exclusion on the grounds of 'different to us' reinforced the need, I felt, to hear more about the situation and how Lynda experienced it.

As a coach, I think this is an important moment that occurs in all sorts of different ways on assignments. It's the kind of moment when I find myself asking the question: 'Is there something majorly dysfunctional about the environment that might mean that anybody coming in from outside, or who had no part in creating it, might experience similar difficulties?' As coaches, we hear of 'impossible bosses', 'bullies' at work and direct reports who 'won't listen to reason'. We coach individuals from the perspective, most of the time I would say, that the individual needs to change to better handle a 'normal', albeit challenging, situation. Occasionally though, and we have probably all experienced this, we are coaching an individual to cope with an unreasonable situation.

When this is the case, I think we have two main options: address the situation or, if we can't or won't be allowed to do that, coach the individual to cope, which might mean counselling them about whether they want to remain in this place. Of course, first we must be sure that the situation is dysfunctional.

In this particular instance, I had some critical questions in my mind: the make-up of the senior team hadn't really changed and yet Lynda talked as if the 'boys' club' had only recently started to impact on her. It wouldn't make its possible existence right, but it was the change that was important. It implied that Colin had in some way facilitated or encouraged this, even if unconsciously. What was different now? In addition, was this a convenient explanation for other, broader interpersonal issues? It can be 'easy' to say 'they hate me because I'm a man, white, a church-goer, a Real Madrid supporter and quiet' or any other category that differentiates us from others, but this can sometimes stop us from looking more critically at what we do and how we do it, and the impact this may have on others. I was concerned that Lynda should not be subject to discrimination (Gattiker and Larwood 1990, Melamed 1995, Morrison et al. 1987, Stroh et al. 1992), but also needed to ensure that there were no other issues causing her colleagues to distance themselves from her.

I wanted to understand how she experienced the group and how they had reacted to Colin's style as CEO. Lynda saw this as an opportunity to criticise the other members of the senior team. They were variously described as 'opportunist', 'putting the knife in', 'now involved in areas they know nothing about', 'not bright enough' and other derogatory descriptions. Asked how she had come to this conclusion, the 'away-day' that Colin had set up was cited several times as her database. It struck me that Colin's attempts to bring others in closer to the business than they had been before had been taken by Lynda as alienation of herself. She had moved from being the 'right-hand woman' once removed, if you like, to simply one of the team, and she didn't like it.

In this description, there were a few references to 'male' behaviour and this seemed to be prevalent during social rather than work moments. For instance, when they took breaks from work meetings, some members of the group would talk about sport, often golf, and Lynda had no interest in this. In the evenings, such as when they had gone away as a group, there would be late drinking in the bar which Lynda did not want to do. These to me, rightly or wrongly, are issues that we all face when spending time with work colleagues with whom we have little else in common other than work. I tend to find myself listening with decreasing interest when people talk about golf courses they have played, their best shot ever and how they have decreased their handicap or had it increased. We can all talk about subjects boring to others. It may be insensitive to do this, and do it consistently, but it is not illegal.

Similarly, working in the field of personal development on residential courses has given me an almost 'binary' reaction to late drinking, or perhaps just talking, in bars at hotels. At times, with a group, their company, and discussion, is so engaging that we find ourselves there in the early, or later, hours of the morning, when the poor staff would like to close up. At other times, drained by giving everything I've got to a group during the day and the prospect of another early start and particularly challenging day tomorrow, heading for my bed is the favoured option. You risk being called 'boring' or 'antisocial', but you have to do what you think is right at the time whilst avoiding obvious offence to others. These, I felt, were choices facing Lynda, they just happened to have a 'male' connotation to them.

It will start to sound, I'm sure, as if I had convinced myself to ignore possible issues around sexual discrimination and, to a degree, I had. I knew the environment within which Colin had worked and discrimination of any kind simply wasn't tolerated. This didn't mean he couldn't possibly have acted with prejudice – after all he'd left that organisation, this could have been one reason why. But it did mean that he was aware of the implications of acting in this way. More, I started to feel from Lynda's explanations of her recent experience that this was not the major issue at work here. It would have been almost impossible to make the case, perhaps with Colin, that it was a 'discriminatory environment', given that reference to her sex or anything other than 'social exclusion' simply hadn't taken place. In fact, I did mention to Colin that it 'couldn't be easy for Lynda working in this all-male group'. He acknowledged this and in fact he cited examples of where individuals had backed off from arguing a point with Lynda when a male colleague might have been treated differently. Colin was adamant that he didn't want this to happen either. All I could do was make him aware that conversation might veer into a style and, certainly, focus that Lynda might find 'macho'; at this point she would opt out.

For me though, the onus was on Lynda to manage the situation, which meant she might have to address directly those matters that caused her offence, at the time, and work on her own input to ensure that this was not the cause for excluding her.

Assessment

We needed to get some more data to work with and, as had already been arranged, Lynda was to go through a developmental assessment. This was an 'individual assessment centre' where the participant was interviewed, completed psychometric tests and questionnaires, undertook in-basket and role-play exercises and reviewed the output of a 360° report. Lynda went through the day and, amidst the comments about 'I hate playing games', found some elements, such as the in-basket, very stimulating. The report was to be compiled and then reviewed by us in two weeks' time, with Colin joining us for a follow-up session.

At our next meeting, I asked Lynda how things were going and for any further thoughts about the day. She kept to the same line about the assessment as before but mentioned that at work things had got worse because Colin was having even less to do with her. We moved on from the report to the feedback in order to keep to our prearranged meeting time with Colin. What emerged was a picture of someone who was bright, but not as bright as Lynda liked to think, diligent and conscientious, hard working, results-oriented and loyal: in fact a replay of all the feedback she and I had received. On the downside, she was found to be blunt and brusque, aggressive in two of the role plays and generally perceived as 'not suffering fools gladly', an English term for lacking patience when dealing with others, especially if they were felt not to be as intelligent as oneself, slow to assimilate information and muddled in their thinking.

Lynda's reaction to this was general acceptance without regret, and she cited the examples that had generated the feedback: 'I wouldn't have a member of my staff take that attitude with me', 'I expect someone in that position to know their facts'. I observed that it was a 'fairly unforgiving' way of dealing with people and Lynda accepted this as a fact about her – and not for changing.

However, the 360° report was something of a trial for Lynda. I knew she was expecting the worst, as she'd already stated her expectations about what would come out and why. Having told me that she didn't get on with most of her peer group, she expected, or had prepared herself for, low ratings. Of course, it didn't mean that if that was what she was given that she wouldn't be hurt. She was, however, expecting more from Les because they had worked together so long and so closely; I also suspected she might be hoping that Colin's ratings would be significantly higher than those of her peers because she had committed significant effort to meeting his needs.

Overall, the feedback was very positive about task delivery but poor on factors concerning interpersonal skills. The former was pleasing to Lynda as her effort had been recognised and with regard to the latter she'd 'expected that'. The surprise for Lynda came in Les supporting the comments of others on interpersonal skills. This, she explained, was not because she thought it was wrong, just that she thought her relationship with Les might have influenced his scoring. Unfortunately for Lynda, Les had not only noted her attitude with others but was also able to be objective about it. Something else that could be deduced from the scoring of the 360° report was that the majority of Lynda's effort went into servicing Colin and Les in their activities, whilst work for the team always came second. Although it could be argued that this was priority, and later Colin confirmed this, it raised questions about Lynda's ability to build and develop an effective relationship with her peer group. We talked about what was happening, in very general terms, and the implications. My summary was:

> Colin's way of working is very different to Don's. You are no longer going to be working with the CEO in the way you have up until now. You don't have solid relationships with your peers and will have to work hard to change this. The question is, do you want to do this?

I think Lynda was a bit shocked at my candour; she looked a bit hurt that I didn't seem that empathic about her situation. This was revealed when she asked me if Colin wanted her out of the business. I said that in any discussion I'd had with Colin he had been very positive about her contribution but reiterated the areas that were causing him, and others, some difficulty. In addition, Lynda had the 360° results to work from; in my mind I thought that the ratings given by Colin, which included an overall 'doing a good job', indicated that he valued Lynda's work if not aspects of her style.

However, I wanted to make it clear to Lynda that, although this overall view might be positive now, if things continued in the same vein her position might not remain secure. Although in some ways I had no hard evidence to suggest this, I felt it right to make Lynda aware of the potential implications rather than allow her to believe that her performance really was good enough to forego any development activity.

Lynda expressed doubts about the impact that any change she might make would have on those around her. She believed others would be suspicious if she 'suddenly was really nice to everyone' but of course, as I told her, this was not what was going to be asked of her. She wanted to know what would be required. As a coach, the temptation here is to reel off a list of 'good' behaviours that you think would be desirable, and in keeping with one's own style. Fortunately, on this occasion, I stopped myself on the 'recommendation trail' and asked Lynda what it was she thought she might do differently, given the feedback she had received. In keeping with her style, Lynda replied 'keep my mouth shut when people make stupid comments!' I have to say Lynda's style had me irritated, so my question to Lynda was 'how do you want to be treated if you make a stupid comment?' I might have guessed the response – 'I expect to be told.' 'Well Lynda, I think your last comment was a stupid one.' I'm not sure if many manuals recommend that you trade insults with your coaching partner; I could say I was 'showing I'm human' or that I wanted to demonstrate to Lynda how that sort of comment comes across but, actually, I just needed to get it off my chest. I thought it would make me feel better; I'd listened a lot to Lynda going on about all the problems with others, I wanted to 'shake' her out of this 'self-centred' view and make her see that her style was a real pain at times and had got to me.

We managed to get the discussion back on course by looking at some specific occasions when Lynda met with peers and with Colin. We reviewed some recent meetings and Lynda's interpretation of how they had gone. With peers, she was frustrated that they did not understand some of the technicalities of what she had been doing. She dismissed this as 'stupidity' and also rationalised away the need to tell them by saying they 'didn't need to know'. I found myself constantly pointing out two things to Lynda:

1. As members of the top team, they had a right to understand everything that was happening in the business, even more so if they asked questions of a colleague.
2. Colin had deemed it necessary for them to be involved. He was the CEO and whether Lynda liked it or not, thought it right or wrong, they would be involved because that's what he wanted.

Agreement

We then went through a period of two meetings covering six weeks when Lynda talked about the possibility of leaving the organisation. She admitted applying for and pursuing a potential job option some weeks after Colin had joined the company and she had started to feel 'on the outside'. In exploring this, Lynda had come to realise how good her role was; the potential employer she'd met with could not offer the same level of involvement in the business, nor would Lynda continue to have some of the benefits she presently enjoyed because of her length of service – such as taking time off in lieu when work had been particularly hectic (by this I mean periods of working for seven days with some all-night sessions).

I think this is typical for executives who find themselves at a point in their lives when they have to make choices about finding the next big challenge or enjoying what they have achieved. This is not simply a matter of 'opting out', as they sometimes express it, but, I think, a realisation of the advantages of having amassed a wealth of experience in a role that still offers sufficient challenge, when up to this point the emphasis has been on trying to 'progress my career'. Doing this has generally involved seeking out new roles with greater responsibility, often in a different organisation that competes in an unfamiliar field. The pressure is on to 'prove oneself' and this is sometimes re-examined by individuals who have pursued this almost without thought of the strain this has placed on them and, where applicable, their families. For me, Lynda was at this point.

We talked about what Lynda enjoyed outside work. She had 'show dogs', special breeds that she would take to dog shows around the country. In the absence of children, and a partner, these were her family, although she had two brothers for whom she had little time. The sortie into the job market had brought home to her that she had established herself in a position that gave her some flexibility in her lifestyle without her commitment being questioned. This was not to say that she had created an 'easy life' for herself, merely that going elsewhere would demand she commit even more.

This raised an awkward point: was Lynda going to stay with this company just because she'd get less flexibility elsewhere? When we talked this through, Lynda insisted that she still enjoyed her work, she just felt that she was not so involved on the exciting projects and was being called upon less than she would have been used before. I pointed out that this 'alienation', as she experienced it, would probably only increase if Colin felt uneasy about her style. Lynda cited Colin's declaration that 'I want people to be honest with me' and how this just seemed like empty words. Again we went back to the feedback from the 360° report, the assessment and my own observations. I volunteered that perhaps Colin still really did want honest opinion and views, but that he just might be able to work with it more effectively if delivered more palatably. Therefore, our broad agreement was that she would stay with the company and our work together would focus on how she could deal most effectively with both Colin and her peers.

Action

First we worked on how Lynda might phrase some of the points of view she wanted to put forward. After three attempts on some, we got close to phrasing that didn't make me wince. We also discussed the need to ask questions of others in the group meetings instead of assuming that they were 'dull'. I encouraged Lynda to think of why individuals might not seem to understand concepts or decisions. It became clear that they occasionally used simple terms to describe technically sophisticated processes and Lynda took this as evidence of complete ignorance, rather than lack of knowledge of esoteric terms. We talked about this approach as the refuge of the technical specialist. The best in their field would be able to describe what they did or were doing in lay terms. Attempting to do this would have two distinct advantages for Lynda: first, individuals would appreciate her willingness to help them understand this technically complex field and, secondly, she would be less likely to be classified as a technical specialist, unable to contribute to broader business issues and discussions. The use of questions and careful listening was therefore included in Lynda's development plan, which also focused on 'thinking' and rephrasing before delivering 'cutting comments'.

As an aside, it was also around the time when we were discussing Lynda's thoughts about leaving the organisation that we got further into a discussion about her upbringing and her relationship with her father. I raise this as an aside because I think this is the type of conversation where workplace coaches find themselves heading towards the limit of their experience and expertise, such as they might have. At times, we tread the line between coaching for improved work performance and counselling for emotional disturbance. In extreme cases, I and other colleagues have had coaching partners wrestling with the challenges of alcoholism, imminent or recent break-up of their long-term partnerships, low self-esteem, abuse as a child, contemplation of suicide, determining their sexuality or deciding their gender. These are not issues that sit easily alongside matters of 'making more input to meetings' or 'asking more questions of direct reports'.

As a psychologist, I have completed courses in 'clinical psychology', 'abnormal behaviour' and 'counselling psychology', which has taught me that this is a specialist field, and you may not even be aware when you have entered it. My concern is always that my ego, and fascination, will seduce me into going deeper into issues with individuals, despite the fact that I am ill equipped to truly assist them with what is there. A poor analogy it may be, but it's a lot easier to take a car engine apart than it is to put it back together. Therefore, in discussions I tend to:

- Make sure that I acknowledge the issue raised rather than ignore what's been said simply because it could be awkward for me, or the other person
- Let my coaching partner explain as much or as little about the situation and its impact as he or she wishes – having made the decision to raise it, he or she obviously wants to talk about it. This is exactly what I would do for a friend. As long as my questioning is open and I respect and check signals that he or she does not want to continue, he or she controls the disclosure
- If he or she calls a halt to discussing the issue, either because it's too painful or he or she feels they have let me in too far or because he or she believes that this is not the place to discuss this sort of matter, then I accept this but remind him or her that whatever it is that has caused him or her concern will not yet be resolved and will probably surface at a later date or in some other guise

- If he or she seeks my advice, I make it clear that this is outside my area of 'expertise', or familiarity (if it is) and that I would recommend he or she seeks more professional input if he or she is going to continue to be troubled by what has happened.

So, back to Lynda: she told me about her father who was now deceased. She had spent a lot of time with him when she was growing up and it was obvious from what she said that she both loved and admired him a great deal. He was a vet in a rural area and she would accompany him on visits to farms and stables. His ability to influence her or her willingness to be influenced by him or to accept what he said so as not to upset him was no better illustrated by the fact that he forbad her to study to become a veterinary surgeon, which is what she wanted to do. Instead, she acquiesced and became a chartered accountant, a profession he approved for her.

She then talked about her ex-husband and drew parallels. He had been in the military, and pursued his career as a pilot with some success. However, she had felt that his life, and needs, dominated and they had split up. For Lynda, this was creating something of a self-portrait. She saw an individual who sought approval from a strong male, and let him be the arbiter of whether she was doing a good job or not. I hasten to add this was her analysis not mine, but it sounded plausible to me.

Working with this idea in mind, she felt that this was an opportunity to break away from a pattern she had seen with other bosses. I asked her what 'breaking away' might look like. I was encouraged that although this contained some elements of 'standing up to the person', an almost aggressive reaction, it also meant to stop treating them as though they were 'above her'. Part of our discussion had focused on expectations of others and indeed Lynda expected her boss to be 'perfect'. She felt a boss had to be able to foresee all difficulties both for their people and the business, to know everything about the organisation, customers and products from day one and generally develop a strategy to leapfrog competitors and sustain growth at unprecedented levels.

Once we started to explore what it must be like to be in the CEO's shoes, the concerns he might have and the limitations under which he was operating, it became clear to Lynda that rather than orchestrating everything to be exactly as he wanted, Colin was still having to feel his way in many aspects of the job. Not least of these was operating as a CEO, as this was his first appointment into a position where he was in charge of the whole business. Whereas I feared this might have caused Lynda to despise Colin as someone who was ill-prepared or even ill-suited to this role, in fact it made her better able to take him down from the metaphorical 'pedestal' on which she had put him (maybe to see him fall further). She was able to reposition Colin and adjust her own view of the equity in the relationship – from her point of view Colin was no longer instrumental in everything he did and indeed potentially shared some vulnerabilities that she felt.

We continued to work on the actions that Lynda would take when working with Colin and with her peer group and reviewed these at each session. According to Lynda, there was a more team-oriented approach amongst the senior group in general, thanks to Colin's focus and encouragement, and this had helped Lynda to implement new behaviours. She had also enlisted the assistance of a trusted colleague who had worked with her for a number of years to provide feedback on how she had performed in the meeting. My own assessment of this colleague, through the process outlined earlier, was that Lynda might intimidate him and not always get candid feedback, but at least Lynda was making the effort. Eliciting feedback that was generally positive might encourage her to ask others who might then provide more 'formative' feedback.

Another Issue

As seems to be the case when things on coaching assignments appear to be starting to go well, we hit a mini-crisis, from Lynda's point of view. She learnt that Colin had engaged a headhunter to find someone to work specifically on acquisitions, an area in which Lynda had been heavily engaged in up to now and which captured her interest more than any other aspect of the job. This process was in fact well advanced and, ironically, the same week that I met Lynda, I was contacted by Colin to assess the prospective employee.

As part of my discussion with Colin about the focus of the assessment, we discussed the impact that this individual coming in, if successful, would have on Lynda. It was clear from discussion that Colin did not really feel this was Lynda's area, although he did envisage her having continued involvement in some of the acquisition projects that were already underway. My own view was that this was a message that hadn't been given to Lynda, but she was, quite rightly it seemed, drawing her own conclusions.

My question for Colin was, if Lynda was not going to be involved in acquisition work, what then? Colin's view was to use Lynda in a more focused treasury role rather than continue with the kind of roving role she'd enjoyed to date. He intended to strengthen the area with the appointment of a deputy treasurer, something Lynda had requested, and saw this as a positive indication of how he regarded Lynda's field.

We also discussed any observations Colin had of Lynda and in general there was a positive view about input and, more importantly, attitude within meetings. In her dealings with Colin, Lynda had also been more patient and made time to explain her position and view without resorting to some 'trademark huffing and puffing'. Colin, Les and the rest of the senior team viewed this positively. It seemed as though Lynda was making progress. My sessions with Lynda continued with us focusing on recent and upcoming meetings, tasks that Lynda needed to tackle with others and the management of Lynda's people; something that, up to now, had occupied us very little.

However, another major hurdle was about to present itself: the appointment of Nigel following the assessment. I hadn't spoken to Lynda about Nigel and his assessment at all, as this was of course completely confidential and concerned only myself, Colin and Les. They were satisfied with Nigel's technical ability, although he did not have vast experience, and they liked him personally. The assessment had raised some concerns, mainly over intellectual capacity and some aspects of his people skills and maturity. He was a 'little arrogant in presenting himself', I had written, 'sometimes without good reason'. However, he was appointed.

This very appointment, as indicated above, was something of an affront to Lynda, who regarded it as invasion of her territory. However, it was made worse, in her eyes, by the nature of the appointee. Lynda was probably (my assumption) not exactly in the frame of mind to welcome whoever came on board with open arms, but this seemed to have been exacerbated by the fact that Nigel had not arrived and demonstrated instant and superior knowledge and competence to Lynda. Because of Lynda's experience and knowledge in the company, Colin had asked her to 'show Nigel the ropes', and this had been taken by Lynda as adding insult to injury. In her view, Nigel was being brought in to oust her from her favourite work, couldn't actually do the work and Colin had the nerve to ask her to teach Nigel what to do.

We were back to a discussion about where Lynda fitted in with the team and the changing nature of her relationship with Colin. This was not about learning new skills or applying acquired skills in new circumstances; this was about Lynda adjusting her 'mindset' about where she was and what she was, and about whether she could accept the change and work effectively with it.

Again Lynda mentioned moving from the company and I challenged her about whether she was serious or not; was this a threat or a promise?

She had been approached recently about a role that was quite local, should she pursue it? We discussed the reasons why individuals leave organisations and what her reasons might be. As is well documented, more individuals tend to leave a business because they are frustrated by their current role than because they spot an excellent opportunity elsewhere; this tends to be rationalised in hindsight. Lynda was certainly 'fed up'; she thought she'd been treated badly and saw no prospect of this changing. This might be good reason to leave, but would going somewhere else resolve problems or simply generate new ones? Lynda decided to go to the initial interview 'out of interest' to see what they were like and what was on offer.

This type of event can obviously place the coach in a difficult position, for example when asked how things are progressing with your coaching partner. 'Oh fine, I'm just coaching Lynda on how to prepare for an external job interview!' My view is to treat this like any other piece of information given in confidence. My client is the coaching partner and in my experience the commissioning party may not use information like this to progress development but prepare the ground for departure, which may then be accelerated. They can be informed when individuals are very unhappy and make up their own mind about what they want to do. But I have never seen statements like 'I'm thinking of leaving' perceived and treated as anything but threats or bargaining ploys.

Lynda went for the interview and we discussed it at our next meeting. The upshot was that it was now clear to Lynda that she was going to find it hard to obtain a post as good as the one she presently occupied. She had been to a medium-sized engineering company that wanted a new finance director and was setting up a treasury function. However, it had no overseas plants and was focused on organic growth. The prospect of joining this solid but less dynamic organisation simply did not appeal. My feelings at this stage were ambivalent. Lynda had at least investigated another avenue and found it wanting; therefore she could feel much better about where she was and regard it more positively. On the other hand, she might be more depressed because nothing had changed about her current circumstances and now she might feel trapped.

I put it to Lynda that she had a tough decision to make: either she had to accept that the situation wouldn't change but she must (or risk becoming unhappy at work and leave eventually), or she had to take action to find another post and be extremely positive and proactive about this. I was more depressed when Lynda started talking in terms of how close her retirement could be, if taken 'early'. This was not necessarily a real prospect, but she was still in the frame of mind to consider any 'escape route'. I likened this to serving a jail sentence, crossing the days off and literally wishing one's life away. Lynda needed to talk this through and we spent that session discussing where she was and the options open to her. Several points emerged:

- Nigel was grateful for the assistance Lynda had provided (even if done under duress) and they were starting to work together more effectively
- Lynda's involvement in some of the acquisition work had not really diminished, it was just that she was no longer the leading individual on new projects
- Things had become easier with Colin, and with some members of the senior team
- She still enjoyed the organisation and its business
- She had opportunities for taking on other challenges.

On this latter point, Lynda had mentioned that she would like to see about becoming a non-executive director at a small company in the area. This was one of the most positive statements Lynda had made in the seven months we had now been working together; I was keen to make the most of it. Lynda had already decided that Colin would refuse permission. We discussed why, and what the problem might be with just asking. Lynda decided to do just that and we worked on how she would present this to Colin, what rationale she would give, what reactions might be possible and how she, Lynda, might deal with them.

Just before our next meeting, Lynda approached Colin on the subject. Colin was generally supportive. He made the case for Lynda perhaps to pursue this in six months' time, once a particular acquisition had been completed but wanted her to explore possibilities in the meantime. This was very positive for both parties. Lynda now had a personal example of how dealing with Colin in the 'right way' could achieve a good result from her point of view.

Exit and Evaluation

It was soon after this that Lynda and I met for what turned out to be the last time. I say this because it was an unplanned 'exit'. It was not even because of the positive result above, as this was a glimmer of hope but not indicative of much of their relationship. I found it harder to arrange meeting times with Lynda and the acquisition referred to above became the reason for lack of diary space; so we drifted apart.

I contacted Lynda to check where we were: are you now done with coaching from me? This prompted a meeting, where Lynda explained that she now thought she had established a better relationship with most of the key players and with Colin in particular. She was not 'happy' with how things were but 'accepted' them. We therefore agreed to halt our regular sessions; I would keep in touch to check how things were going and Lynda would contact me if she felt she could benefit from talking through issues at work.

In the months that followed, I met Lynda again to carry out assessments for two new hires and she focused on discussing these individuals rather than herself when we met. I felt as though she believed she had 'survived' coaching and there was no need to revisit areas that her boss no longer 'complained' about. These are very much my feelings. I think Lynda benefited from having someone to listen to the issues causing her concern, but maybe never really took on board the need for change other than to get others 'off her back'. She did change, but I remain unconvinced that she 'revelled' in the different results and reactions she was able to generate as a result.

My follow-up conversations with Colin and Les confirmed that 'things are better than they were', which I suppose was the objective at the outset. But Les took me aside on a subsequent visit to explain that he thought Lynda had made progress but was always going to be a problem to others and Colin, and predicted that she would be sidelined in the future. To date this has not happened.

My Review

In review, I find this a strange assignment. I did not immediately find rapport with Lynda when we started and had difficulty empathising with her on occasions when we worked together. Maybe I should have discussed withdrawal from the assignment at an early stage. When I mentioned this to colleagues at an early stage, no one volunteered to take my place. Lynda had upset staff in our office over several visits.

In conversations with Lynda since, I still find her style quite demanding, energy sapping. Today, we experience relatively brief exchanges. I deliver feedback more directly and more quickly. This is designed to stop her in her tracks and point out when she is replaying old conversations that are now in the past. Below I outline the learning for me from this assignment:

- Identify early when working with the coaching participant may not suit you personally and when rapport is not easily (if at all) achieved
- Give more feedback quicker about the compatibility of styles between coach and participant, and how it impacts on both parties
- Call a halt, time-out or at least challenge the situation, when you feel you are merely acting out the 'coaching script', going through the motions. This is particularly relevant if you suspect that either party is not committed
- Ensure formal review, evaluation of progress and feedback on completion of each assignment. Progress may be reviewed against agreed development goals and milestones.

Review Questions

1. What were your thoughts at the outset of this assignment?
2. How would you have focused discussion and action planning?
3. What were your feelings about the potential discrimination issues?
4. What would you have done the same and why?
5. What would you have done differently and why?
6. When would you have terminated the coaching relationship? Why? How?

CHAPTER 9

Executive Coaching in Action: The MD as Team Coach

John decided that he needed some help. Only after some searching did he engage an executive coach. After 18 months in post as incoming MD of a nuclear technology division of Rolls-Royce, he knew he should be making more progress. His brief was complex and company-wide. He had interviewed two previous coaching candidates prior to our meeting and had found neither suitable. According to his comment subsequently, 'I felt we just clicked – it was more about chemistry than anything tangible, but I felt we could work together.'

His brief as incoming MD was to build substantially the portfolio of existing contracts and imbue his executive and management teams with a more commercial approach to business. A main client was the UK Ministry of Defence (MOD) and the era of cost-plus contracts was ending. Competitive commercial contracting was the name of their new game, a culture shock for many of the highly specialised engineers and scientists in the organisation. John felt that he was responsible for a change to the culture which would align it with the recently defined strategic business goals. Prior to his appointment, the organisation of around 2500 employees had been part of a programme to develop the culture for several years.

Cultural Characteristics

Dependent on largely cost-plus military contacts, the organisation was replete with highly qualified British scientists and engineers. John discovered that they represented a highly talented but reactionary group, whose mindset towards doing business and managing their organisation was compatible with their approach to product and technology development – zero-defect, highly proceduralised and risk-averse. Several senior leadership figures had been recruited from the military services and felt little adjustment in aligning with the corporate culture. The challenge for John was to reform the current culture to develop a mindset that was more commercially focused, embraced the notion of competition and enabled more innovative business proposals to flourish. Although John was an engineer himself with a formal university education, he was seen as an outsider – the first CEO to be recruited from outside the company.

We faced an initial brief that referred to executive coaching, but we quickly recognisd that the challenge for the coaching agenda was much more demanding. The coaching agenda involved the development of the MD, his executive team and the middle management population.

Slow delivery, missed project targets and poor morale were all symptomatic of the business. Whilst returns were not high, the financial performance of the company was seen as 'steady and regular', based on cost-plus projects with a built-in profit element. The leadership vision was to make the business more competitive, building commercial skills to manage the changing nature of the customer demands (even the MOD was becoming more demanding of suppliers and cost-plus projects were becoming obsolete). Whilst some business results were slowly improving, John was not satisfied with his leadership or that of his immediate executive team. Although our initial coaching conversations focused upon John's leadership behaviour and effectiveness, we soon moved to the composition and capability of John's executive team, all of whom he had inherited.

We discussed the results of John's 360° feedback, which largely reflected his own view that he could be more effective. He was in his words 'propelled to find a coach because I needed to become a better leader and wanted to find out how'. He felt he had yet to build trust in an effective executive team and communicate his vision effectively further down the organisation.

John faced an organisation unused to executives appointed from outside the company. Up to that point all the previous MDs had been 'home-grown'. John came with an impressive track record achieved in ICI and later BNFL (British Nuclear Fuels). However, his description of the cultural characteristics he encountered was highly critical. What he met was a family or club culture which, dominated by the engineering mindset pervasive throughout the corporation, was infinitely accommodating. John said his mission to change the culture felt like 'trying to move jelly. There was invisible and passive resistance everywhere you looked.' He described his feelings of little support from his boss, and split loyalty from some executives in his team. 'It was a deeply authoritarian regime with little care for the people within it.'

We agreed a coaching programme as the result of our first few meetings. John's coaching was self-determined and he remained his own sponsor throughout, although we did meet together with his boss, Tony, on occasions. After completing a 360° leadership survey, combined with a personal style analysis, John was clear that he needed to develop in key areas of his leadership:

- Developing a better communicating style: transmitting a vision for the business
- Building and leading his executive team.

John was never comfortable in describing his feelings about his situation but he accepted the feedback, although it was easier for him to accept his weaknesses rather than his strengths.

Over the next few months, John slowly re-engineered his team. He moved out those he felt were ineffective or unwilling to change and invited new members to join the executive team. I was reminded by John subsequently that I asked him that difficult team membership question when we first met. Now one of my early enquiries in any prospective leadership coaching assignment, 'Have you the team you need to meet your business goals?', evoked some difficult thinking. (If you're an executive coach, try it when you next meet your client, if it's unfamiliar territory. If you're in a leadership role, try to be ruthlessly honest when answering it.)

His next action was to surprise myself and his team equally. At the end of a conventional board meeting, John had added another item, his own development plan. In open and eloquent terms he presented the feedback he had received from his executive colleagues and invited their further comment. In our experience, here was probably the best, and most courageous, example of an executive moving from the *private to the public domain*. It supports the explosion of our next myth.

Myth: Executive Coaching is Performed Most Effectively Within the Privacy of a One-to-one Meeting and Relationship

On the contrary. Here was a dramatic example of inclusivity in a coaching assignment netting multiple benefits. The response was clear from John's team. They were surprised by his openness (atypical of boardroom behaviour) and impressed by his courage. Their response was to further inform his feedback about the impact of his leadership behaviour and areas for development focus. In hindsight, the process accelerated the building of trust in the team, but it had to be two-way. The next step for executive team members was to voluntarily prepare their own development plans for presentation and review at the next meeting. The sequence ended with the MD and his top team publicly sharing a review of their current strengths and development needs as well as their emerging actions plans. Not surprisingly, several co-coaching contracts were agreed among team members. For example, the engineering director needed to become more strategic in his appreciation of the business and the commercial director more informed about the operations side. Interestingly these were strengths in the other, so reciprocity was achieved and a co-coaching contract possible. This was further enabled by their attendance at many of the same meetings, allowing post-meeting feedback to occur regularly.

Overall, John was seen to have made a huge gesture toward his executive team. The practical outcome was substantial; improved levels of trust and quality of communication among the team members, and even their customers began to notice the change and were favourably impressed. Unfortunately, this was not so further down the management hierarchy. Middle managers felt threatened by the new MD who, to them, was an unknown quantity.

Several initiatives were taken to help the change required in the middle management population and throughout the organisation. These included regular but informal meetings, akin to the familiar 'town hall' meetings so popular in GE, between the executive team (or part thereof) and a random sample of managers to discuss issues regarding change raised by them. A series of 'skip-level' board meetings took place which allowed junior managers and recent graduate entrants to observe board decision-making in action. Executive secretaries were empowered to design and monitor the organisation of executive offices. Collectively they agreed on clear goals and metrics and transmitted them to the executive team. This was one initiative that was to be successfully implemented and sustained beyond its early phases of existence. This further helped to transform the image of the executive team and the MD from one that was distant, aloof and intimidating to one more accessible and supportive. Workshops were conducted by the managers to design the values and behaviours most appropriate for the leaders in the business. A few managers took this practice and applied it in their own functional areas. Some progress was achieved in helping the managers to change. John scores the result of this change initiative as '4 out of a possible 10. Whilst we would never achieve a 10 rating, I felt we could have made it to 8.' Coincidentally, these internal initiatives were mirrored by those emerging from corporate headquarters to be applied across the business. This provided further momentum to accelerate the rate of change but it was short-lived. Lack of sustained follow-up was largely responsible from John's perspective.

Myth: Smart People Learn More Quickly Than Others

Chris Argyris (1991) suggests that 'smart people' may have a particular challenge in learning and development due to their intellectual abilities. In this case, this phenomenon was manifested frequently when members of the management team, mainly highly qualified engineers and scientific specialists, described their role. Typically, when invited to describe what their job was and how they performed it, many would describe their role so objectively as to give the appearance of something distant, alien, outside themselves, as though they were describing someone else acting as the role incumbent. This became more clearly apparent when they received feedback about their behaviour, often dismissing the value and occasionally the accuracy of others' perceptions. It seemed as if they objectified their own behaviour to the point of taking no responsibility for its outcome.

Only when within the tight confines of a technical judgment did this management group become engaged. Not surprisingly perhaps, as this was the criterion upon which their status, recognition and promotion had historically depended. This had created a further challenge for the MD as he wanted to break the mould. It was also noticeable how many of this group engaged in hugely demanding out-of-work activities. One manager was head of a local drama and operatic society and chairman of a local debating society and a local chess club, which left little energy and commitment for his work. He was not unusual. We wondered what was happening at work that so many applied so much creative energy out of work yet so little internally. It's a good question. It wasn't immediately apparent on a cursory inspection, but as John became more familiar with more junior levels of management, he discovered what others described as a 'cosy conspiracy'. Bright young graduates found little incentive to progress as a result of attractive overtime payments at their level, providing no encouragement to their more senior colleagues, a comfortable life was enjoyed by all. In addition, encouraging engineers, who were primarily concerned with quality and a zero-defect approach to products, to accept that an '80 per cent right' approach may be acceptable to management, to improve timeliness and speed of implementation, was an uphill struggle – seen by those resisting change as delivering 'crap on time'. Indeed, management and leadership themselves were seen as 'black arts' practised by senior figures in the organisation, demanding that one sells one's engineering integrity to gain membership of the club.

Management and leadership, to them, was (and is) replete with ambiguity. There were never any 'right answers', unlike science and engineering where problems had discrete solutions. The organisation at this time was about 40 years old, having been created at the emergence of the nuclear industry and employing leading industry experts within its staff. Over time, engineers and scientists had been promoted to positions of leadership responsibility as a result of their success in achieving engineering projects and resolving technical challenges. Their position often bore little reference to their capability as managers or leaders. People management was regarded as residing in the domain of the personnel function and made little impact on the daily operation of the business.

Engage the Management with a Compelling Vision

John had read the relevant business journals on change. He knew the checklists off by heart. How to engage the management population further down the hierarchy? He crafted a powerful speech, invited the entire management population, and took the stage. He described his view at the time:

> I wanted to demonstrate I was open to feedback. I knew I was typically a closed person, I don't confide in anybody normally but I wanted them to understand me and the vision more clearly.

His executive was fully supportive by this time. John began by describing his and the executive's own development journey, exposing his own values and principles, reflecting how they did (or on occasion did not) align with those of the organisation. He presented a powerful message of the change vision to the group. He invited managers to rewrite 'procedures' which they felt impeded their progress in delivering the changes necessary. They were of course the historical authors of these very same procedures too. John invited personal representation to the group to identify irrelevant or obsolete practices. Out of 100 managers, one came to see him to discuss changing the way they worked.

Progress was emerging, but slowly, too slowly for the MD, who felt that speed was the key to achieving the changes necessary. This attacked one core value of the 'engineering culture' of the business – the value of quality. Rolls-Royce is one of the world's most powerful brands and is based in some considerable part on sustained engineering excellence. The reaction of the change resistant managers was to promote a counter-story. The communication grapevine reported that executives now demanded the business deliver 'crap on time'. This resistant element in the management group, which became known as 'the asbestos blanket' as a result of their ability to absorb energy, became a major block to changing the culture. Many didn't want to change and, despite attempts to mobilise opinion around, above and below them, the group resisted until a major corporate restructuring took place and many had no jobs in the new structure. They were overtaken by the environment changing around them. In hindsight John commented:

> While we made substantial progress, increased speed of implementation would have helped us. Timing is one area I could have improved but we are an organisation full of 'monitor evaluators' – people who double-check before even a small change can be made and then only with the guarantee of a predictable outcome. Change in organisations isn't like that. Our culture, like all other companies, has both strengths and weaknesses. In our case, our excellence in engineering mindset has helped build and sustain our global brand but can inhibit rapid leadership and organisational change.

Doubly unfortunate, John experienced a serious injury which kept him away from work for some time. However, overall, the financial results had improved markedly, a 60 per cent improvement in revenue over John's tenure and improved profitability. But the culture change programme hadn't worked beyond the senior executive team. John had developed visibly as a leader but still reflects on the power of the collective middle management group who provided such a powerful block to change initiatives.

Lessons Learned

Not everybody can change, not everybody wants to change. Despite evidence that if you don't, you will fail, many logical, rational people choose not to. There is too much emphasis on senior level development. All change literature encourages the focus of change to reside at the leadership level. We have all been involved in change programmes which started at the bottom or in the middle of organisations. They always seem to fail. There needs to be some clear incentive to change, maybe discomfort too. This group experienced neither.

The quality of the executive teamwork was outstanding. Even staff unions and customers commented on the improved levels of teamwork at the executive level. Today, six years later, the executive team members still comment on the team as the best they have ever worked in, before or since. The entreaty from Kotter (1995), 'build a broader coalition or alliance for change', is easier said than done. The critical alliance with middle managers was unattainable at this time. Blaming the senior managers' lack of engagement is inappropriate in this case. John's final comments recently recaptured his feelings at the time:

> I felt there was much success and wish I'd started the process of coaching sooner, engaging my boss and the people above him more in the process. I realise now that it is not a mechanical process too.

Going public with his executive board was a powerful and effective step towards openness for John. Whilst executive coaching agendas invariably lead to behaviours and skills which are visible to a wider society, few are as courageously presented.

A final contemporary comment from Chris Mead, then Commercial Director, reflects the sustained impact on John's executive team:

> Although John Glanville is the best manager I have worked for, leadership was not his natural strength. However, his sheer intelligence and self-awareness made him realise that he needed help to improve in this area and to improve the performance of the RRA Executive team.
>
> He devised a programme with professional help from ECC and took some big personal risks in terms of openess with his team, and invited us to do the same. The process of self-discovery was not easy but, as they say, no pain no gain. Each member of the Executive will have his own story to tell but for me it was an invigorating experience that helped me understand how I was perceived and what more I could deliver to the Executive team. It encouraged me to be more open and to contribute more in areas that were not my natural comfort zone. It encouraged all of us to be less defensive, accept feedback as valuable and to think of the team more. It has also helped me assess the performance of other teams that I have either been a member of or worked with. It was an unforgettable experience and is an invaluable management tool.
>
> *(Chris Mead, Vice President, Government Operations Europe and Africa, Kellog Brown and Root)*

Review Questions

1. How do corporate cultures change and develop?
2. What is the role of senior leadership teams in facilitating change?
3. What are the key ingredients for successful culture change ?
4. How would you have coached John to help him achieve his ambition?

CHAPTER 10

Building a Multicultural Leadership Team: The Case of the GM in Jeopardy

This is the case of a Latin American executive in a US multinational located on the Iberian Peninsula. Corporate management struggled with the situation, given the poor market conditions and inadequate performance. They questioned whether the experienced general manager could succeed with this business. They knew the team had to come together for the good of the business but were puzzled and disturbed by the lack of progress.

The Situation

The business was located in Seville, Spain. It became part of a US multinational consumer products firm via an acquisition 35 years earlier in the 1960s. Several of the brands owned by the firm at the original time of acquisition were still important in the market today. Growth came in several ways, including organic growth stimulated by the marketing expertise of the American parent, strategic acquisitions of competing brands in Spain and also the penetration of selected brands from other country operations in the multinational organisation.

The market in Spain had been insulated from the rest of Europe for many years. The Spanish economy remained far weaker than most other Western European countries throughout the 1960s and 70s, and had only begun to close the gap slowly during the 1980s. In those conditions, purchasing patterns stayed rooted in local, lower cost preferences and brands. Tastes were uniquely Spanish, with little interest in exotic tastes and habits of other parts of Europe or North America. Street markets and small shops were still central elements of the distribution system in Spain. It was in this environment that the firm had established a strong market position in Spain in most of its product categories.

The 1990s brought unprecedented prosperity to Spain and a large portion of the Spanish people emerged into middle-class affluence. Finally, poverty became a condition of a minority of the population, concentrated in the urban slums of the great cities such as Madrid, Barcelona and Toledo, as well as in the small, rural villages dependent on agriculture in a dry, inhospitable land. The majority were now in the middle class, aware of and attracted to Paris fashions, US pop music, fast-food restaurants and Italian cars, among a dizzying array of goods from all over the world.

While the street markets kept a place in the weekly shopping habits of many, the small shops headed down the path eking out a marginal existence, unable to weather competition from the great European hypermarket chains. Carrefour, in particular, entered the Spanish market with vigour and aggressive pricing in the late 1980s. It led the way in establishing sophisticated buying, logistics and promotional marketing in the Spanish market through the 1990s. It demanded similarly aggressive pricing from all its suppliers, and dictated terms of business. As in its home market in France, Carrefour built up sufficient volume that every consumer products manufacturer had to knuckle under to the pressure applied by them.

The business in question struggled with the transformation to this hyper-competitive environment. It was used to premium pricing, relaxed terms, business granted as an outgrowth of multi-generation relationships with shop owners and a similarly loose, familial management style in the factories. Recently, margins collapsed in the face of pricing pressure from the hypermarket chains, delivery pressure became more intense and both inventory levels and manufacturing productivity suffered as a result. The parent firm had recently merged all the operations on the Iberian Peninsula into one, thrusting together the two disparate cultures of Portugal and Spain. They reasoned that cross-boundary markets were emerging and additional volume would bring economies of scale.

Unfortunately, the new team wasn't coming together. It comprised Spanish, Portuguese, French, Italian and Central American members. Surprisingly, English was their common language, consistent with the corporate policy of the parent US multinational. More spoke Spanish, but that language would never be acceptable to the Portuguese or French. Cliques had formed in the team, based on old relationships and cultural affinities. A Spaniard managed the sales organisation, and he led a clique including all his Spanish sales managers, the engineering director and numerous supervisors in all functions who remained aligned with the old Spanish organisation. Another clique was led by the Portuguese manufacturing director, and included the purchasing director, plant controller, the Lisbon site manager, the Portuguese sales manager and a similar contingent of Portuguese supervisors throughout the organisation. The Italian HR director had lived in Spain for several years, and generally aligned with the Spanish clique. The French marketing director was relatively new to the team and stood apart from all the cliques, allowed to without interference, because he brought knowledge and expertise that everyone knew they needed – how Carrefour built up its business in France, and how the manufacturers learned to cope profitably in France.

Real decisions never took place in the management team. Power lay in the two rival cliques, one Portuguese and one Spanish. Of course, the Portuguese felt the decision to make Seville the headquarters of the Iberian operation slighted them. They secretly resolved to resist any overt leadership coming from any Spaniard. Conversely, the Spanish contingent swelled with pride and superiority when they initially learned about the headquarters decision. The real decisions took place in private, informal networks where national rivalries played out alongside the pressing needs of the business. For example, a monumental decision had been reached to close the Portuguese factory after a careful analysis of all the factors involved. The plant near Seville had relatively new equipment, more flexible in design, and able to absorb the products and volume from Portugal. All members of the management team supposedly had agreed, after much debate and careful deliberation. Yet, the Portuguese clique had been plotting to preserve their existence all the while. They had leaked the possibility of the plant shutdown to a well-connected local politician in Lisbon, who in turn leaked it to the media.

Shortly after the supposedly final decision was announced, an official contact from the Portuguese ambassador to the US to the CEO of the American parent carried with it a complaint and not-so-veiled threat. Over 20 years ago, large sums of government funds were provided to build the factory in Portugal. Even though it had been many years, a loophole in the agreements between the parent and the Portuguese government left the possibility of a reclamation of the investment funds. The ambassador made this quite clear in his meeting in New York. Needless to say, the carefully thought-out and prepared decision by the management team had been foiled by the underground, 'real' power clique.

The Leader

Where was Juan, the general manager, in all of this? Despite his title and substantial experience in the multinational firm in other countries, he was essentially powerless. He didn't fit into either clique, yet unlike the French marketing director, he offered no perceived special knowledge to the team. They played him like a political fiddle, foiling every initiative of substance that Juan proposed.

Juan is an attractive, charming and articulate man, naturally drawn to the role of marketing and sales. Yet his surface charm goes much deeper. A sincere and caring leader, he easily attracts followers and cements their loyalty with attention and support. He serves as an ambassador for his organisation in the local and regional community, interacting with national leaders as easily as local merchants and mayors.

Juan grew up in Costa Rica, son of an influential political and business leader there. He attended university in the United States, and considered that country his second home. Nevertheless, he maintained the historical family home in Costa Rica, and I learned during the course of this engagement that he hoped one day to return and spend his retirement in public service. He joined this organisation shortly after completing his university studies, and had built his career there over a 30-year period. He was a core member of the informal team, the transnational leaders, who moved from one country to another, bringing corporate culture along with their performance track records and growing sophistication in multicultural marketing and leadership.

Over the course of his career, Juan occupied key leadership positions on three different continents: Europe, South and North America. To each role, he brought a strong sense of duty and loyalty to individuals and the corporation. He had also established a virtually unblemished track record of strong performance and success in each assignment, the past three as country manager in South America and Europe. He had reached the stage of his career where he knew that corporate leadership was a long shot. In fact, his fondest hope was to retire in roughly five years to his native Costa Rica.

So, on the surface, Juan was the ideal candidate to rebuild a performance culture, market share and profitability in the recently merged Iberian Peninsula operations. He was fluent in Spanish and Portuguese, as well as English. He knew how to run a country operation successfully. He brought a Latin sensibility to the job and his relationships. He brought deep marketing expertise to a role demanding new marketing thinking in response to a changed competitive landscape. But something was missing. Business results continued to decline. The new team wasn't functioning effectively. The new Iberian Peninsula organisation wasn't a real organisation in any way except on paper. Competitors solidified their market share gains. These signs raised alarms in both European headquarters in Brussels and in the corporate offices in New York.

The European human resources director met me, briefed me on the situation and asked if I could help. I had met him several months earlier as part of a global client review. His organisation used consultants from the US offices of my firm in a variety of situations and he wanted to evaluate us as potential resources for them across Europe. After that initial contact, I met with him several times to help him think through the various challenges he faced and to learn more about his organisation and its business.

The Process

In partnership with the human resources director, I designed a process intended to engage the team and the general manager, together and separately over a six–eight-month period. We wanted the GM to feel ownership of the entire process, so I offered to present my action plan as a first draft, and use an initial discussion with him as a both a diagnostic session and a working design meeting. The only strict requirement that the HR director left with me was to report back periodically on the progress of the intervention, evaluating the strength of the team and, in this particular context, the general manager.

Armed with only an introduction from the HR director, I contacted Juan and discussed his situation. He presented himself as an open, curious leader looking for help. In particular, he took suggestions from the corporate hierarchy seriously. They had a reputation for leaving general managers alone to execute their plans, intervening only for planning, budgeting and remedial action in cases of lagging performance. In that 'hands-off', 'deliver your numbers' culture, any direct overture from top management was taken as very serious and worthy of immediate attention.

Knowing about the culture from colleagues helped me to avoid most mistakes. I let Juan take the lead in the initial meeting, knowing that he didn't feel he had any real choice regarding the engagement. I needed his full support, so I made room for him to exercise significant choice. Under the broad outlines of a combined team and individual intervention, I followed Juan's lead in shaping the particular interactions according to his energy and preferences. Juan had experience in working with outside consultants in team-building processes, so he came to our discussions with definite ideas about what would work with his team. His strong ideas could have led us down the wrong path, so I asked him what he wanted to accomplish and what barriers or problems he saw in the way. I probed around those issues and objectives, helping him to clarify what was really going on with the team as well as educating myself about Juan and his leadership style and competence. In discussion with Juan, I learned of his frustration with this team, business and assignment.

In retrospect, that initial meeting with Juan contained my biggest mistake in this engagement. I was charmed by Juan, as are most people who meet him. Soon, I saw the world through his eyes and focused my attention and resources on helping him to achieve the goals he set for the organisation. The brief I had received from the European HR and business leadership was subordinated to my loyalty and service to Juan.

He had taken this lateral move (or even a slight demotion) in order to prepare himself for a later move to Central America on his final company assignment. Top corporate management knew of his desire and offered to make it happen for Juan if he could make a success of the Iberian Peninsula market over, at most, a five-year assignment. Nevertheless, he felt that this job was slightly beneath him. The business was half the size of his previous assignment and was in two fringe countries of Europe for the US multinational. His previous assignment was as country manager in Brazil, a large market and core to the entire South American strategy for his organisation.

Yet, he had not yet found success. He couldn't get the team to rally around his leadership. He had applied all the tools learned over a long, successful career in forging a strong, focused team, but had yet to see worthwhile results. He had just about concluded that several individuals were in over their heads and blocking the progress of the team and the organisation. He would remove them after my engagement with them, if my findings proved his point that basic competence was an issue with the team. I convinced him to allow his leadership style and impact to be included in the potential sources of low performance of both individuals in the organisation and the organisation as a whole. With that in mind, we agreed on a general design including several team meetings with some form of diagnostic, coupled with action planning as an action-oriented approach to building trust and an achievement mindset into the team. In addition, I would meet privately with Juan for up to half a day after each team session, debriefing the meeting and his participation as the leader. I anticipated a series of four or five such interventions with Juan and his team over an extended period of more than six months.

Sequenced Interventions

Personal style and preferences and their impact on team effectiveness

This leadership team needed a common language. They were from multiple cultures and had formed rival factions, one Spanish at its core, the other Portuguese. They represented what had been two separate country organisations within the parent firm. They didn't know one another well – styles, preferences, personality, capability and track record – none of the most relevant characteristics.

The first team intervention focused on getting to know one another. Initially, I asked each person to give a profile of him/herself to the rest. I asked them to emphasise their life outside work. While this self-disclosure ran counter to the local culture in both Spain and Portugal, the GM and I agreed to take a risk in order to break down the barriers dividing the team members. Self-disclosure with lower barriers between work and family was typical of the organisation at large in the US, and had become the prevailing style across most European countries. The session started slowly, with halting self-descriptions. But, as that first morning wore on, we all could feel the barriers falling. The degree of disclosure surprised everyone, including each individual as he/she described his/her life outside work. My role shifted from prodding and urging each to participate, to supporting and protecting each person and the group as they uncovered vulnerabilities and intensely personal qualities.

In my view, this technique raises legitimate questions of manipulation and coercion. The participants couldn't really choose to avoid taking part. To decline would be to implicitly declare their unfitness for leadership or membership in the team. Consequently, all joined in, despite obvious reservations. In many cases, the exercise violated their sense of personal boundaries and cultural norms. How can it be appropriate to subtly coerce participation in an activity like this? Despite these concerns, the exercise worked marvellously to reduce tensions and establish more open, genuine communication among the members. This type of exercise is one among many difficult ethical dilemmas facing coaches in their practice.

That afternoon, I distributed results of several psychometric instruments used with each team member, including the Myers–Briggs type indicator

(MBTI) and the fundamental interpersonal relations orientation form B (FIRO B). These tools uncover differences in how each team member prefers to interact with others and the team. After the morning session, they were ready to put some structure around the powerful lessons they had learned about one another. When the general discussions about the instruments and their interpretation was complete, I took time to review the results individually with each person while the remainder jotted down questions, observations and new insights about their own results. When I opened the conversation up to all, they jumped into a free-flowing, light-hearted exchange about their stories from the morning, performance on the job and a wide range of specific work situations. They consciously noted where the test profiles helped them better understand themselves and the rest of the team.

Towards the end of the day, I summarised much of what they had said. Then I facilitated a discussion in which they defined and agreed upon a 12-point list of behavioural standards for the operation of the team. The points ranged from open, consistent communication with the rest of the organisation to respect for the other members of the team, allowing each to complete his message before moving on to other points. Juan took responsibility for preparing the 12-point contract in a form that could be posted in each member's office and Juan's reception area. They all saw this as a concrete step of progress from the session. I reminded them that this symbolised a new, common language of leadership for them. If they remained committed to its use, it would be a major step forward for them as an effective unit. With the group's permission, I agreed to review their performance against the new standards at the beginning of the next session.

Organisational feedback on leadership team

At the beginning of the second session, six weeks after the first, we discussed the progress each had made in living the 12-point leadership contract. Generally, they found it helpful to see it every time they sat at their desk. They all felt that the civility and respect among the leadership team had improved markedly since the first session. Two of the members had used the contract as a discussion item with their teams, allowing them to use it to monitor continuing progress of the team.

We also conducted a brief survey questionnaire about leadership and organisational effectiveness on all managers, supervisors and professionals. In addition, I interviewed 15 of this group as a follow-up to the survey. The general themes were clear: the leadership team couldn't be relied upon for clear direction; conflicts were avoided; decisions were frequently delayed unduly long; politics and cultural differences occupied most of their time and attention, as opposed to the needs of the business; and people worried that jobs could be in danger if business results didn't improve quickly. I was surprised to learn that the European headquarters staff seemed to know the pulse of the organisation so well.

In that second session, I presented this information and conclusions to the leadership team. In preparation for the session, I met with Juan to make sense of the feedback and chart a course for the direction and priorities of the session. Juan openly criticised the leadership team with me, and saw the results as unacceptable for any leadership team, and especially one facing turbulent change and marketplace pressures such as they were experiencing. I acknowledged that the business circumstances and personalities of the team both played important roles in generating the harsh criticism from the employees. I also suggested that Juan's own leadership should be included in the mix for determining root causes and charting corrective actions. Juan accepted very generally and broadly that his leadership must be included in the analysis, but he deftly avoided making it a serious concern. He argued with me that he had successfully handled very similar situations in much larger organisations for the firm in more strategically vital countries. He refused to believe that he didn't have the situation under control. Rather, he was convinced that the relatively low competence level of several members of the team, coupled with difficult cultural conflicts, were the core causes of this crisis of leadership. The more he heard, the more he was convinced that he needed to change several members of the team to break through the performance malaise. Based on his resistance, I intended to use the reactions of the team to help overcome his arrogant overconfidence in his own leadership.

This was easier said than done. In this session, I observed most clearly a distinctive behaviour pattern of Juan's. In order to encourage free-flowing lateral communication across his team and the organisation, he frequently 'sat out' during intense discussions. He would observe the proceedings and periodically monitor the agenda or objectives for the meeting, but allow the debate to rage amongst the participants without his comment. In many situations, this did indeed provide 'space' for the members to engage with one another and actively debate critical points without feeling censored by the leader. But, in this meeting, I saw Juan use the technique in another way. He used it to distance himself from the discussion. If he disagreed with the direction of the debate, he would withdraw from the discussion, only to enter it later, giving him the opportunity to 'veto' any progress and shift the direction. If he felt attacked or pressured, he would withdraw into passivity, leaving others with the impression that he understood the points and tacitly agreed to an action or decision. In fact, he was disengaging in order to avoid the conflict or pressure and avoid tension. I saw it as subtle, yet powerful resistance.

Yet, in the workshop, the leadership team resonated to the feedback. It shocked them, causing them to stop and reflect on the business and their role in new ways. They didn't reject the feedback, but rather were energised by it. The highly critical nature of many of the points seemed to draw them together. It served as a clarion call to action. They now knew that they needed to overcome their power and faction-driven differences for the good of the organisation and all the employees.

A critical moment occurred mid-morning. The Spanish sales director and Portuguese manufacturing director (the two informal power bloc leaders) began supporting one another's points. This dynamic began with the manufacturing director agreeing with the sales director's contention that better information flow was essential to make the forecast more accurate, reliable and less political. After that breakthrough, the two regularly echoed and supported one another and the rest of the group came along in achieving a common, positive view of the challenges they faced in leading the organisation. They wanted to know what to do to change the negative perceptions of them as a group across the organisation. We spent the better part of the afternoon charting out a course of action. It was during this morning feedback session that I observed Juan's disengagement most particularly. He remained silent most of the time, and when he interjected comments, they were almost always defensive of the plans and actions taken thus far.

We held a broad discussion on the health of the business, in light of the harsh feedback from the organisation. Over the lunch break, I asked Juan to remain silent during this discussion. I felt that he would be tempted to pull out his corporate presentation on the strategies and objectives of the new Iberian Peninsula organisation and try to impose those views on the group. The team was coalescing in a very positive way, seeing the performance of the organisation in a new light, and I didn't want Juan to disrupt this positive momentum. Rather, I wanted him to observe it under way. Much to my chagrin, Juan announced that he would not attend the afternoon session. He indicated that his reason was to avoid dominating and steering the discussion to his own views. Privately, before we commenced the afternoon session, I told Juan that his presence would be the best solution, so long as he would remain a silent observer. He persisted in wanting to sit out. I ultimately agreed that his silence was important, and if he felt he couldn't stay on the sidelines, perhaps not attending was best. In hindsight, this was a major error on both Juan's and my part. The team was growing stronger and coming together in a common cause to improve the business and their reputation as a leadership team, and they were doing it without Juan.

The team quickly reached a consensus on the actions most critical to improve overall business performance and eliminate perceptions of negative politics on the executive team:

1. Marketing needed significant strengthening to combat the increased competitive threats.
2. The two manufacturing facilities needed to be combined into one, necessitating the closure of the Portuguese factory.
3. Sales required a strong large-account programme to profitably serve the emerging hypermarket customers, most urgently in Spain, but also in Portugal before long. This didn't exist and would entail new roles and support activities.
4. Integration and team building was important in virtually every function and at most levels in order to overcome the cultural differences and conflicts of organisational interests created in the merger of the two country operations. Early efforts had begun among certain staff functions, including HR, finance and engineering. But nothing was under way in the largest line functions – manufacturing and sales.
5. The leadership team needed to live out the 12-point contract, most importantly to: make clear, timely decisions; support them across the organisation outside the meetings; and communicate openly and frequently about status and progress of the overall organisation.

We agreed to present this agenda to Juan, and use it as a centrepiece for the next team meeting. I asked each member to come to the next session with a presentation from their function, showing existing initiatives supporting these five priorities, along with recommended new initiatives. They each agreed with enthusiasm. I walked away from the meeting with a dark sense of foreboding. Juan wasn't part of this watershed session. Would the team remain his? Or, would this session amplify their concerns about his leadership and further diminish his role?

That evening I met with Juan for dinner. I shared the progress and process of the afternoon. He showed mild support of the team and then reverted to a discussion of the plans and objectives which he had prepared at the beginning of the year and presented to both the European and corporate headquarters staff. He contended that the team was doing nothing more than finally embracing the plans that they had all agreed months ago. When I brought up my concerns regarding the team coalescing without his presence, and also his pattern of disengagement when he felt direct pressure, he deflected my messages and dismissed them (denial was in the air). He expressed pleasure that he finally had the team supporting his plans and was looking forward to the next session.

He felt that the next meeting focusing on skill feedback for each team member would clearly demonstrate the weaknesses with several members and give him further evidence for removing them. I urged him to avoid using the feedback in this way. We both had encouraged their participation, with the promise that the feedback should and would be used only for their development and that their own results would be as confidential as they chose to make them. I warned him that using the information to support decisions to terminate any of the members would severely damage his credibility as the group's leader. It was at this moment that my relationship with Juan faced its sternest test. He grew angry with me and accused me of not supporting him. I restated my commitment to helping both him and the team achieve success. I asked him whether the anger was a sign of deeper concerns on his part about his own leadership. The question heightened his frustration with me. After venting his frustration, he began to describe his concerns. He didn't have a deep commitment to this Iberian Peninsula unit. He had taken the assignment as a means to an end – his ultimate move to Central America in advance of his retirement. Increasingly, he had found himself wondering about that future, rather than intensely focusing on the challenges facing him in this job. Before arriving in Seville, he had genuinely thought that the problems would be easy for him to solve, given the much broader scope of challenge he had had in his previous assignment in South America. He had begun harbouring doubts about his own leadership as a result of the persistent difficulty in making real progress here. Nevertheless, his dedication to working it through successfully was undiminished. He was deeply loyal to the firm and its senior leadership, who had provided him with so many opportunities over the course of his career. He could not imagine an unsuccessful outcome, and would not consider leaving Seville until his duty had been fulfilled. As we ended this intense dinner meeting, I asked Juan to consider his objectives and motivations before we met for the next session, scheduled for four weeks hence.

I sought out Peter, my European region HR contact, and gave him a progress report. I frankly wondered whether the engagement had a chance of success, given the latest interactions. Peter reassured me that he had heard very positive comments from the Iberian Peninsula HR manager, as well as other comments floating around the European organisation. The word was that a breath of fresh air had been infused into the leadership team and they were finally dealing with the 'real' issues. Therefore, Peter was delighted with progress. He told me that Juan's motivation and focus issues were not unknown to senior management, and in fact had been a central reason for my engagement, coupled with the genuine business challenges. When the engagement was under consideration by him with his management, they all realised that Juan would reject any intervention unless he could bond with the consultant and feel in control of the process. Therefore, they chose not to give me the full brief on the situation. Should I have withdrawn at that point? I seriously considered it. I confronted Peter with my reaction. He reinforced the importance of strengthening the team in the face of its business challenges, independent of Juan's ultimate fate. On that basis, he gained my agreement to continue the engagement through to its designed conclusion.

360° feedback on skills

In the next session, we spent half a day dealing with feedback on skills for each member of the team. We used a 360° feedback instrument to gather perceptions from colleagues, subordinates and bosses. For most of the team, this was their first use of such a feedback tool. In particular, they were very apprehensive about the commentary they might receive from peers and subordinates. Once the results were distributed and I had spent time reviewing the overall presentation with all members, and talked through each member's results privately with him or her, the barriers and apprehension virtually disappeared. Much like any group of managers, they found most of the feedback confirmed things they knew about themselves already, and there were a few surprises for all.

Contrary to Juan's expectations, I found that the group was seen by their colleagues (peers and subordinates) as a competent group of leaders. Although there were striking weaknesses for several of the individuals, and a couple of important themes for the group, overall, these leaders were seen as capable and competent. The two themes standing out as development needs for the group were teamwork, both demonstrating it themselves and encouraging it across the organisation, and managing disagreements. None of the members was surprised to see these emerge as consistent themes of improvement for most of them. Nevertheless, the overall results encouraged them to face up to the challenges. Their people saw them as capable and they felt a responsibility to lead the organisation through the competitive business challenges facing them.

Over the lunch break, each member set out to write a development plan. I urged them to pick two, or at most three, areas in which to focus their attention. They had the enthusiasm of the converted, and I had to help them establish a practical, realistic approach. Meanwhile, Juan and I ate lunch privately to review the morning's outcomes. Initially he didn't want to accept the overall conclusion that the group was seen as capable and competent. I spent a good deal of time reviewing the progress of the whole engagement thus far. When Juan heard my observations and the obvious progress the team had made, he finally capitulated. He realised that the group wasn't the problem. They needed to embrace change, but their actions over the past several months demonstrated that they could do it with the right encouragement and clear standards. They needed to be accountable, but had shown repeatedly that they were willing to accept this. They needed to overcome cultural biases, and even in this most difficult area, they had shown substantial progress away from political intrigue to positive leadership action.

Juan ended up taking on the failures of the business and the leadership team as his personal responsibility. It was a breakthrough moment. But I had to remind him that tough new competitors and a challenging, cross-culture merger just might be small contributing factors, as well. Even so, I was gratified to watch Juan gain new insight into the situation and his role in it. The question we agreed to begin addressing over dinner was, what to do about it?

Operational challenges and tactics

That afternoon, we provided each team member with the opportunity to present his initiatives in support of the organisation-wide high priority issues identified in the last session. They really moved into action during this session, reflecting hard work and a much higher level of cooperation than ever before. Several subgroups had met between the sessions on this very topic and had refined their ideas and plans to address the five priorities. Juan observed, but also added his own observations, helping to make several actions clearer and more aligned with corporate strategy. The momentum and direction was truly impressive. Everyone engaged fully in the session – they really looked like a team, perhaps for the first time.

I found myself tempering their enthusiasm, encouraging them to let the ideas settle in for some time before making final commitments. I cautioned them against 'group-think' in which everyone gets caught up in the energy of the group dynamic and subconsciously subordinate their own ideas and concerns in order to avoid dampening the spirit of the moment. In another part of my mind, I was wondering, 'Why do I find myself taking an opposing view so frequently?' An engagement starts and I'm presenting new, challenging information and concepts, striving to help the client to gain some new insight into his or her issues – hoping on hope that positive change will take place. Then, just as the client finally embraces the new view, I take a more cautionary stance, urging reflection and balance. Perhaps it's my upper midwestern US upbringing and Scandinavian heritage. Is it an important part of the coach's role? Seeing another person or group adopt new information or frameworks that you have proposed, and then make positive change, is powerfully seductive. I think coaches must ensure that the change is not taken as a result of undue influence by us. The client must truly own their actions, and not create a dependency upon us.

For this Iberian Peninsula management team, the controller played the 'devil's advocate' role, as do many financial executives. He took up my cautionary concerns and started to play that role more broadly. Juan reinforced this by requesting that the controller continue to monitor their plans to ensure practicality and achievability. When the afternoon session ended, the team had completed a new framework for action to improve the business and had established ongoing processes to execute those plans and monitor their progress over time.

That evening, Juan and I both basked in the positive changes in the team over a glass of wine. The fundamentals of the business hadn't yet changed, and the market conditions were deteriorating somewhat. Nevertheless, Juan sensed genuine optimism that this team finally had come together in a common cause, and that they had a very good chance to succeed. We talked about how these changes had occurred at least in part without Juan's presence and, to a certain extent, in spite of his leadership tendencies. In that light, what direction should his next career step take? We both knew the eventual answer – he wanted to return to his native Costa Rica and engage in community leadership, possibly in the political arena. His motives were laudable – to improve the lot of his people. He had been very fortunate in his life, growing up in affluence, gaining an education in the US, working around the world in highly paid, senior management positions. Juan's devotion and sense of duty led him to a powerful motivation to give something back to his home country and people.

His motivations, as we explored them, were more connected to his personal legacy than to the success of the business. He was fulfilling his duty to the firm and, more importantly, to the president who had been his sponsor for many years. How could Juan move forward in his current situation? He felt compelled to soldier on and make a success of the Iberian Peninsula organisation in order to fulfil his responsibility to the firm. At least he now felt an optimistic sense of possibility, rather than hopeless doom. He declared the intervention a success, and felt my continued engagement would bring diminishing returns. I encouraged Juan seriously to evaluate his own position. Perhaps an earlier retirement or a move to another country operation would better suit him, assuming that a smooth transition could be arranged in Seville? He promised to give it consideration, but felt the likelihood quite low of anything happening for at least two to three years.

Outcomes

The engagement ended. I felt unfulfilled. Certainly, the management team was in a much better place. They had coalesced into a strong unit, implementing difficult organisational changes, including consolidation of operations between Spain and Portugal, an action requiring both cultural and political savvy. But what of Juan? My initial contract had been with him. His motivations and aspirations were more clearly under active consideration by him, but he didn't really change, even though change was called for in this particular situation.

The organisation did improve its market and financial performance successively over the ensuing three years. The eight months I worked with them was a pivotal time for them, whether I was there or not. I take some measure of pride in their prosperity. I suspect that the organisation would have struggled through somehow, but I'm quite sure they achieved a unity of purpose and clarity of direction much more quickly at a very crucial time. Juan left the Iberian Peninsula operation within ten months, and also left the parent organisation in an early retirement. He returned to his native Costa Rica and has settled into his legacy career with enthusiasm, albeit three to five years earlier than his original plan.

Perhaps all is well. Everyone involved seemed pleased with the outcomes. As a coach, I learned more from this engagement than any other. My professional ethics were challenged several times, and my decisions have remained object lessons for me to this day as I approach my practice. I regularly question whether I made the right choices. I never felt that Juan's needs were met well, yet all parties came away satisfied with the ultimate outcomes. While frustrating for me as a coach, this type of situation is all too common. The world of large organisations in complex and unambiguous wins are rare.

The cultural differences and historical envies ran deep with this group. Yet, they quickly overcame those differences at work when they were forced to face a common cause – the survival of their business and the jobs of hundreds of people. And the new language of leadership that emerged from this crucible of change retained a remarkable persistence. Somehow, a work culture emerged that allowed everyone to let go of their ancient rivalries, at least while they were at work.

CHAPTER 11

Cross-cultural Coaching: A Case of Cultural Disruption in Europe

Europe has created a new reality over the past half-century. Today, we see the emergence of a more united Europe, which began with the Common Market, through to the EU and now the issuance of the euro currency. Of course, the real changes wrought by the unification of Europe are only beginning to emerge. Regional cultures have taken on greater importance for the typical citizen, even while national cultures become blurred with pan-European urges. For example, Wallonia and Flanders drift towards more autonomy within the Belgian state; Scotland seeks and wins support for more autonomy and external recognition from the UK; and Catalonia places a renewed stamp of its independent thinking on the Iberian Peninsula.

This is a story of forging a unified management culture linking Britain and the Continent. On one hand, it's a problem faced over the ages by many organisations, yet it's new in the context of an economically unified Europe. In eras gone by, multinational organisations established relatively independent operations in every country, mirroring the distinct political economies in each. This story is of a German CEO in a British–German joint venture, with its headquarters in Germany.

The Situation

The client organisation was a German–British joint ownership firm comprising certain operating units from both a German heavy industry firm and a British firm. Both had strong roots in advanced technologies in several fields. The impetus for the joint venture was extraordinary, but a frequent occurrence during the last years of the twentieth century. Customers in each sector of the business had begun seeking suppliers on a global basis as early as 20 years ago. In response, competitors from other regions had largely completed their own transformations. First, the industry leaders had all established profitable, growing operations in multiple regions around the world. Second, any government ownership or protection was largely a thing of the past. These firms competed, sometimes ruthlessly, for every bit of business and had earned reputations for technical excellence, business-like operations and reliable performance.

In order to survive in this harsh, unprotected environment, the respective British and German parents took a great step joining forces through the structure of a new firm, jointly owned by the two, with nearly equal contributions of people, technologies, facilities, customers and contracts. If successful, this new firm would bring capabilities unparalleled in the marketplace. In several heavy equipment and infrastructure segments, the combined capabilities would immediately position them to win. However, after nearly two years, the two organisations were not coming together as one business. Each organisation retained great pride in its heritage and culture and saw itself as an asset of its home nation. Often, that attitude superseded the attention and requirement to achieve satisfactory business results.

For example, early on, a business opportunity arose in which a very large, multi-year infrastructure project came up for bid. Historically, the British had used its own stable of subcontractors to bid on those elements of the project that they couldn't deliver themselves. The German partner operated a world-leading business in an area that would have been subcontracted in the past. The CEO intervened and asked the two organisations to join forces, rather than compete, as they had done previously. Initially, managers on both sides quickly agreed that working together on the bid response would benefit the corporation. Then the resistance and delays began. First, the British insisted on a non-disclosure agreement with the German operation, so deep was the historical mistrust. Then, the initial meeting could not get scheduled for over two months, leaving only half the time available until the submission of an initial proposal. Both groups sent relatively junior people from their respective proposal teams to the meeting. Predictably, neither side would make the necessary commitments to the final proposal – the people attending were not empowered to do so. Ultimately, the British-led project team wrote their German counterparts into the proposal with inadequate information, and lost the bid to a competing French consortium. Examples like this abounded in the early months of the new organisation's life.

This did not happen because of bad intentions or an unwillingness to act in the best interests of the corporation and its strategic goals, but because of an accumulation of the small, seemingly inconsequential behaviours of many executives, managers and technicians that naturally emerged out of the attitudes and culture each carried with him. The British operations functioned just as they had under the former British ownership, while the German operations did likewise. From the British side, the old view that Great Britain is an island nation reared its head every day in the business. Cooperation with their German colleagues rarely happened. The British saw their technologies or strategies as proprietary and shunned any sharing with the Germans. It would violate their independence and unique island status as European, yet not quite. The Germans acted in a similar fashion, seeing the British as just a bit inferior. After all, they reasoned, the German industrial machine had regained its position as the engine of growth for Europe shortly after the end of World War II. And the skill, industriousness and wit of the German people had sustained its position for more than two generations. They were quite happy to leave their British colleagues to their own devices.

Management activities at the corporate level looked like a political bureaucracy and contributed little to the business success of the combined organisation. Every engagement of leadership required careful negotiations just to allow the intervention to occur. Technical advancements were not shared until the relative contributions of the two sides had been valued and the positions of the respective leaders adjusted to reflect the 'value.' Almost every human resource policy, practice or programme remained strictly 'off limits' for corporate activity. The labour laws varied dramatically between the UK and Germany, after all. In this environment, formal conferences, coalition-building and reluctant engagement were the operating reality for any corporate initiative. Everything was political, as might be expected. Diplomacy seemed to be the most critical skill for the corporate leadership. But diplomacy rarely delivered profits.

The Leader

The CEO was fundamentally a diplomat as well. He was chosen for his astute diplomatic skill, as it was needed to hold this unlikely organisation together. Educated in a leading German university, he had travelled widely during his university years and throughout his career. He excelled in every step along the way. He was very intelligent, well read, sophisticated, urbane and worldly in his outlook. While thoroughly German, he travelled easily on a global stage. But the spotlight could be reserved for others. He preferred a quiet, well-reasoned discussion to an intense, charged debate. He generously allowed others, including subordinates, to occupy the centre of attention while he remained in the background, pulling the levers of power far removed from public scrutiny. Nevertheless, the CEO recognised that the firm was not competing successfully. Diplomacy would never win out in a vastly more competitive world than the one in which the two parts of this new firm had grown and developed. Its primary competitors now operated as unified organisations across multiple global regions, and achieved lower costs, more rapid response and better coordination in bidding on and delivering major contracts.

This emergent new organisation, created from bits of two, very unique, political and strong organisations, needed to pursue a strategy of global marketing, cross-boundary coordination (across both political and functional boundaries), investment in people and aggressive competition. The new strategy required collaboration, more people-oriented leadership and rewards aimed at elevating leaders with these capabilities. The CEO was driving this change, even as he realised that he himself did not exemplify the new leadership much better than anyone else on his senior team.

The Process

Sequenced Interventions

Internal executive development staff recommended an entirely new set of policies and systems for leadership development. Only a complete remake would enable the CEO to implement the dramatic changes in strategy and management style that he envisioned. These would include compensation, performance management and goal-setting programmes aimed at creating more emphasis on corporate performance and common goals. A new management and executive development initiative would prepare leaders in new ways, and provide for refreshed succession management disciplines geared towards the identification and preparation of a new generation of leaders all aligned with the new model. Underpinning all these systems, programmes and initiatives would be a new and clear definition of the requirements and demands that these leaders would face. The internal group selected a consulting team, including me, to research and redesign the role of senior leader in the firm consistent with the altered direction.

My initial intervention with the CEO was a series of interviews, examining the business and strategic context of the organisation. The method of the first meeting was simply a structured interview. The purpose was to gather information from the CEO (and a wide range of other senior executives) to help to shape the competency model that the client had requested. I varied from the 'structure' in order to help the CEO find and clarify his sources of greatest energy.

The first interview uncovered a restless dissatisfaction with the performance of the organisation, along with a distinct view that no more than a third of the current leadership were appropriate for the challenges facing the firm. Another third would never make the transition and would ultimately leave the organisation. The remaining third was critical; they were the 'fence-sitters'. Competent and able to work across boundaries, this group was nevertheless sceptical, preferring things to remain unchanged. If he could move this group to embrace change, he felt that the organisation could weather the turbulent shift to a more competitive, global, cross-boundary type of firm. If these fence-sitters could not be moved, then the resistance from them and turmoil caused by their eventual likely replacement could potentially paralyse the organisation and lead to its failure and break-up.

Towards the end of the interview, the CEO began disclosing the political nature of the management in the firm. He began to see me as a valuable 'sounding board' and was now discussing one of the more sensitive and difficult challenges he faced as a CEO, one he thought of as taboo for any open discussion. We agreed to explore it more fully in a planned second discussion, as well as discuss the initial draft competency model proposal. His willingness to enter the ground of taboos left me convinced that the second interview would be even more fruitful.

Several weeks later, we met a second time. In that discussion, we explored the political genesis of the organisation and the limitations placed on the CEO by the essentially political joint venture partners. Both joint venture partners retained substantial ownership by their respective governments. Therefore, the interests and objectives of the partners sprang from national interests as strongly as commercial ones. Governance at the board level involved the interplay of political figures expressing national interests and manoeuvring to strengthen their positions based on the interests that they each represented. The CEO felt, and I concurred, that this dynamic is common and makes up a significant portion of the group dynamic in any board. But, the unique circumstance in this particular case was the government ownership and express national interests competing at the board table.

I helped the CEO to express and clarify several paradoxes inherent in the situation he needed to confront. My purpose was not for him to choose a course down one path or the other to resolve any paradoxes, but rather to help him fully understand the new, shifting pressures he was creating in the organisation, especially for the leadership team he cherished, but criticised at the same time.

Collaboration in an increasingly competitive environment The firm faced stiffer competition in every line of business. Every employee, starting with senior leadership, was forced to adopt a more aggressive, competitive approach in order to meet the competitors successfully. Yet, at the same time, the merging of the two organisations, coupled with more cross-boundary work, demanded a more collaborative, collegial approach to coordination of work across functional and geographic boundaries. How will these two new styles reside in the same leader and organisation?

Task focus and results orientation in a profoundly political firm Much of both businesses had lived under the umbrella of 'cost-plus' government contracts as a major source of revenue. Bureaucratic methods of project management were the norm. Disciplined cost or schedule management took a back seat to agency relations, contracting officer management and parliamentary lobbying. These business dynamics would not change quickly, yet the combined joint venture firm could not expect competitive success without an intense focus on deadlines, costs, quality and deliverable outcomes. How can 'cost-plus' contracts coexist with a net profit margin mindset?

The politics of national interests in a firm facing private competition The interests of the German and British nations played profoundly important parts in the business of both joint venture partners. Each devoted entire organisational units to ministry relations, housing staff virtually permanently in the offices of the various client ministries. Lobbying efforts are a primary means of marketing in that environment. Senior executive transfers from board to ministry and back helped to maintain the web of relationships needed to win projects and programmes. At the same time, the emerging competitive environment called for strong, arm's-length competition for bids, proposals and projects. How could the same programme directors execute both well?

Stability of long-term projects during a period of radical change Projects or programmes in these businesses require an investment of 18 months to four years to develop the business and win a contract. Then the production and delivery period may range up to five, ten or fifteen years. Stability of organisation, project staffing and quality of delivered product are vital characteristics of any successful supplier. Yet the change envisioned by the CEO would generate turbulent instability for several years, with possible echoes of that turmoil lasting many years into the future. How could the leadership maintain stability while fomenting turbulence and rapid change?

Creating a common business culture during a time of renewed national and regional cultural values On the one hand, the emergence of the European Monetary Union coupled with expanding globalisation had created a fertile environment for common business cultures cutting across national boundaries. Yet, at the same time, people in their own community were (and still are) seeking a renewed emphasis on their local, distinct culture. Leaders need to acknowledge and support these urges yet still forge a common set of values and beliefs for their organisation. How could the organisation acknowledge distinct local cultures while forging a new, cross-boundary corporate culture?

Demanding accountability and short-term results in a business with long cycles Projects frequently play out over periods up to 20 years, from business development through to final production. Leaders must see the long term and manage client value creation with that long view. Yet, at the same time, a successful transformation of this organisation required a new focus on immediate deadlines, goal attainment and 'hitting the numbers' every fiscal year. How could they maintain a long view and demand disciplined, short-term performance management at the same time?

As we discussed these paradoxes, we both realised that they captured a central part of the leadership challenge. The CEO needed to exercise all of his skill in identifying these paradoxes, showing the importance of both sides to success and encouraging his leadership team to find their own way of living with and embracing these paradoxes. I helped him to recognise the risk of others seeing him as 'two-faced' or 'speaking out of both sides of his mouth'. Nevertheless, dealing with the tension in these paradoxes would generate the change needed in his organisation. This insight reinforced my value to him as a sounding board and foil. He had never conceptualised leadership as wrestling constructively with paradox before, and it energised him.

Next, we explored the nature of power and how these dynamics played out in his organisation. The 'rules of engagement' for power politics were unspoken in both the German and British sides of the new firm. As we explored these, the CEO concluded that the rules varied quite a bit between the two sides, based on the two national cultures. I helped him to realise the importance of codifying the rules of engagement. Such clarity would acknowledge the reality of political action, reinforce a new common corporate culture and minimise the presence of personal politics based on personal interests and ambitions.

The outcomes of this second interview, an understanding of the new set of paradoxes facing leadership and clarity about the nature of power politics in the firm, helped the CEO to create an agenda for his personal involvement in change management. The emergent leadership competency model emphasised typical changes in competency for a successful competitive enterprise. As I presented the draft model, the CEO expressed several needs. He needed some sort of mechanism to:

- Create a broad impact on his leadership team
- Help to evaluate leaders on their ability to change towards a new set of competencies and achieve success for the firm
- Generate change momentum throughout the firm.

The vehicles for meeting these diverse needs came through a series of organisational interventions with the extended leadership team (a population of 160 senior managers drawn from German and British units) and several personal interventions with the CEO.

Organisational Interventions

Once a new leadership model was approved, the first intervention was to create a feedback instrument and development process for leaders. The instrument's design provided for specific feedback on the behaviours identified as essential in the new leadership model. The use of this tool helped to establish a new common language of leadership, helped senior managers to gain greater insight into how others saw them, evaluated them against a new set of standards and generated a new sense of openness in communication across the organisation. Each of these outcomes helped to bridge the cultural gap between the Germans and British by forging a new, shared leadership model.

Individual development interventions with senior leadership

All the senior management population used the feedback tool to solicit observations from their colleagues – peers, subordinates and bosses. The consulting team facilitated individual interpretation and development planning sessions with each leadership team member. The objectives for these sessions included:

1. Understanding the feedback and identifying additional questions to answer.

2. Prioritising a development agenda, that is, identifying which strengths to leverage and which weaknesses to improve would form the basis for initial development activities.
3. Helping to shape career questions for the leader (for example am I suited for top executive leadership? Does this feedback foreshadow derailment for me?)

A significant minority of the leaders resisted the use of the feedback instrument for their own development. They raised many reasons ranging from lack of time to participate, doubts about the validity of the instrument, concerns over the involvement of subordinates, preferences to exclude peers, cost of intervention, lack of development support and mistrust over the intentions of the organisation.

Design and implement a performance management process emphasising the new requirements

The internal human resource staff took the responsibility to design the reward systems and performance management processes needed. They requested assistance from our consulting team to help to shape these systems. The criteria of greatest importance included:

- Behavioural measures as well as business, financial and milestone outcomes
- Rewards linked to the measures, including the behavioural measures
- Ease of use in the process, to help ensure compliance and consistency
- Inclusion of process participation measures in the goals for leaders
- Design consistency with the firm's succession practices
- An appropriately balanced emphasis among business goals, behavioural competencies and developmental progress.

Train internal consultants and managers to carry the change initiative throughout the organisation

The consulting team designed and conducted training courses, practice sessions and on-the-job observation and coaching with internal trainers,

HR professionals and managers in the use of the tools, methods and systems designed and implemented. It became their responsibility to carry the change processes forward into the organisation. Only with the ongoing involvement and commitment from these groups would the changes envisioned by the CEO come to fruition.

Personal Interventions

One-to-one 360° feedback

The feedback meeting I held with the CEO took on a different flavour from similar sessions with other leaders, not unlike the free-flowing form of the interview meetings held earlier. We had now established a comfortable relationship – one that allowed me to question his most deeply held assumptions and him to disclose and explore alternative views safely. He wanted to accept the data without question and act on it promptly to show a good role model for the entire organisation. I cautioned him about that approach. His position as CEO coupled with the political nature of the organisation made the ratings of him highly subject to many biases, most unknown to the raters themselves.

I helped him to explore the degree to which he was 'told the truth' in any situation. My question created a difficult moment between us. He was offended by the notion that anyone would 'lie' to him. After discussing several situations and probing to understand the specific actions, the CEO realised that almost every communication he received was couched in careful terms, rarely giving him direct, complete information.

Political constituency analysis and action planning

With that conclusion in mind, I suggested that we conduct an analysis of his political constituencies before identifying behavioural strengths and weaknesses. Together, we identified the following constituencies:

- Board members
- Executive committees of the joint venture partners
- External financial community
- Key government ministries in the German and British governments

- His leadership team and, within it, several important subgroups representing the original organisations, the different lines of business, the staff functions and so on
- The broader management team of the combined organisation
- The entire, collective employee population of the firm.

We began the analysis together, and I left him with the assignment to complete before we met again in a month's time. In the analysis, we agreed to answer the following questions for each constituency:

1. What were the group's primary interests, that is, what did the group hope to achieve vis-à-vis the joint venture?
2. What external factors affected the group most heavily?
3. Was this group an enemy or friend of the joint venture organisation, and why?
4. How much power did the group hold, that is, to what degree could the group accelerate or disrupt the performance of the business?
5. What actions could the CEO take that were both possible and appropriate to deal with the political posture of each constituency?

This exercise easily fitted into the CEO's mindset about the organisation. As a natural diplomat, he thought in political terms. This exercise helped him let go of the assumption that he needed to rid the organisation of politics. Instead, he formed clear agendas on how to deal with each constituency in a constructive political manner.

Development planning

In our second feedback meeting, we reviewed his political constituency analysis, then moved on to behavioural development planning. I asked the CEO to describe his personal view of his distinctive strengths and development areas. To that, I would add my observations from three in-depth meetings thus far. We had agreed that the feedback data from the survey would be filled with biases. With that in mind, we used that data only as a check of his and my perceptions, rather than a primary source of potential conclusions.

Defining his strengths became a tough exercise. The CEO rarely personalised the causes for his successes. For him, strong parents, superb education, good connections and luck together conspired to provide him with a wonderful series of opportunities over his lifetime. I told him that humility was good, but that perhaps he was being too self-effacing. He had excelled throughout his career by being analytical, but then coming to decisions based on sound, intuitive judgment. He comfortably balanced facts with instincts. He always used a distinctly strong strategic view to shape the direction for whatever organisation he led. He had exercised discipline in driving results and maintaining consistent performance over time. When faced with obstacles, he had acted with determination and persistence to sustain the course. Finally, he had always brought others along and engaged organisations through unusually canny diplomacy, recognising the ebb and flow of power and differing interests. I think he was genuinely surprised to see this list of deep strengths compiled in one place. He showed well-deserved pride in his own capabilities and accomplishments, humble but not with false modesty.

His weaknesses were easier for him to identify. The CEO had always been introspective and self-critical. My role was to leaven his own harsh judgment, remind him of his successes and point out the positive feedback from others. Even so, as a private man, he primarily trusted his own judgment in making decisions. This made collaboration difficult. He wasn't sure he wanted to collaborate with those whose intellect and analytical capability he doubted. To best exemplify the new model he espoused, the CEO would need significant improvement as a collaborator. He was a private, analytical and logical executive. Emotions had no place on the job for him. He genuinely believed that emotions would cloud his judgment and leave him prone to poor decisions and even open to attack. While a detached, logical style suited him best, his lack of emotional connection with people left him similarly detached from the organisation, in ways which made it more difficult for him to unleash the full energies and drive of people. This new organisation cried out for an inspirational vision, a direction and purpose extending beyond the humdrum, day-to-day activities. This CEO was uncomfortable expressing his ideas about the future in ways that would stimulate inspiration across the organisation.

Finally, coaching and developing other leaders did not come easily to this CEO. When faced with a performance challenge or a new opening, he used one of three approaches, in sequence:

1. Replace the leaders with the biggest performance or capability gaps

2. Use a political process to determine the next in line for the opening
3. Go outside the organisation to fill crucial competency gaps.

He believed that, at the most senior levels, inadequate performance could not be turned around and replacement was the only real solution. Furthermore, he questioned the belief that leadership could grow in individuals throughout their career. He truly felt that upbringing, education, connections and luck made careers. Yet he also realised that such assumptions ran contrary to the leadership he knew was needed in the organisation going forward.

In a particularly vulnerable moment as we talked about these weaknesses, he confessed that he doubted whether he was the right leader for this emerging organisation once it truly established itself as an independent body. I shared the concern. After that moment, I suggested that we skip the step of prioritising development needs for the purpose of crafting a development plan. I felt we should more carefully explore his fit with the role next.

Personal evaluation of CEO's leadership fit with new requirements

We entered into a very open conversation about his fit with the demands facing the new organisation. His credibility with the joint venture partners was essential for navigating the transition to an integrated, independent organisation. This process would not be completed until the firm entered the public stock markets, allowing the joint venture partners to reduce their respective ownership stakes substantially. But, once this transition was complete, the firm needed an energised, inspirational leader who could tap into the emotional energies of the entire organisation. The CEO had been allowing such thoughts to ramble around his mind without form for over six months. Our dialogue helped him to reach the conclusion that he should plan the transition to a new CEO shortly after the firm's IPO.

Such a plan would require the full understanding and support of the board, and would inevitably involve delicate preparatory discussions with key financial market players and important client ministries in the British and German governments. These sensitive diplomatic overtures played to his greatest strength as a leader and he was convinced that he could handle these steps over a two-year or longer period without creating any negative impact on the organisation or its clientele.

Legacy planning

In our last meeting, I again structured the agenda to follow his greatest interest and energy. Based on the previous meeting, the CEO felt the most energy on the issue of legacy planning. It took very little exploration to identify the qualities and accomplishments he wanted to be remembered for after his retirement. He had given this serious thought since our last meeting, and named several descriptors and accomplishments he wanted attached to his reputation:

- A new, public firm – a leader in its field
- A unified culture in the firm, with free-flowing ideas and resources across all boundaries, without regard to nationality
- A robust, resilient leadership team, equipped to carry the business forward without pause
- A European leader in the twenty-first century sense, who established a truly great European firm with global impact and visibility.

He saw these as within his reach. The timeline would be over the ensuing two years or so. That time, added to his two-plus years already in office, meant a very short period over which to establish such a grand reputation and legacy. Nevertheless, he could envision it.

Outcomes

So, what has happened in the two-year period since this engagement ended? The CEO committed to replace himself after:

- Successfully unwinding the German and British partners' controlling interests
- A successful IPO of the new, independent firm
- Rebuilding the leadership team with the right talent for an intensely competitive market.

The business has spun out from its original joint venture partners and is now traded publicly as an independent firm. But the leader remains in place, with no visible plans to change. The management team has substantially transformed itself. In fact, almost the entire senior team is new since the time of this case. For some time, the firm was seen as an increasingly competitive entity. Unfortunately, the firm fared poorly, along with many other organisations, during the economic downturn of 2001–02. The markets have judged the firm harshly and analysts have blamed management.

Was the coaching engagement a success? I see it with ambivalence. The coaching served as a catalyst and support mechanism for the CEO to sustain his commitment to transformation. He came to see the challenge of change in new ways, particularly regarding the new set of paradoxes facing them and the role of power politics in the organisation. The firm did indeed navigate a tremendously turbulent period in its history, forging a new, cross-boundary organisation. It now functions as a unified, cross-boundary firm with a global footprint. It shows the potential for long-term success, although it's not a guaranteed thing. In these regards, the engagement must be deemed successful.

The degree of change in senior management positions ended up being severe and the ensuing tumult has been difficult. The changes happened in much the same way as in the past, with little visible evidence of more development of senior talent rather than changing them out. Active development of talent is much more evident at lower levels. This bodes well for the next generation of leaders. The CEO recommitted to lengthen his own stay, although I felt the decision we had made for him to replace himself was the right one. Who knows what pressures he faced from the financial markets to maintain stable leadership and follow through on his change vision? The management culture has moved, especially in seeing itself and operating much more as a cross-boundary organisation. But the movement has been limited, and it remains a deeply political firm, with unclear rules of engagement, leading to continuous jockeying for position at all levels. In these ways, the engagement did not fulfil its promise.

CHAPTER 12

Cross-cultural Coaching: Coaching in the Middle East

Anyone who teaches me just one letter,
then I will be his slave.
THE HADEETH *(Thoughts of the Prophet Muhammad)*

Background to the Gulf States

When many observers talk of the Middle East in terms of the world business map, they usually are referring to the Gulf and the states that comprise the Gulf Cooperation Council. These six countries (Bahrain, Kuwait, Oman, Qatar, Saudi Arabia and the United Arab Emirates (UAE)) share the waters of the Persian Gulf (more commonly referred to in the area as the Arabian Gulf), an area of economic and political interest. They range in geographical size from the largest, Saudi Arabia with a landmass over four times that of France, to Bahrain, which is the smallest. They also vary in the nature of their political frameworks, population and economies. However, one strong factor that they have in common that shapes behaviour is the dominant religion of the Gulf, that being Islam. The religion has a strong pull on the way in which people behave, relate to each other and work together and will be explored later.

Political and Economic Context

Traditionally, the political nature of the Gulf has been one of autocracies, foreign domination and a recent growth to a more democratic stance. For centuries, the Gulf was a part of the Ottoman Empire and then it attracted the attention of European powers, notably Great Britain, due to its strategic importance. During the early twentieth century, the move for self-determination and the decay of the power of the Ottoman Empire led to the emergence of new nation states (the most notable being the birth of Saudi Arabia as a nation in 1932). In the latter half of the last century, there had been slow growth to a more democratic atmosphere in the Gulf states. This has continued with Bahrain becoming a constitutional monarchy with an enlarged franchise (February 2002).

Economically, the Gulf is still dominated by oil. Until oil was discovered in the 1930s, the economic base of the Gulf states was largely a mixture of subsistence farming, pearl fishing and acting as a trading post between Europe and Asia. The advent of oil changed the fortunes of the Gulf and gave the states a vastly different position in the world economy. However, less than 50 years later, with some of the countries' oil reserves almost gone, Bahrain and the UAE (with the exception of still oil-rich Abu Dhabi) were forced to look in other directions to maintain economic growth and prosperity. This has led to a more open-door policy and an encouragement of the IT and banking and finance sectors in the two countries. It is this factor that has led to a changing attitude to 'outside' influences in Bahrain and the UAE. In the countries still sitting on vast quantities of oil (Saudi Arabia alone has nearly one-quarter of the world's known oil reserves), the need to be so outgoing is less so. In addition, oil can be very 'forgiving'. Despite massive fluctuations in oil prices over the last 30 years, the power that oil gives to those who have it allows them to be a little blasé about the future.

Cultural Influences on Attitudes and Behaviour

> The stable routines and habits of thought and perception that we call culture.
>
> *(Schein 1996)*

Attitudes to coaching and to being coached are subject to the same multi-faceted cultural influences as all other aspects of life in a society, both corporate and national. In addition, in the Gulf, there is the third strong influence on culture; religion. The wide-ranging spread of company types with their own cultures makes drawing any blanket conclusions about the influence of corporate culture on attitudes to coaching somewhat futile. Certain companies have a clear and genuine desire to continue being, or becoming, a true learning organisation in which employees will develop through all avenues, including coaching. At the other extreme, there are organisations in the Gulf that wish to draw as much from staff members in the short term and have no desire to invest in their development and thus any coaching that takes place is in spite of the corporate culture and not because of it.

In a major work on national cultures (*Culture's Consequences*, 1980) Geert Hofstede investigated 50 countries and three regions in respect of their cultural orientation. This work continued in *Cultures and Organizations* (1991). One of the regions is 'Arab speaking countries' (ASC), comprising seven countries, two of the major ones (Saudi Arabia and the UAE) being in the Gulf. Therefore, we can make a reasonable assumption that many of Hofstede's findings relate to a large extent to the Gulf. That is certainly borne out by my experience and that of other management development professionals that I am in contact with in the Gulf. So what are the cultural factors, how does the region rate on the factors and what are the implications for coaching in organisations in the Gulf? Hofstede (1980) drew up four factors which can define a culture:

1. *Power distance* (the psychological distance between a boss and subordinate).
2. *Individualism* versus *collectivism* (the prevalence of the individual or group interests being served).
3. *Masculinity* versus *femininity* (competition and assertiveness versus nurturing and caring).
4. *Uncertainty avoidance* (the level of need for rules and structure).

How do these factors impact on the attitudes towards and the implementation of coaching in the workplace in the Gulf countries?

Power distance – can be defined as the extent to which the less powerful members of an organisation within a country expect and accept that power is distributed unequally. In the survey, Hofstede's respondents not only expressed how they saw their relationship to their boss but also their preference of how it should be. There is a strong correlation between how the relationship is and how it is desired to be. So, this indicates that subordinates are happy with the state of affairs.

In ASC, there is a high level of power distance. Of the 50 countries and three regions, it ranked seventh in the table. This indicates a high level of dependence on the boss by the subordinate. As a result of this, bosses assume a more directive style of management and the expectation of both parties is that power will be in the hands of the boss. In countries with a high rating, as power is prized by people, then it follows that those with it will wish to retain it.

Interestingly, in a high power distance culture, the way in which the concept of coaching is understood can be very different to accepted models of the principles and practice of coaching. An American manager I know working in the Gulf was pleased when he found out that his new company conducted 'a high level of boss to subordinate coaching'. His later experience proved the mismatch of definitions of 'coaching'. What to him was telling and instruction was seen by his Arab colleagues as good quality coaching! Many managers in the Gulf feel uneasy about relinquishing or sharing power. In a coaching context, this manifests itself in the 'if I tell you what I know, you'll take some of my power away' mode of thought. So, although lip service can be paid to coaching, in actuality, it can be delayed, diluted or distorted. As subordinates in such cultures accept to a great extent what their boss does, then it is unlikely that they will complain about this approach.

Individualism versus collectivism – individualist cultures are ones where ties between individuals are loose and collective societies are ones where individuals are integrated from birth into strong cohesive in-groups, which throughout a person's lifetime continue to protect them in exchange for unquestioning loyalty. The rating for ASC puts the region towards the collective bias. This collective bias can be seen in ASC, particularly in Saudi Arabia, where many business activities are based around relationships and formal links. The group all of us first enter is the family. In Saudi society, the family is a highly extended one, as tribal affiliations are exceptionally strong in the country. The tribal aspect of the collective society is given a further twist by the local phenomenon of *Wasta*. The Arabic word does not translate fully into English but in simple terms it is networking, connections and advancement on the basis of who one knows rather than what one does. But unlike the 'old school tie' in the UK or *Guanxi* in Chinese societies, *Wasta* is more pervasive and is something you are born into (by tribal links) rather than acquire during life. Having or not having *Wasta* can be a strong influence on the career path of an individual. If you have good *Wasta*, you may be looked on more favourably in a company than a colleague in the same area who does not have the same connections.

The implications of this advanced level of collectivism are clearly demonstrated in organisations in the Gulf. As a manager, you would be more inclined to coach and develop a person who is connected to you or someone who has good *Wasta* that you want to tap into. As the person who is potentially receiving coaching and advancement, you can expect career progression not from what you do but from who you are connected to. So, if you have good *Wasta*, you can progress; if not, then progression will be more difficult. At the extreme level of *Wasta*, your career can move forward no matter how well or badly you do your job if you are connected, so why do you need any coaching and development? Similarly, if you have little or no *Wasta*, what is the point in personal development (including coaching) as you are not going anywhere anyway. In organisations, this can mean that the attitude towards coaching can be negative, being a case of 'it doesn't matter whether I do it or not, my career is determined by something other than ability'.

On the positive side, individuals in cultures with a collective bias generally look to build personal skills and look for ways to use those skills. The person being coached sees it as a good opportunity to build skill levels. To capitalise on this, many large companies in the region with training and development facilities conduct coaching workshops for managers to enable them to coach effectively and some have training professionals who conduct individual coaching sessions with staff members. The attitude of the person receiving coaching is generally very positive. There can be a real appetite for personal development and coaching is seen as a good way to satisfy that appetite.

Masculinity versus *femininity* – the ASC as a region shows a marked bias towards masculinity. This means that in such cultures there is a greater importance attached to: the opportunity to earn more; career advancement; recognition; and having a challenge. In addition, the gender roles traditional in the Gulf reinforce the assertive/aggressive and competitive approach to most activities (which if you have ever driven a car in Saudi Arabia or Bahrain will be self-evident). The 'masculine' thought process believes that the strong should be supported and that the job of the strong is to control and correct the less strong. This outlook can affect the coaching process, making a manager less likely to undertake coaching as it is not seen as congruent with a strong, driving, masculine image of someone in command. At the same time, if the coachee sees the society in which they live as a corrective one, then the coaching process can be perceived as a sign of weakness and to be avoided.

Uncertainty avoidance – feelings of uncertainty are not just personal but may be shared with others in the society. The feelings and associated coping mechanisms become part of that society and become reflected in the values and behaviour of its members. This can lead to patterns of behaviour that may seem incomprehensible to an outsider. Extreme uncertainty creates intolerable anxiety; societies develop ways to reduce the uncertainty. Technical advances help to prevent uncertainties caused by nature; laws and rules control uncertainties of behaviour by people; and religion helps to accept uncertainties of the future life. In company life, uncertainty can be reduced by having a set of rules and adhering to them and by seeing a long-term future with the organisation. Individuals with a high need for certainty will gravitate to stable, rule-driven companies where they can look forward to a long stay.

The ASC region shows a marked preference for certainty and the avoidance of ambiguity. The strong factor in the Gulf that gives certainty is the religion, Islam. The strong faith and conviction inherent in the religion gives certainty. Praying five times a day at closely delineated times gives a personal and collective structure and discipline. Islam also gives a feeling of certainty to its adherents that overcomes the ultimate uncertainty – what happens after we die? One of the fundamental aspects of the religion also gives a feeling of 'if we cannot control the uncertainties, then someone will do it for us, so there is no need to be concerned'. That someone is Allah. The concept of 'inshallah' (if God wills it) is used in many settings but generally is a fatalistic acceptance of things outside one's control. If one accepts the phenomenon of inshallah, then one's path is determined by a higher being. Thus, it is God's will if you progress in your career and, to an extent, anything you do, including being coached and developed, is secondary in impact.

The avoidance of uncertainty in a culture gives a structure to life in many ways, one of them being how people learn. In strong uncertainty avoidance cultures, the student is comfortable in structured learning situations and is concerned about having the 'right' answers. Also, the teacher is supposed to have all the 'right' answers. From a coaching perspective, it makes sense to recognise this and have a format that caters for this tendency by giving a very clear 'purpose, content and outcomes' statement at the start of a coaching process and again at the start of each session.

The 'Traditional' View of Personal Development and Career Advancement

In the Gulf, the changes experienced in economic development and working life in the last 50 years have been almost beyond belief. The transition from pearl fisher to banker and subsistence farmer to oil company manager in two generations has changed views hugely. If there ever was a 'traditional' view of development, then it was one of short-term opportunism and the hope that things will work out in the long term. Having lived an almost hand-to-mouth existence for centuries leaves little room for deep thought about career development. Again, whether an individual succeeds or fails, a lot of the influence on the outcome is Allah's, rather than the individual's.

The Changing Socioeconomic Dimension

The changes in the economies of Gulf states continue to move at a high pace. The image of oil-rich, big American car-driving Arabs, that is prevalent in the West, is changing. In Saudi Arabia, for example, although the energy reserves are high (and with recent oil and gas field discoveries, getting higher), they have to be shared among a rapidly growing population. The encouragement for Saudi married couples to have big families (families of six or more siblings are very common and double-figure families are by no means unusual) in the past is now having its impact. The per capita income is getting lower; unemployment is running at 15 per cent and growing.

Many graduates of local universities are leaving college to find they have no ready-made jobs to go to and now have to make a shift of mindset from that of their fathers, where turning up was enough to get a salary. The need to fight harder to get a job and progress is hitting the current generation of potential managers and the need for personal development is no longer being regarded as an optional extra. In fact it is not only individuals that realise the need for a change of mindset. One of the largest companies in the region designated last year as the 'Year of Self-development' to encourage its employees to take charge of their personal progression.

Added to this is a gradual social liberalisation in the Gulf. Bahrain became a constitutional monarchy in February 2002 and held elections with a much wider franchise. The UAE has the highest percentage of female undergraduates in its universities of any country in the world. Opening up to other economic opportunities has inevitably led to the influence of other countries and their management styles. As in most countries in the world, the use of English is spreading and is increasingly becoming the lingua franca of the Gulf (for example if you want to learn from the Internet, it is almost impossible without the ability to speak

English). This has led to an ever-increasing desire to learn English and be educated in an American, Canadian or British university.

Attitudes to Personal Career Development

Due to the changing conditions in the Gulf, the attitude to career development is shifting. It is moving from an attitude of a job being an entitlement, to one where it is seen as something individuals need to work at to get and develop themselves to retain it and advance to higher positions. So the younger generation in the Gulf has a very positive attitude towards their career development. They realise that they need to seek out every opportunity to make themselves more competent and have a desire to learn from others, whether they are management development specialists in formal courses or their more experienced colleagues. For many of those in the later stages of their career, the attitude towards career advancement ranges from a genuine desire to learn from any source to one of 'you can't teach an old dog new tricks'. As in many such settings, it is dangerous to make assumptions and the coach can fall into the trap of dividing sheep and goats inaccurately. My experience of coaching in the region is that adopting an open mind until it is informed by what happens in a series of one-to-one sessions is the best path to follow.

Approaches to Coaching Own Members of Staff

As mentioned above, there can be a strong element of 'knowledge is power' when it comes to the prevailing attitude of many Gulf managers towards coaching their staff. Too many feel uncomfortable with the whole coaching scenario, as it runs counter to much of their preferred way of relating to staff as conditioned by their cultural background. Coaching can simultaneously mean to the potential coach: a shortening of the power distance between themselves and their staff member; a meeting that can be used by a staff member to bring up other issues (for example grading given on the last appraisal review); a show of concern for a colleague (a feminine trait in a masculine culture); and the simple fact that many managers may feel uneasy exposing their lack of experience in certain areas. In a strong uncertainty avoidance culture, of course, the teacher (coach) is supposed to have all the answers. For these reasons, managers acting as coaches often do not feel really committed to the coaching process. Although at an intellectual level they know all the good points in favour of coaching and staff development, at the subjective level they see it as a potential source of conflict, embarrassment and the reduction in personal power.

Coaching Experiences in Large Organisations

Many of the larger companies in the Gulf have an appreciable Western influence. Some companies have had exposure to North American and European methods as a feature of joint venture operations (oil companies); some by longstanding political affiliation (Bahrain); and others by increasing their economy's mix to bring them into the 'Western' preserves of media and information technology (UAE). This influence has led to the introduction of many Western management practices, coaching being one of them. The range of experience has been mixed and the general story is one of less rather than more successful. Facilities to develop managers as coaches are in place and many managers go through the process. But the rate of transfer to spend time on a regular basis coaching subordinates is low.

A regional survey showed that, on average, only about 8 per cent of all managers conduct regular coaching sessions that would be seen by coaching professionals as fitting most of the criteria for a successful session. On following up many trained coach managers, many reasons are given why coaching has not taken place (time, pressure of other work, 'they' don't want to be coached). Most companies expect that their managers will coach. A smaller number will provide programmes to develop managers as coaches and expose them to the risk of coaching their staff, while an even smaller number will actively challenge their senior managers to develop their successor. One large oil company made it a prerequisite for advancement that each senior manager should groom at least two of their staff to take over from them before being considered for promotion themselves.

The experience of companies who are trying to get managers to act as coaches and staff to expect to be coached is generally a story of success in the latter and failure in the former. However, it is unlikely that many of the larger organisations will give up on the challenge of spreading coaching within the corporate culture. It is seen as a necessary component in the growth of the company and, although it is a long process to embed it, the process will continue.

Case Study

Development in the Desert

Mohammad Al Ghamdi is the head of a department in the engineering services division of a large oil production and refining company in the Gulf. He has a team of 38 staff members, six of whom (senior engineers) report directly to Mohammad. They in turn manage small project teams of junior engineers. Both Mohammad and his six direct reports are highly qualified as engineers with degrees and doctorates from both local and North American universities. Mohammad has also taken the management development programme at Harvard and has found it useful in his transition from a technical specialist role to one of managing a team.

However, he finds that the pressure of his technical work allows little time to spend with his senior engineers. But, as qualified people, he is confident in their ability to manage their projects. He holds a review meeting every two weeks to update all of them on the progress of projects. Normally, the meetings deal with purely project-related technical matters. But at one meeting, one of the senior engineers (Abdullah Dossary) reacted uncharacteristically angrily to what he saw as unjustified criticism from Mohammad. One of Abdullah's junior engineers in his team made a mistake in a specification he drew up for a project at one of the company's smaller refineries. The refinery manager complained about the delay caused by the error to the head of engineering services (Mohammad's boss). Mohammad felt it wise to discuss the matter fully with Abdullah outside the meeting and during their discussion several key issues came to light, most of them related to the lack of development within the department. Abdullah said that he and the other senior engineers felt lost when it came to managing their staff. In turn the junior engineers had to hope they were doing their job correctly, as they got little or no guidance from the senior engineers. Also, Abdullah and his peers were unwilling to ask for help from Mohammad due to the nature of their working relationship, in which they felt comfortable discussing the technical issues they faced, but not the 'soft' areas of development of their management competence. However, the senior engineers desper-

CASE STUDY cont'd

ately need help to make them good people managers as well as being technical experts.

The discussion started Mohammad thinking about his role in relation to his senior engineers and the department's staff in general. He personally felt unqualified to develop his direct reports. That was always something that had been handled by the company's training department. He then contacted the training people to see what management courses they could provide to get his senior engineers more competent at managing their staff. The head of training, John Dixon, suggested that he and Mohammad meet to plan how to manage the situation. During their meeting, John listened carefully to what Mohammad had to say about the situation and how he would like John to train his department to be better people managers. John suggested that training alone wasn't the solution. An element of formal training needed to be blended with a lot of work in Mohammad's department to make any lasting and appreciable difference to the management abilities of not only the senior engineers but Mohammad himself. John pointed out that generally the best development results in the company have come when there has been a commitment to coaching from a head of department, and time to undertake coaching with members of staff is seen as an important activity to enable that department to operate more effectively.

Despite his misgivings, Mohammad agreed to put his weight behind a schedule of activities. The plan they agreed had the following five elements:

1. Participation by Mohammad and his seniors in a 'coaching for performance' workshop run by John and his staff.
2. Compilation of a 'code of conduct' to embed coaching as an accepted part of the department's operating practices.
3. Booking time on a quarterly basis for Mohammad and his seniors to undertake one-to-one coaching sessions against an agreed coaching schedule.
4. Coaching review meetings in which Mohammad and the senior engineers report on the progress of each person involved in the process.

Case Study cont'd

5. Introduction of a competence evaluation system to estimate the progress shown by each person receiving coaching. This took the form of a simplified appraisal document being completed quarterly by the coach and those being coached.

The five initiatives were completed and yet it took nearly nine months for the coaching practice to start to function well. Some of the early snags experienced were:

- Initially coaching was not seen to be important ('it's more training courses we need') and it got shelved when more 'important work' came in
- Senior engineers felt uncomfortable sharing their limited management experience with junior staff (the power distance factor in operation)
- Junior staff initially felt uncomfortable sitting with their boss
- Mohammad had to 'sell' the initiative hard to his boss, who firmly believed that development equated to training courses.

A year after their initial discussion, John Dixon and Mohammad met again to review the results of the work that had been done. John also wanted to use the experiences of the past 12 months to develop a coaching template for other department heads in the company.

The three major points from Mohammad's point of view were that: firstly, he didn't realise how much work was involved in the planning and implementation of a coaching programme. In fact he said that if he had known in the first place what was involved he probably wouldn't have done it. Secondly, he realised that it needed a deep personal commitment to the process on his part. Without that, Mohammad recognised that the coaching process could have been yet another company change initiative that had failed and would have worsened the motivation level in his department. Finally, Mohammad was pleasantly surprised by how well the process had worked, although he mentioned to John that it took a lot of doggedness and persistence on his part to 'encourage' his senior engineers to keep faith with the process.

However, on a positive note, both Mohammad and John agreed that the hard work and persistence on both their parts had paid dividends.

Case Study cont'd

Although the benefits of the initiative could not be measured precisely, they decided to see how the individuals and the department (and in turn the company) had gained from the coaching activity that had taken place. John conducted a series of informal interviews with both the senior and junior engineers to gather anecdotal information on the impact of the activities. Many of the comments centred around the following points:

- The quality of teamwork was improved as the coaching led to a greater understanding of the scope and pressures of the boss's role by the junior engineers and vice versa
- Junior engineers commented that they felt less anxious about a step up to a people management role in the future having been able to start to explore it with their manager
- Senior engineers said the fact that they were coaching staff on both technical and management issues had helped them to keep more up to date with technical changes and also to be more critical of their own performance as managers
- Those senior engineers who had participated in management programmes during the year would then hold briefing sessions for their junior engineers when they returned to the department to pass on the concepts and learning from the course
- As head of the department, Mohammad had made a conscious effort to be more closely involved with the individuals throughout the department, which enabled him to be more critical about how much of the technical detail of projects he got involved with. By seeing the coaching initiative as a project that he was championing, it led him to become more adept at seeing the function of the department at a strategic level. He became less enmeshed in the actual day-to-day work and more focused on what he wanted to create in the department as a vision within the company's mission.

The benefit for the company has been a much higher level of motivation, commitment and ability in the department. John Dixon is now introducing a 360° feedback process to produce a 'before and after' report on the

Case Study cont'd

progress of those involved in future coaching interventions to give a stronger link between the activities and the improved personal and departmental performance.

Based on the joint experiences in the engineering services example, John Dixon was able to draw up a checklist of things to take into consideration to make other department heads aware of the key factors for success when setting out on the coaching path:

- Be aware of the cultural factors that will impact on the process, especially when working with a group with a variety of cultural backgrounds and approaches
- As in many initiatives in an organisation, it needs the full commitment of the head of the operation to drive it forward. This is vital in the early stages of the coaching process, when resistance to change can be at its height
- Ensure that coaches have the required skills to devise and conduct effective coaching sessions. If they don't feel competent to coach, then there will be a natural resistance to taking part in a process that will probably expose their own lack of skill
- Have a clear programme of activities and ensure that the purpose of those activities is clear to everyone involved
- Commit time to the process; resist the temptation to postpone sessions when an 'emergency' job comes in. The coaching activities may not be urgent but on most occasions it is much more important
- Be patient and share early success stories to encourage others to commit to the programme.

Lessons Learned for Wider Coaching Context

From the point of view of introducing coaching into a Middle Eastern company, the implications are that it should be positioned in a way that will be acceptable to the prevailing cultural norms. Those introducing it should recognise that coaching in its accepted sense is not a natural part of 'traditional' management style in the area. This certainly holds true for the Gulf. Looking at experiences here and the lessons for coaching in general, many of the points are widely seen in many parts of the world. Managers in the UK may feel uncomfortable with the one-on-one structure; the typical Chinese manager will feel that his power distance has been diminished; and a manager in Uruguay will be uncomfortable with the loose format, as he sees it, of coaching. However, in conclusion, the lessons learned in the Gulf are essentially:

- Be patient if introducing managers to coaching; you may think it's a great benefit to the company but many managers are focused on what's good for their part of the company
- Understand where any resistance to coaching is coming from and what is motivating it
- Explore the cultural factors where you are going to tailor the approach to make it as acceptable as possible to those coaching and being coached
- Expect it not to work and be prepared to relaunch an initiative if and when it falters
- Be prepared for a long process that will need extensive support in its early stages by either internal or external HR development specialists.

CHAPTER 13

Cross-cultural Coaching: Coaching in the Asia Pacific Region

My personal journey into coaching was no road to Damascus revelation. Rather, I enjoyed a meandering journey down a fascinating road to find myself heading the Executive Coaching Centre in New Zealand. As a consulting partner in my own firm, I ended up spending nearly eight years in Hong Kong working in most of the countries in Asia. I have experienced much about the complex cultures of Asia and conducted many fascinating cross-cultural team-building exercises. I know I am only beginning to understand these cultures. Coaching provides an ideal channel for the skills I have learned over the past 25 years as psychologist, consultant and business leader and today I enjoy running the New Zealand sister organisation to the UK Executive Coaching Centre in Auckland.

Background to the Peoples of the Asia Pacific Region

Coaching in the Asia Pacific region has a number of unique challenges that are imposed by the cultures and people of the region. The total population of Asia is in excess of 3.2 billion, with East Asia alone comprising 1.3 billion people; in addition, Australia has a population of 20 million and New Zealand 4 million (Microsoft's Encarta 2001). The Asia Pacific region contains a very culturally diverse population, perhaps more so than those of any other region in the world. The range of languages in the region reflects this cultural diversity. More than 1 billion people speak Chinese dialects, 125 million people speak Japanese and 70 million speak Korean. Southeast Asia contains no dominant language, with Thai, Malay, Khmer, Burmese, Lao and Vietnamese all being spoken. In South Asia, millions of people speak Urdu, Hindi, Tamil and Telugu, while in Southwest Asia, Arabic is the dominant language. English is the principal language of both Australia and New Zealand and the use of English is increasing throughout the region, as it is the primary language of business. The main challenges of working in the Asia Pacific region are largely as a result of its cultural diversity. It commonly presents many practical challenges to organisations transferring staff from Europe or the USA to Asia Pacific.

Understanding and Tolerating Cultural Differences

Many people in organisations, or indeed out of them, struggle with the practice of tolerating differences. Review any world newscast any day and we find examples of intolerance of differences. As a coach, it is not enough for the coach to merely understand the nature of cultural differences, he or she also needs to be tolerant of them. A key requirement of any coach working in Asia Pacific is to have an understanding of these cultures. Geert Hofstede, the founder of the Institute for Research on Intercultural Co-operation, has provided many useful insights into cultural differences in the region and elsewhere. His book *Culture's Consequences* (1980) used surveys to provide comparisons in over 50 countries on the impact of culture in the workplace. Many cross-cultural insights can also be gained from *Riding The Waves of Culture: Understanding Diversity in Global Business* (Trompenaars et al. 1998).

Hofstede developed four dimensions, which now represent a kind of cultural filter for the world. He later added a fifth dimension. These dimensions were researched using questionnaires completed by IBM employees and the results produced scores that can be used to compare different countries. Knowing one's own cultural profile assists coaches in understanding others and how business transactions may differ according to the five dimensions. Hofstede's (1980) four dimensions of culture are: uncertainty avoidance, power distance, masculinity versus femininity and individualism versus collectivism. A fifth, Confucian dynamism, was added later (Hofstede and Bond 1988). I have found Hofstede's terms difficult for many coaches to grasp easily and apply and I have therefore simplified them as follows:

Hofstede's term	*Simplified term*
Uncertainty avoidance	Need for clarity
Power distance	Accepting power
Masculinity versus femininity	Relationship focus
Individualism versus collectivism	Group focus
Confucian dynamism	Long-term focus

Need for clarity – this refers to how comfortable people feel when issues and ideas are unclear and/or ambiguous. Cultures with a high need for clarity prefer clear formal rules because uncertainty will generate uncomfortable levels of anxiety. Cultures with a low need for clarity have few formal rules and feel relaxed with uncertainty. High need for clarity cultures include Greece, Japan and Korea while the low need for clarity cultures include Singapore, Hong Kong and the UK.

Accepting power – according to Hofstede and Bond (1988), the original term 'power distance' is defined as 'the extent to which the less powerful members of institutions and organisations accept that power is distributed unequally' (p. 419). I prefer the term 'accepting power', which means that people in cultures high in this dimension are much more comfortable with large differences in status between the senior and junior members of a work team. People from low accepting power cultures prefer egalitarian work teams. Countries that are high acceptance of power cultures include Malaysia, Philippines and Indonesia. Low acceptance of power or egalitarian cultures include New Zealand, Germany and the UK.

Relationship focus – in the original work by Hofstede, this dimension referred to the relative degrees of achievement or task versus nurturance, or what I call 'relationship focus'. This dimension also has been applied to the so-called relative masculine and feminine influences in the culture. It is sometimes referred to as the expected gender roles in a culture. Cultures high on relationship focus rate caring for others and the quality of life as more important than achievement and success and vice versa. At a practical level for the cross-cultural coach, some cultures place more importance on relationships while others place more importance on achievement. High relationship focus cultures include Sweden, Norway and the Netherlands, with high achievement cultures being Japan, Austria and Italy.

Group focus – this refers to the degree of individual versus group orientation. Cultures high in individual orientation value freedom of the individual and tend to dislike conformity, while those with a group focus like teamwork and interpersonal harmony. Highly individualistic cultures include the USA, Australia and the UK. High collective focus cultures include Indonesia, China, Taiwan and Korea.

Long-term focus – Subsequent to Hofstede's original work, Hofstede and Bond (1988) produced a dimension that partly explained the rapid economic development of many Asian countries, the so-called Asian Tiger economies. This dimension is based on several values found in Confucian teachings. The emphasis in these cultures is on thrift, persistence, a sense of shame and following a hierarchy. It is usually called Confucian dynamism but I prefer the simpler term, 'long-term focus'. At a practical level for the cross-cultural coach, some cultures place more importance on long-term results while others place more importance on short-term achievements. The countries with the highest long-term focus are China, Hong Kong, Taiwan, Japan and South Korea, while countries such as Australia, New Zealand, the USA and the UK have the lowest.

Using the Cultural Dimensions in Coaching

The cultural dimensions can act as a useful map that can help coaches to understand their own cultural preferences (and prejudices) and that of their clients and colleagues. Understanding cultural differences helps the coach to show respect for others' differences and to accept these as natural. The five dimensions can help to create realistic expectations of coaching goals and sessions.

In each of the examples below, I present complex information in a simple way. I realise that this simplification may miss some of the subtlety of the many different cultures in Asia but hope that it provides some practical foundation for further exploration by coaches.

The Issue of Clarity – A Case Study

Jane was a UK training consultant working on a three-month project with a major Japanese manufacturing company. The project involved introducing a Western approach to training design and development. The methodology was to be used to train Western managers who worked for the company in the UK. Jane was finding the project very difficult. The Japanese trainers she was working with seemed so vague to her. They had endless meetings, never made decisions and treated plans and deadlines with indifference. To make matters worse, many decisions seemed to be made by senior managers who were not part of the agreed decision-making process and had little knowledge of the issues.

Jane's cross-cultural coach was able to explain that, for the Japanese, the uncertainty and ambiguity that Jane hated was normal and comfortable. Matters needed to be widely discussed and thought through before real decisions could be made. Once these were eventually agreed to, the plans and deadlines could be easily met.

For coaches and their executive clients whose cultures differ in their need for clarity, the following will be useful.

Coaching someone who has a low need for clarity	*Coaching someone who has a high need for clarity*
The executive may seem difficult to understand, as the conversation is indirect, meandering, very tactful, rather aimless or even evasive.	The executive may seem overly direct and to the point so that it may seem blunt or rude.
■ Take time, be patient and remember that there is no one right way to do business	■ Try to be as quick and to the point as possible
■ Do not force the meeting process but let it flow and sometimes gently encourage progress	■ Try to structure the meeting as much as is comfortable with an agenda and timescales
■ Show clear respect for a person's age, job title and position, no matter what issue is being discussed	■ Do not use titles or recognise skills unless they are directly relevant to the matter being discussed

The Issue of Power – A Case Study

Sarah was a New Zealand human resources consultant who was transferred to the Malaysian office of a multinational consulting company. After two years in the job, she had learned a lot about the culture of the Malaysian firm and how very different it was from home. Her most painful lesson had come at the end of her first year in Malaysia. She was in the middle of a project with a key client when she found her team members were temporarily transferred to another project and another department. The managing partner announced the change in a management meeting without any consultation with Sarah. She was dumbstruck and could not find the words to argue at the time. Later she came to understand that in this culture the power of the managing partner is paramount and for local staff orders simply have to be obeyed. The managing partner did a superb job in explaining the situation to Sarah's client and there was no real damage despite the project being delayed by one and a half months. Sarah had the emotional maturity not to take the situation as a personal attack and while she never agreed with the decision, she did understand that this was the nature of power in this culture.

People from cultures with a high acceptance of power are much more comfortable with a larger status differential between the senior management team and the front-line workers. People from low acceptance of power cultures prefer an egalitarian workplace.

Coaching someone who has a high acceptance of power	*Coaching someone who has a low acceptance of power*
■ Accept that for this person management are held in high regard because of their position	■ Understand that the person is not disrespectful and that challenging management is a natural part of the culture.
■ Do not encourage criticism of senior management	■ Try not be offended by the lack of courtesy

The Importance of Relationships – A Case Study

Sven worked in a Swedish–Japanese joint venture mobile phone project. He found the attitudes of the Japanese executives strange. They appeared to be happy to be in Sweden away from their families for months at a time. They worked extremely long hours and even when they had leisure time they seemed more interested in talking about work than phoning their wives and families. To the Japanese executives, Sven seemed more interested in his family and friends than he was in getting the prototype of the new mobile phone agreed upon and finished. For the Japanese executives, working hard and being successful was equally important for themselves as it was for their families' sense of pride. Yet both parties had enough respect and understanding to see that neither attitude was the right one – just that their two cultures differed in the importance they placed on achievement versus relationships and family.

Executives from high relationship cultures place much more importance on family and personal relationships and less on achievement as compared to those from low relationship, high achievement cultures.

Coaching someone who has a high relationship focus	*Coaching someone who has a low relationship focus*
The executive may seem to lack drive and be overly concerned with selfish pursuits.	The executive may seem obsessed with work and achievement to the detriment of his or her family and personal life.
■ Understand that the critical issue is how well the job is performed.	■ Understand that respect for a superior in the hierarchy is seen as a measure of commitment
■ Be sensitive to the relationship by respecting the status and influence of the executive	■ Respect the knowledge and information of the executive

Group Focus – A Case Study

The Indonesian factory managers were surprised by the behaviour and attitudes of Peter, the American buyer who came to negotiate long-term contracts for sports shoes. At first, the Indonesian managers thought that Peter was arrogant and self-obsessed, as he continually talked about himself and rarely gave any credit to his colleagues for achievements. He also seemed to prefer to work alone rather than in a team, despite the fact that when asked he would talk endlessly about the importance of teamwork. Slowly the Indonesians came to understand that for Americans conducting business alone means that this person is highly respected by his or her company and considered fully competent. While they never got used to Peter's behaviour, they did came to see it as normal in the American culture and not as arrogance.

Below are some practical steps you can take when working across difference in the level of individual or group orientation. For example, the coach may be from a highly individualistic culture such as the US, Australia and the UK, while the executive may be from a highly group focused culture in such as Indonesia, Taiwan and Korea.

Coaching someone who has a high level of group focus	*Coaching someone with a low level of group focus*
The executive may seem to be self-effacing and always assume joint responsibility for achievements and tasks.	The executive may seem to be self-centred and egotistical and personally assume responsibility for achievements and tasks.
■ Show patience for the time taken to consent and consult	■ Be prepared for quick decisions and sudden offers not referred to headquarters
■ Understand that conducting business when surrounded by helpers means that this person has high status	■ Understand that conducting business alone means that this person is highly respected by the company
■ Understand that the aim of business is to build lasting relationships	■ Understand that the aim of business is to make quick effective deals
■ Respect the authority of the group	■ Respect the importance of individual responsibility
■ Hold up team goals for all to meet	■ Understand that the person admires people who take individual initiative

Long-term Focus – A Case Study

Bill Brown was an Australian executive working with Taiwanese computer manufacturing executives. Before coming to work in Taiwan, Bill was proud of his direct 'no-nonsense' style and his ability to get to the heart of the issue. However, after six frustrating months, he came to see that his Australian style was totally inappropriate. His typical approach generated suspicion, mistrust, even passive aggressive behaviour and avoidance. With some very skilful coaching and considerable courage, he came to understand that gentleness, perseverance, graciousness and enduring patience achieved better results. Bill came to see that having a long-term view of the importance of his relationship with the Taiwanese managers was the key to success.

Here are some steps you can take when working across difference in the level of short or long-term orientation. For example, the coach may be from a short-term culture such as Australia, New Zealand, the USA or the UK and the executive may be from a long-term culture such as Taiwan, Japan or South Korea.

Coaching someone with a long-term cultural orientation	*Coaching someone with a short-term cultural orientation*
The executive may seem unnecessarily soft, persistent, polite and extremely patient. ■ Never embarrass or shame the executive ■ Agree future meetings in principle but do not fix deadlines for completion ■ Do your homework on the history and traditions and past glories of the company and the culture	The executive may seem unusually demanding, results-focused and insensitive to the long term. ■ Expect the person to be exacting and want rapid achievements ■ Agree specific deadlines and do not expect work to be completed unless you do ■ Do your homework on future prospects and the technological potential of the company

The Importance of Language

We have seen how useful it is for cross-cultural coaches to have frameworks to understand their own and others' culture, however, sometimes it is not the culture but simpler issues such as language that cause problems.

Case Study

Peter Johnson was a systems integrator for a major UK-based IT consulting company who had been sent to Shanghai to head part of a large client project. When he arrived, he was delighted to find that most of his team, while Shanghainese, spoke excellent English. The team members

Case Study cont'd

were smart and had an excellent knowledge of company consulting procedures and IT systems. He quickly became confident that his part of the project was going to be completed ahead of time and below budget.

However, two months into the work, he started to have serious doubts about the project and the intelligence level of some team members. They could understand the technical side of things very well but failed to follow agreed procedures and even seemed to avoid personal responsibility for outcomes. The project started to slip behind schedule.

It was while discussing these issues with his boss that Peter became aware that his language was the cause of much of the problem. While many of the Chinese consultants spoke excellent English and understood the technical terms, they were often utterly confused by Peter's colloquial language and his broad Manchester accent. Over the next month, Peter made a concerted effort to speak slowly and clearly, using shorter sentences and simpler words. After three months of persistence, his English peers commented that he had started to lose his accent. Peter also learned to avoid using his football terms like 'off side' and 'stop dribbling and start shooting'. This was easier to do when he realised that these expressions were completely meaningless to the Shanghainese.

As a result of these changes, the project picked up and the team caught up with the project schedule. Peter still occasionally fell back on his old ways but the blank stares from his Chinese team members were a useful reminder that while they spoke good English they were certainly not from Manchester.

Language barriers are obvious blocks to effective coaching. While English is usually the common business language in Asia Pacific, it is certainly not the mother tongue for over 3 billion people in the region. Language problems can create many difficulties, including a breakdown in trust, and it is the prime responsibility of the native English speaker to help overcome this problem using the following tips.

Use simple sentence structure and vocabulary – effective coaching depends on establishing clear patterns of communication. The coach should use simple shorter words such as 'big' rather than 'gargantuan', 'fast' rather than 'expeditious'. Whenever possible, use the same word consistently to mean the same thing. Use short simple sentences and avoid double negatives, for example 'I would certainly not stop doing that'.

Be careful of the different versions of English – there are real differences between British, American, Australian and New Zealand English. For example, stating that a project is a 'bomb' is very positive in the UK (where a bomb is a spectacular success) and very negative in the USA (where a bomb is a catastrophic failure). The word 'tinnie' means a can of beer in Australia but means poorly made in New Zealand. There are literally hundreds of English words that mean different things in different cultures and for this reason these words are best not used in cross-cultural coaching.

Avoid jargon – much jargon comes from a sporting context such as baseball that is unknown to many non-English speakers, for example 'out of the ball park', 'covering all the bases', or from rugby ('fumbling', 'scrum', 'off side'). Other unhelpful jargon comes from a military context, for example 'off the radar screen', 'blow them away', 'blast them out of the water'. Three-letter acronyms are also popular but often confusing, for example PBR, TQM, MBA and so on. These letters mean virtually nothing to people who do not know the cultural or business context in which they are used. Such jargon should be avoided until the coach is sure that the other party understands.

Building trust – trust and the ability to confide in a coach are critical to success. Trust varies greatly between cultures; in some, trust is built as the coaching work progresses, while in others, it must be established before any progress can take place. In many Western countries, trust is built up gradually over time as the coach and the executive get to know each other. In many Eastern cultures, trust is a prerequisite for useful interactions, and building trust can involve lengthy discussions on non-professional topics, for example sports, food or family. In these countries, effective coaching discussions only start when your counterpart has become comfortable with you as a person.

The assumptions about the level of trust between strangers vary from culture to culture. In many Anglo-Saxon cultures such as the UK or the USA, people generally assume that other people can be trusted, until proven otherwise. Strangers in business typically regard the other person as reliable and that they can be depended on. These assumptions are not as common in Western countries like France or Italy or in Eastern cultures. These cultures tend to believe that strangers' intentions are negative until they have a chance to find out that this is not the case. The cross-cultural coach must be aware of the assumptions about trust in his or her own culture as well as those assumptions in the executive who he or she is working with. The coach must be prepared to put in time building a relationship before any intense discussions take place, if this is the cultural preference of the client.

Know yourself – if there is one key point about successful cross-cultural coaching it is that the coach must know his or her own self. Ignorance of one's own cultural preferences, attitudes and characteristics can lead to serious misunderstanding. Sun Tzu (1994), the famous Chinese philosopher and military strategist said 'know yourself and you will win all battles'. Without a sound knowledge of yourself, other people's styles and characteristics can often be strange, bizarre and even threatening.

Does Coaching Work in the Asia Pacific Region?

Research undertaken in the Asia Pacific region by Stephenson (2000) suggests that coaching works well when provided to:

- Executive staff
- New staff
- Existing staff entering new roles
- Whole work teams.

To be effective, coaching must be a structured process focused on improving effectiveness and keeping talented staff. It works best if both individual and organisational needs are clearly set out and actively pursued. Cook (1999) suggests that coaching has the following benefits:

- Developing competence
- Diagnosing performance problems
- Correcting unsatisfactory performance
- Developing productive work relationships
- Focusing on appropriate and deliberate guidance
- Developing a self-learning orientation in those being coached
- Improving performance and morale.

There are three types of coaching:

- *Feedback coaching* which usually involves working with a staff member for one to six months, providing performance feedback and creating a development plan to address specific needs.
- *In-depth development coaching* which usually involves working with the staff member for six to 12 months in a close relationship. Data collection usually involves 360° feedback and psychometric testing such as the FIRO B or the NEO PRI (Costa and McRae 1992). Once the data is produced, the coach meets with the staff member on a regular basis to produce a plan and motivate the person to implement it.
- *Content coaching* which involves the coach being an expert in a particular content area, such as global marketing, and addressing a specific learning need. The learning process often involves personal research, reading, role plays and videotape feedback.

Executive Development Coaching: A Case Study

During the course of the content coaching with the HR director of a large corporation in Hong Kong, it become clear that major organisational improvements could not be made without developing the individual members of the executive team.

An interesting project involved management development coaching with a young and ambitious information services director. Ivan had been recruited from the UK to work in Hong Kong to assist with the implementation of an enterprise management software package. He had a reputation for being task and deadline-focused and this was one of the main reasons why he was selected for the job. Yet it became clear after some months that he needed to learn to become more open and warm to his staff if he was to get the best from them. The goal of coaching was to enable Ivan to see that his task focus was a real strength but that it also had limitations and he would only progress if he were able to be more expressive and empathic.

The coaching began with a very frank discussion in which Ivan recounted a discussion with the CEO about his strengths and limitations. He was pleased the CEO had recognised his achievements but felt that his task-oriented management style was simply part of his personality and unchangeable. We agreed to work together for the next three months and use the CEO's judgment about Ivan's management style as the indicator of success. The work began with the administration of the NEO professional development report. This indicated that:

- A low level of emotional reactions with few worries, little frustration or sensitivity to stress
- High levels of assertiveness and activity but lower levels of warmth
- Average levels of openness to change
- Mixed levels of agreeableness, with lower levels of trust in others, candour and sympathy
- High levels of work ethic including sense of competence, orderliness, sense of responsibility and need to achieve.

Ivan felt that this was an accurate picture of his work personality and subsequently showed the profile to his wife who thought it was extremely accurate. In the next session, the profile allowed us to discuss the issues of lack of warmth and candour in a very open and helpful way. We spent some time looking at Ivan's family history and how his personality was partly a product of this. However, we also discussed how Ivan could vary his work style a great deal depending on the circumstances, so that he could be more concerned for others and open if he wanted to.

The next series of sessions consisted of spending time talking about a wide range of work and home issues that had some emotional impact on Ivan. This allowed Ivan to talk about his feelings in a safe environment. While this initially seemed rather strange to him and not very 'work-focused', he quickly come to see that understanding how he felt was the first step in being more open and empathic with others. We also spent time identifying or creating opportunities where Ivan could be more open. The easiest tasks involved expressing more enthusiasm for the work of his staff, while the harder tasks involved expressing not only his opinions but, more importantly, his feelings about matters that arose in senior management meetings.

At the end of the three months, we reviewed progress with the CEO, who felt that Ivan had made considerable progress. His ability to show concern for others and be genuine in his expression of feelings were seen as his greatest achievements. Ivan also felt that he had made considerable progress in his management style and that the work had improved his relationship with his wife.

The coaching scorecard

Below I have set out my views on what went well in this coaching project and what I could have done better.

What went well?

The psychological test results provided an excellent basis for the coaching as they identified the most critical areas quickly and gave both Ivan and I a clear vocabulary to talk about them in a non-threatening manner.

What could I have done better?

While the coaching went very well, I failed to help Ivan establish a coaching climate in his team. He made excellent progress but I am not sure that he learned to coach his staff as effectively as I expected.

Coaching as a Source of Competitive Advantage: A Case Study

Background

The client was a medium-sized chartered accounting firm in New Zealand with a 54-year history, of which the six partners were very proud. However, in the last five years, the firm had started to slip in terms of customer service and profitability. This downturn seemed to stem from the loss of two younger partners who had departed four years previously. These partners had been carefully groomed to be the future face of the firm and take it into the next decade. The reality had been that they were very ambitious and found their older partners too conservative and unwilling to delegate. Their departure left the practice short of staff and as a result some key clients were lost. The remaining partners were left with the unfortunate mix of fewer good clients, fewer good staff and higher overheads resulting from unused office space. This dramatically affected profitability for a number of years. However, the real cost was psychological, as the pain of the departures hit home. For several years after the departures, the remaining partners went into a 'bunker' mentality, where they cut costs in all areas, including training, and became inward-looking and insular.

Peter Mackay had been voted in as managing partner in early 2000 and was determined to reverse the fortunes of the firm. He wanted to move the partners out of the 'bunker' mentality and into a business development mentality. For Peter, the key to better profitability lay in the firm's ability to get better leverage out of the business processes and staff. He was also determined to improve the firm's business planning process with strategic planning and the introduction of the balanced scorecard approach to measure performance.

Aims of the executive development coaching programme

Peter wanted to use the services of an experienced coach who could not only help with the business planning issues but also with process improvement and, most importantly, staff development.

After an initial meeting with Peter, we worked out that the aim of the coaching programme was to increase partner quarterly income by 25 per cent within 18 months of the start of the programme. This was to be achieved by the use of:

1. A sound strategic plan that would develop the underlying business logic critical to better performance.
2. A balanced scorecard of performance measures that would enable the firm to measure a full range of relevant changes in performance.
3. The introduction of a coaching culture in the firm so that the critical progress of delegation of work could mean much better use of junior staff with lower chargeout rates.
4. The use of coaching to facilitate better business processes and so streamline services and improve efficiency.

The coaching culture concept

At a senior management workshop, the following coaching culture change concept was developed. This was designed to spearhead the change from the current culture where personal partner chargeable hours were the supreme measure of performance to one where job and firm profit was critical. It was recognised that this change was not going to happen with a single or simple intervention. Four key changes were focused on to alter the culture of the firm:

1. Introducing coaching as a part of the firm's values – these would be written up, acted upon and displayed through the office.
2. Revising the recruitment criteria for the firm and placing much greater emphasis on learning potential rather than just on technical skills.

3. Training in coaching that consisted of: launching a brief, firm-wide coaching awareness programme which told everyone about the nature of coaching and the benefits it could bring; and undertaking coaching skills training for all those who supervised staff.

4. Using objective measures plus a web-based multi-rater feedback to assess the impact of coaching and implementing a range of incentives for those who achieved sound coaching achievements.

Figure 13.1 illustrates the coaching culture change process.

Coaching as a key firm value – introducing coaching as a part of the firm's values – these values would be written up, framed and placed in the boardroom, all offices and open-plan work areas. This would be a simple, clear signal that the firm saw coaching as important.

Recruit for learning potential – the firm's recruitment policy and practices were revised and all new staff were selected not just for technical skill but for their willingness to learn and coach others. All recruiters were given a half-day training programme in competency-based recruitment interviewing and individual follow-up and coaching was provided both before and after recruitment interviews.

The training in coaching – the training programme for coaches consisted of a one-day intensive workshop followed by a half-day refresher and problem-solving session one month later. Due to the multicultural nature

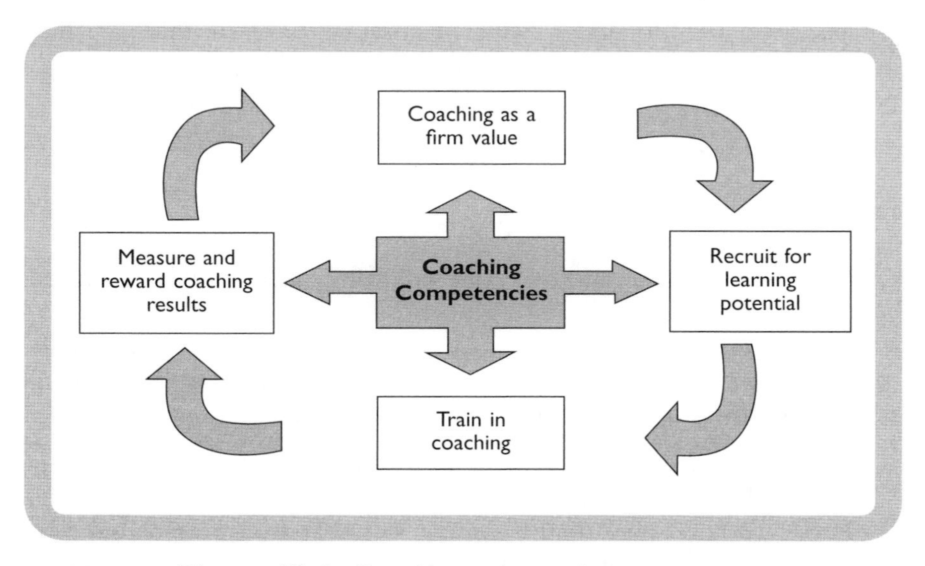

Figure 13.1 Coaching culture change process

of the clients and the workforce, particular emphasis was placed on cross-cultural coaching. The training programme consisted of:

- An overview of coaching
- The benefits of coaching
- Skills training in giving feedback, encouraging, problem-solving and challenging
- Cross-cultural coaching skills
- How to write a coaching plan
- How to gain support and supervision in coaching.

The initial one-day programme was very highly regarded and after reading about the firm's committment to coaching and seeing the publicity about it, many managers were keen to learn the skills. The follow-up programme was equally successful and many practical issues and challenges were discussed and resolved at the session.

Measuring and rewarding coaching – the key objective measures of coaching ability for any manager or partner in the firm was the ratio of staff per manager or partner and the level of fees generated by their team. These measures were selected because they were objective and clear drivers of profitability in the business. In addition, a web-based multi-rater feedback was used to assess the satisfaction of staff with their coaching and skills development. Incentive payments were made to managers and partners who performed to a high standard in all these areas.

Programme outcome

Over a period of 18 months' work, the following outcomes were achieved:

- Introducing coaching as a part of the firm's values was seen by the partner group as a useful start – staff were initially sceptical about what it would mean but later come to see its value.
- Revising the recruitment criteria for the firm was a longer term change and in the initial 18-month period only a few changes were seen. However, the value of the change was that it signalled in a very practical way that the firm was taking the coaching focus seriously.

In the long term, the managing partner considered that this change will have a profound effect on the firm.

- Launching a firm-wide coaching awareness programme was also seen as having a useful effect but not a profound one. It certainly did heighten awareness of coaching and built powerful expectations that demanded satisfaction. Staff reported that they found the awareness programme very interesting.
- Undertaking coaching skills training for all those who supervised staff was seen as highly successful because of its practical approach. Managers reported that they learned realistic, useful skills that they could easily apply with their staff. They found the biggest challenge was to encourage staff to come up with their own ideas for solving problems rather than just telling them how to resolve the problem.
- The objective measures and web-based multi-rater feedback were regarded as very appropriate measures as they consisted of a mix of objective and subjective areas.
- Most importantly, partner income increased by 28 per cent and 31 per cent for the final two quarters of the programme. The partner group was very satisfied with the success of the programme.

The coaching scorecard

Below I have tried to set out my views on what went well in this coaching project and what I could have done better.

What went well?

This project was a milestone for me as it allowed me to develop a successful method of changing a whole organisation and producing clear bottom line results from coaching.

What could I have done better?

I don't feel that the average staff member of the firm saw this project as a clear integrated whole – as it is presented above. I suspect that they saw only a series of vaguely linked initiatives which had the word 'coaching' in common. Next time I would pay much greater attention to ongoing communication of the concept of the coaching culture. I need to develop more colourful, easy to read newsletters or web pages that provide staff with the fundamentals of the approach. These newsletters or web pages need to be very regularly updated.

Conclusion

Coaches in the Asia Pacific region need to deal with a range of complex cultural issues and this is made considerably easier with a sound understanding of critically important cultural dimensions. The case studies provide a useful indication that with careful and sound implementation, coaching can increase productivity and profitability in a wide variety of settings. To summarise the key behaviours for successful cross-cultural coaching, I would propose that the coach:

- Be patient when coaching across cultures. Try to suspend judgment when you are in a coaching session that is difficult. It is easy to think 'Why doesn't this individual just say what he/she thinks!', when the other person is being polite because of his or her cultural context.
- Know thyself. You will be a much better coach if you know your own cultural preferences in the areas of desire for clarity, the use and acceptance of power structures, the importance of relationships, the degree of individuality or group focus and the preference for long-term or short-term focus.
- Integrate coaching practice: whilst coaching is a highly flexible approach and can be used to enhance individual and team processes, it will achieve maximum impact if it is adopted as a company value, people are recruited for their willingness to develop and managers are training, measured and rewarded for coaching results.
- Ensure that coaching addresses concrete business issues and has business outcomes. Always try to link executive development goals with business objectives. This approach will generate ready support from senior managers.

CHAPTER 14

Review of Best Practice

Having presented a cross-section of our collective experience of executive coaching with appropriate models, assembled below are what we believe are the primary elements of best practice in executive coaching. If you have conscientiously worked through the chapter questions and checked your profile against our 'capable coach' model (see Appendix), you will have the basis of your own coaching development action plan which can be completed by following the suggestions in the latter part of this chapter. To remind you of our common model for managing the process of an executive coaching assignment, here is the 'A4' model, referred to in Chapter 2, but shown in diagrammatic form in Figure 4.1.

However, best practice coaching takes many forms. Leadership coaching can be quite diverse, ranging from the direct, 'hands-on' approach to a more indirect style. For example, the Spanish managing director of the Tech Data global high-tech distribution business in Stockholm has engineered and led a dramatic turnaround over the past three years. Largely due to the change managed by its MD, Lorenzo Garcia, and his top leadership team, the business has been revived after inheriting a legacy of poor leadership and people management. Supportive of the comments by Goffee and Jones (2001), not all leaders are naturally good coaches. Whilst Lorenzo himself is now developing his skills as a coach, particularly in coaching his successor, he has designed and implemented a series of development initiatives intended to build commitment to the organisational changes he has initiated.

However, what distinguishes him from many of his peers is his sustained commitment to the development of his people to help achieve business results. From the top team and throughout the management population, he expresses a consistent philosophy about the need to unlock the potential in his staff. This can be seen as a form of coaching, that is,

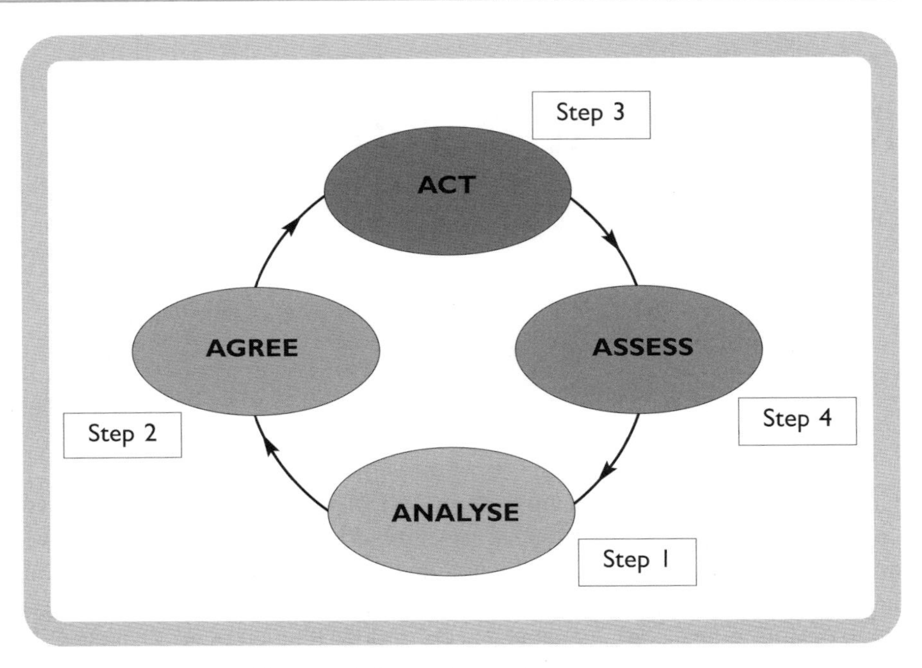

Figure 14.1 A4 coaching process

coaching the development of the organisation. Whilst the management population had received little formal people management skills prior to his tenure, Lorenzo recognised that a priority for the business was retention of talent in a very competitive marketplace. Having 'steadied the boat' and consolidated the organisational structure, his next organisational ambition was to build people and change management skills in his managers, both thought to be critical to the sustained success of the business. The performance of the business has improved dramatically, turnover of key talent is significantly reduced, commitment to the development of people and change management skills have also improved.

The change process Lorenzo leads hasn't stopped because a successful turnaround has been achieved. He may rely more heavily on his top leadership team, but Lorenzo's ambition for his people and the business is undiminished. Here we see the commitment of the leader to a process of continuous improvement. As with a more direct, one-to-one coaching assignment, it requires enormous levels of stamina and enduring commitment.

In a best practice coaching assignment, we have presented this outline process to the relevant stakeholders, walked them through some anecdotal examples and described the practical implications of each phase in the cycle, with particular reference to commitment of resource. Here, perhaps not surprisingly, the stakeholder's primary concern is more often about commitment of executive time and not financial cost.

Our typical executive coaching assignment lasts between six months to two years, dependent upon the nature of the development coaching goals and the availability of the executive. The frequency of coach contact ranges between one and two days per month, excluding all additional preparation work, such as development diary completion on behalf of the executive. Whilst we are aware that other coaching consultants claim significant development achievements in much shorter periods, we have found sustained development benefit demands the level of time commitment outlined above. As we described in Chapter 9, sometimes moving quickly from 'private to public' coaching transactions can save time. For example, including the coaching participant's immediate team in a development process will often reap time-saving rewards, as it can help to move quickly to the implementation of development actions. In transition terminology, we are moving 'fast to 5'.

It is important to emphasise to clients unfamiliar with coaching that it is a process not an event. In our collective experience, it is rarely a 'quick fix' and as a coach you will need to adapt your approach to the individual's learning capacity, rate and style as well as corporate context.

As we describe in the early part of this book, there are almost as many models of developmental coaching as there are coaches. This apparent complexity can be understood once you accept the unique and individual nature of the undertaking. For many executives and managers, developing direct reports through coaching can be the most challenging part of their role. The coaching styles you express will be a reflection of your values but the process you may wish to follow may reflect the A4 model; each step of which is now detailed.

Step 1: Analysis

This involves a careful analysis of the key issues in the coaching assignment, and includes the following aspects:

- Identification of the origins of the coaching need
- Identification of the key stakeholders and commissioning parties in the coaching transaction, their ambitions, success criteria and roles. Who is the client, who are the sponsors, what is their interest?

- Determination of the ability and motivation of the executive to be coached, his or her potential and ambition. Analysis (using multiple sources and multiple instruments) of key strengths and development needs of coaching candidate
- Analysis of executive role, team context and corporate culture. Build understanding of the position of the role in terms of business process
- Determine level of compatibility with coach and level of support and resources available post-coaching.

Account for any necessary changes resulting from company-wide initiatives. Development needs are often derived and refined by feedback from others in the organisation. In this phase, rapport and trust are built and the important development areas are 'scoped'.

Step 2: Agreement

A critical stage which sets the scene for the action stage of the coaching assignment. Here there may ensue a negotiation with key stakeholders concerning the definition of success. It is at this point that the coaching plan is agreed and appropriate resources committed. In Chapter 10, you can see the dilemma for the coach at the end of the assignment. He asks himself the question 'who was the real client here?' as he is now unsure. This is the phase where agreement concerning outcomes and the coaching programme is established.

In summary, at this stage the coach:

- Presents and agrees his view of the executive development needs and goals, including success criteria (KRIs – key result indicators), agrees expectations
- Identifies and outlines a suitable action plan with all parties, describing the programme of activities designed to achieve the coaching goal(s)
- Invites and proposes suggestions about milestones and metrics, agrees how progress will be measured
- Determines, in consultation with executive coaching partner, the opportunities to practise new approaches or behaviour. For example, these can be new projects or working groups.

Here too agreement about the use of coaching 'tools' can be agreed. Such tools may include planning one-to-one meetings, 'shadowing' the executive at work, team development activities, role play, simulations and keeping a development diary that captures the results of development actions (observations, thoughts, feelings) through the eyes of the coaching participant.

Step 3: Action

In this stage the coach encourages the participant to experiment (see Chapter 2: stage 5 of transition process), to try out new ways of working that are consistent with the agreed development goals.

Implementing the agreed coaching programme may not be a simple action. Some revision and refinement is inevitable as the practical realities of corporate life emerge. Changes in the circumstances of the coaching partner, his or her boss or colleagues can all affect the relevance of the original coaching programme. At this point, the coach should be flexible and adopt the concept of 'equifinality', that is, getting to the same end point by different routes. The coaching programme may require some amendment in order to achieve the same development goals.

The coach encourages his coaching client to seek opportunities to practise new skills and gain feedback about effectiveness, that is, success and failure. The coach needs to support his or her partner by helping to create options for action, looking for suitable projects, 'stretch' assignments, programmes and relationships where new skills can be applied. As mentioned previously, typical coaching tools employed here are work shadowing, role play, experiential events, coaching dialogue, development diaries, feedback, development actions involving the immediate team and case study comparisons.

Step 4: Assessment

The key action in this stage is to help your client to assess the level of development progress achieved. At this stage, we evaluate development progress against set and agreed development goals. It is an opportunity to review progress and identify any remaining (or emerging) blocks to success. Here the coach proposes options to sustain the learning achievements and momentum as well as minimise the common tendency to regress.

One common process for evaluation is the reapplication of an original 360° feedback instrument, checking for areas where changes may have occurred as a result of coaching. Final evaluation should of course involve all stakeholders involved in establishing the coaching contract initially. In addition, successful outcomes are examined to enhance enabling resources for further sustaining coaching progress. In a recent case, this sustaining action for an executive client was to coach his three direct reports.

In terms of best practice, although we have rarely encountered this approach in corporate clients, we would help to construct support processes for the individual in the organisation, identifying what mechanisms may exist internally to help to sustain and extend learning.

Pitfalls to Avoid in Executive Coaching

As part of the process of identifying best coaching practice, it is important to avoid basic, but all too common, errors. Whilst the A4 model presents a collection of best practice distilled from the combined wisdom of the experienced executive coach contributors, it may be useful to consider some of the fundamental pitfalls we have met as executive coaches. As a foundation for those embarking upon an executive development coaching assignment for the first time, we catalogue some potential pitfalls we would caution against. Rather than examples of best practice, here the focus is how to learn from the mistakes we have made. Unfortunately, to summarise these potential pitfalls so far looks like one of those checklists we promised to exclude. In our defence, they are designed to stimulate and provoke coaches and those coached rather than propose a prescription to be applied uncritically.

Most of these headlines below can be as relevant for an internal as an external coach.

Do I know the client(s) and the stakeholder(s)? Do I understand the brief? Is there collective agreement on the development agenda?

There are always at least three stakeholders, the coaching partner, immediate colleagues and the sponsoring organisation. At the executive level, it is not uncommon for assignments to be self-initiated by the prospective coaching participant. More commonly, there is a sponsoring boss and a relevant responsible HR/T&D/education and learning resource too.

Executive coaching rarely resides within the confines of the executive office. As leadership remains a social activity, demanding the influence of others, at some stage the learning acquired through coaching needs to be applied. This brings the executive learning into the public domain and may involve further 'team coaching'.

In common with many other consultancy contracts, the development agenda originally defined may not be the agenda subsequently delivered. Part of this phase is creating commitment and aligning expectations across stakeholders in terms of coaching process and content.

What's my coaching model, my preferences, values and prejudice?
It will come as no surprise to practising coaches that the professional practice of coaching is replete with paradox, as a coach has to balance:

- Being close but keeping some distance (objective versus subjective analysis)
- Being open to create trust but, on occasions, being closed (the coach can't always disclose true feelings or information)
- Managing a private relationship but encouraging more public disclosure with the participant's immediate colleagues
- Empathising but remain challenging
- Building trust but sustaining a caring critic role
- Balancing the 'push' (of an imperfect present) with the pull (of a desired future).

If you have low levels of self-awareness, coaching can be a demanding if ultimately rewarding process. Whilst the best way to build coaching capability is to coach or be coached, it is preferable that the latter practice be engaged first. The coaching process, when effective, always reveals insights for both coach and coaching partner. However, revelationary insights and major surprises for the coach can distract from focus on the coachee's development at a critical moment.

Do I experience the 'executive halo'?
Senior executives often don't have all the answers these days. Too much respect can lead to fear and inhibition (Fitzgerald and Berger 2002). Presuming levels of competence often attributable to the seniority of the role can be misleading. Employees and coaches alike can fall into the 'executive halo' trap. This occurs when one assumes that any executive will possess a clear, coherent, strategic vision for the business. In this period of accelerating rate of change (and therefore uncertainty), it is increasingly possible to discover senior leadership figures with only a hazy appreciation of strategic direction. Meanwhile, more junior members of

the organisation may experience frustration concerning what they perceive as lack of communication of strategic direction from those leaders formally responsible for setting and executing strategy.

In addition, there is often an expectation that executives will learn faster because they're smarter. As Argyris (1991) suggested in his paper 'Teaching Smart People How to Learn', intelligence is no guarantee of speed of learning or rate of development. We would support the proposition that there may in fact be an inverse relationship, particularly as the brighter coachee may have a broader repertoire of defensive and resistant tactics, including well-rehearsed 'smart' language.

Do I seek 'quick-fix solutions'?

Typically derived from a desire to help, many managers developing coaching skills seek to find an instant solution to any coaching problem. This approach seems particularly prevalent in science or engineering-based businesses. They seek to add value with every paragraph and development solutions can be found in one 2–3 hour session. The coaching approach is to assume the role of expert and operate in a prescriptive mode.

Allied to this is the 'quest for the instant solution' style. This approach can often be accompanied by a desire (which can become obsessive) to provide a fast and coherent coaching prescription as quickly as possible, sometimes offering the coaching participant instant solutions to *apparently familiar challenges*. This is likely to be particularly unhelpful on at least two counts:

1. The 'hidden' development coaching agenda, which requires a deeper understanding, may be missed.
2. There is little or no personal commitment to development actions from the coaching participant. Whilst a dependency relationship may be one that is helpful to create where the expert is always better informed (or *right* as we like our doctors to be), in executive coaching, personal commitment to sustaining a development action plan is often the key to successful development. As two leading practitioners (Hicks and Peterson 1996) in executive coaching in the US have noted, a partnership relationship in executive coaching provides the most effective results.

Berglas (2002) is much more critical of the coach seeking instant solutions. He asserts that such an approach can be positively dangerous:

> Many executive coaches, especially those who draw their inspiration from sports, sell themselves as purveyors of simple answers and quick results.

How do I know when coaching is successful?
It is essential to define and agree success criteria early. Ask yourself, how will you know when development goals are achieved? What are the metrics and milestones you will apply to the achieved outcomes? If it is a deep-seated/long-term/well-established pattern of behaviour or challenge, it may take several sessions just to 'scope' the dimensions of the issue, assuming appropriate levels of openness can be achieved. Ownership of the development action should ideally reside with the coachee. When the boss/coach assumes the prescriptive style of the expert, he or she endangers the likelihood of commitment to and ownership of the development action.

Apprentice coaches can also feel intimidated by the need for a level of structure which is prepared in anticipation of a coaching meeting. Planning a complete session is impossible, as at least 50 per cent of the content is unpredicatable (that is, the other person's responses). Coaching conversations can (and often need to) meander, apparently directionless on occasion. The coach's need for certainty and predictability should not be the driving force here. Whilst we both need to achieve a development goal, often within a prescribed timeframe, the route to its achievement is often co-determined, in close combination with the coaching partner.

Is my feedback understandable and actionable?
Jim, an electronics engineer with a leading manufacturing engineering business in the UK, was perplexed. He had received comprehensive face-to-face feedback during a leadership development programme from his colleagues, but feedback from his coach described him as 'perverse in his manner of managing relationships' which did not fit with his self-image.

Despite examples, Jim didn't like feedback, expressed a lack of understanding and would not accept it. It was also a small protest towards his coach who he was finding more critical as the programme progressed. Jim was an amiable person with considerable social leadership skills. An easy mixer, he moved easily across the cultural diversity evident within the programme participants – Spanish, Belgian, French, English and German – who all agreed, Jim was an enjoyable companion.

Jim was probably firmly rooted in denial until the group engaged in an outdoor teamwork development process. It was during this event that Jim, in his terms, moved to acceptance of his feedback. A practical team task, as usual, had elicited some wide-ranging observations and feedback for the group. At an observable level, the group's task was simple: divide into two teams and rendezvous at the top of a nearby hill, solve a task requiring the whole group's contribution, reform into teams and return to a fixed point. Easy? Well, easy until the corporate context is factored into the equation.

The organisation represented was one that had succeeded by setting each European business in competition with one another. Based on some US-derived motivational theories of the 1950s, it was felt that competition in any form was healthy. Recently it became apparent that the business needed to collaborate rather than compete in order to raise performance standards especially in quality terms. It became apparent that some European sites were intentionally sending poor quality parts and information to other sites in order to improve their relative position in the European business league table.

Further compounded by the group's emergence into programme cliques that the exercise had disrupted, some ill-feeling had emerged when the exercise did not run well. Emerging failure provoked some powerful responses, varying from withdrawal (from the failure) and blaming others' behaviour. All very familiar, I'm sure, but what became a legendary act, only revealed during the team exercise review and feedback session, was that Jim had been active during the exercise.

In the review, Jim decided to present his own contribution. It was about his relationship with José, who he wanted to get closer to, so Jim informed us: 'I'm walking behind José, following him up the hill and I want to build a closer relationship with him, I don't try to get alongside or start a conversation, what do I do? I put rocks in his rucksack.' Now, that's perverse!

This short case study indicates the need for clarity and acceptance in an effective feedback process.

Am I adequately curious, open and flexible?

Explore others' world view – models of self, change, learning and how flexible they are (aren't) and be open about yours. Historical models are not always particularly useful as they can be poor predictors of success in the future. Allow your view as coach to be informed by your coaching partner, particularly with reference to his or her potential and what he or she may become. Use a 'working hypothesis' as the metaphor for your view of your coachee. Allow yourself to be surprised by development achievements.

Do I surface early disagreement, coach mismatch or 'chemistry' problems?

Even if a rigorous coach selection process has occurred, occasionally a mismatch occurs. Difficult to discern in advance, sometimes rapport is not established between coach and coaching partner. If you're the boss, coaching a direct report, don't feel disappointed, someone else will be a better match. If you're an external coach, it is more effective to surface early chemistry problems, withdraw or propose a replacement.

Am I in danger of early compartmentalisation or stereotyping?
As Alexandre Dumas said, 'all generalizations are dangerous, even this one'. How useful is stereotyping in understanding and delivering a successful coaching assignment? In our view, not much. Individuals don't behave in simple predictable patterns of behaviour. Maybe there are many national similarities (as there are in personality). But a process designed to help us understand the enormous and diverse amount of information serves merely to obscure what may be the important differences.

Building Your Coaching Development Action Plan (CDAP)

Here we present an opportunity for you to create your own coaching development action plan. As you will have observed at the conclusion of Chapters 1–9, we invite you to review your learning. Having read the entire book, now you may wish to review your development needs as an executive coach. The key first step is for you to summarise your own view of your coaching capability (motivation and potential). Use the 'Capable Coach' model in the Appendix as a checklist for your current coaching performance and rate yourself from 1 (not developed) to 5 (excellent) through underdeveloped (2), competent (3) and very effective (4).

Having determined your own view of your coaching skills, you need to determine how others see you. These may be colleagues, clients or coaching partners. Ideally, use all three to provide a 360° review of your coaching capabilities or just your own and your coaching partners (maybe your direct reports) for a 180° review. Contact details of how to receive your confidential 'competent coach' feedback report are provided in the Appendix. The feedback provides one data point for you to determine your coaching development needs and goals. Referring to the development planning process in Chapter 4, we can apply the same basic model, as shown in Figure 14.2.

Having obtained feedback from various sources (clients, colleagues, psychometric instruments, 360° report), you now need to interpret the data, factoring in your own ambition (best national/international/global executive coach or perhaps something more modest, for example 'best executive coach I can be').

Next, identify one or, at most, two development goals that are achievable in the short term. Make these practical, tangible steps which can be

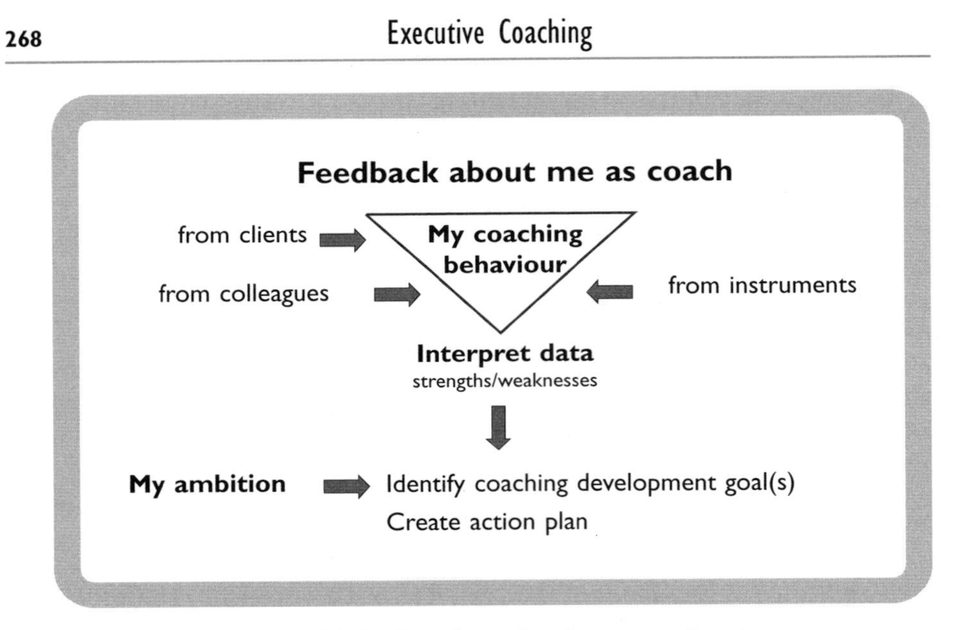

Figure 14.2 Coaching development planning

measured. Describe in detail the actions necessary to achieve these goals, as these form the basis of your coaching development action plan. Now identify the resources required to achieve them, who will support you in their achievement and how long will they take to complete? Finally, find someone who is a proficient coach, who you trust, and present your plan. Invite comments about practicality, implementability and level of ambition. Refine the plan accordingly and, as soon as possible, start coaching!

APPENDIX

The Capable Coach Model

As outlined in Chapter 3, one way of assessing our coaching competence is to review our practice against a competency framework. This can be done by self-review alone, or through self-review as part of a 360° (or 180°) process. On the pages that follow, you will find a questionnaire that you can use to rate your own performance. In addition, you can collect useful feedback from other sources by giving them the same questionnaire to complete about you.

Self-review

Once you have made your ratings on each of the behavioural items in the questionnaire, it is a simple matter to review how you have scored yourself. You will undoubtedly be interested in 'highs' and 'lows' and any pattern that emerges. The purpose is obviously to identify where you are particularly effective, and think about why this would be and also to take note of areas where you might improve. Checking both of these out with other parties is extremely important even if you feel unable to complete the full 360° (or 180°) review. We trust this exercise will help you in constructing a meaningful development plan for you to enhance your coaching delivery.

180/360° review

Whilst the self-review can be conducted exactly as outlined above, in carrying out the 360° (or 180°) review there are some points you may wish to consider:

1. Who will you give the questionnaire to and why? Select those who know your coaching style well; current or previous coaching partners are ideal. Do not simply pick people with whom you get on well.
2. Think about how you will ask others to complete this for you. Some individuals may appreciate your openness to feedback and give it accordingly. Others may be suspicious of your motives and be reluctant to complete it as honestly as they might like.
3. Have the report processed independantly by ECC[1] as assurance to your chosen raters that their input will be treated anonymously and confidentially, unless you have made a different arrangement with them about this.
4. Consider what you will do with the report you receive back. Will you share it with those who completed the questionnaires? Will you share it with your boss, if applicable?
5. Think about how you will handle the feedback you receive; what support mechanisms do you have in place?

THE CAPABLE COACH: A COMPILOR©® FEEDBACK INSTRUMENT

The following competency model applies to both the 180° and 360° versions of the 'Capable Coach' *COMPILOR* questionnaire. Respondents are invited to consider the behaviour of the coach in question and rate him or her against each item below. On each questionnaire,[1] under each competency heading, there is room to write verbatim comments illustrating the perceptions of the respondent. These comments are collated and presented in the final feedback report alongside the numerical ratings.

Self-management	**Rating**
Does the coach:	
1. Demonstrate high levels of personal integrity: act in a way consistent with espoused values?	☐
2. Sustain commitment to direct report's/others' development in the face of setbacks, uncertainty and stress?	☐

3. Evidence a high level of self-awareness; is the coach open, easily disclosing own personal strengths and weaknesses? ☐

4. Pursue personal development goals; seek regular feedback from clients and colleagues and act upon it? ☐

5. Maintain the level and frequency of contact necessary to satisfy the needs of the coaching partner and commissioning client? ☐

Communication

Does the coach:

1. Listen actively; check own understanding and probe for meaning? ☐
2. Deliver clear and constructive feedback? ☐
3. Provide support, encouragement and motivation for implementation of development actions and practice? ☐
4. Balance the ratio between talking and listening in coaching meetings? ☐
5. Communicate confidently at all levels within the organisation? ☐
6. Present the 'case for coaching' persuasively and with conviction? ☐

Coaching craft

Does the coach:

1. Identify appropriate development goals for direct reports and plan actions to achieve them? ☐
2. Determine relevant metrics and milestones to measure and review coaching progress against agreed goals? ☐
3. Consistently provide support and encouragement for achievement of agreed coaching goals? ☐
4. Establish a clear coaching agenda with the coaching partner before commencing assignment? ☐
5. Identify measurable success criteria for each coaching assignment? ☐
6. Develop practical development action steps to be implemented by coaching partner? ☐

7. Explore alternative options for development action to be undertaken by coaching partner? ☐

8. Adopt different role styles to maximise effectiveness in the situation, with the individual or at the particular stage in the coaching process? ☐

9. Motivate individuals to pursue their development and to take on challenges to realise their potential? ☐

Interpersonal skills

Does the coach: ☐

1. Recognise and act in ways that place the coaching partner's development first? ☐

2. Build rapport quickly with others; show interest in people and demonstrate empathy with them? ☐

3. Create and sustain relationships of trust with others? ☐

4. Manage conflict effectively; initiate/facilitate the successful resolution of disagreements? ☐

5. Create and propose options for coaching practice? ☐

6. Treat all individuals with respect? ☐

7. Detect changes of mood and motivation in others and respond appropriately? ☐

Breadth of experience

Does the coach demonstrate:

1. Experience of a wide range of corporate development projects and coaching assignments across a broad industrial and cultural base? ☐

2. An in-depth appreciation of executive roles, associated role demands and pressures as well as corporate politics? ☐

3. A wide-ranging network of development providers that can be called in to enhance coaching programme if required? ☐

Technical skills

Does the coach demonstrate:

1. Practical experience and capable application of an appropriate range of assessment tools? ☐

2. A sound knowledge of alternative and complementary models of development and learning? ☐

3. An extensive array of development action and development opportunities to offer coaching partners? ☐

Rating scale:

1 = *Not developed.* Undeveloped in most aspects of this behaviour/skill

2 = *Underdeveloped.* Lacks consistency in this area. A potential weakness if critical for coaching success

3. = *Competent.* Adequate in all key areas. Considerable room for improvement

4. = *Very effective*, but still some room for improvement

5. = *Excellent.* An obvious strength. A model for others to follow

Note

1 Contact Dr T. Chapman, ECCLtd@globalnet.co.uk for information about processing and the 180/360° questionnaire packs

References

Adams, J., Hayes, J. and Hopson, B., *Understanding and Managing Personal Change* (Martin Robinson, London, 1976).

Anderson, N.R. and Harriot, P. (eds) *International Handbook of Selection and Assessment: 1997 Update* (Wiley, London, 1997).

Argyris, C., 'Teaching Smart People How to Learn', *Harvard Business Review*, May–June (1991): 5–14.

ASE, *AH Series* (NFER-Nelson, Windsor, 1984).

ASE, *The 16 Personality Factor Questionnaire*, 5th edn (NFER-Nelson, Windsor, 1994).

Bellow, S., *Humboldt's Gift* (Penguin, Harmondsworth, 1976).

Bennis, W. and Thomas, R., *Geeks and Geezers: How Era, Values and Defining Moments Shape Leaders* (Harvard Business School Press, 2002).

Berglas, S., (2002) 'The Very Real Danger of Executive Coaching', *Harvard Business Review*, June: 3–8.

Blinkhorn, S.F., *Graduate and Management Assessment* (NFER-Nelson, Windsor, 1985).

Boyatzis, R.E., *The Competent Manager* (Wiley, New York, 1982).

Boyatzis, R.E. and Kolb, D., 'Feedback and Self-directed Behaviour Change', Working paper, Sloan School of Management, Massachusetts Institute of Technology, 1969.

Bradley, C., 'Turning Anecdotes into Data: The Critical Incidents Technique', *Family Practice*, 9(1992): 98–103.

Bridges, W., *Transitions: Making Sense of Life's Changes* (Addison-Wesley, Reading, MA, 1985).

Briggs K.C., and Myers I.B., *MBTI Step 2,* (Oxford Psychologists Press Ltd, Consulting Psychologists Press Inc, Oxford, 1992).

Briggs, K.C. and Myers, I.B., *Myers–Briggs Type Indicator* (Oxford Psychologists Press Ltd © Consulting Psychologists Press, 1998).

Bruce, M., 'Managing People First – Bringing the Service Concept to British Airways', *Journal of Industrial and Commercial Training*, March/April (1987): 21–6.

Business Week, 'The Business Week Global 1000', *Business Week*, 15 July (2002): 39–40.

Chapman, A.M.P., The Work Motivation of the Industrial Supervisor, unpublished PhD Thesis, Cranfield School of Management, CIT, Bedford, England,1982.

Clark N., *Team Building* (McGraw-Hill, London, 1994).

Consalvo C.M., *Outdoor Games for Trainers* (Gower, Aldershot, 1995).

Cook, M.J., *Effective Coaching* (McGraw-Hill, New York, 1999).

Cooper, G. and Hingley P., *The Change Makers* (Harper & Row, London, 1985).

Costa, P.T. and McRae, P.R., *The Revised NEO Personality Inventory – Professional Development Report*, (Psychological Assessment Resources, Odessa, FL, 1992).

Deming, W.E., *Out of the Crisis* (Massachusetts Institute of Technology, Cambridge University Press, 1988).

Dotlich, D.L. and Noel, J.L., *Action Learning: How the World's Top Companies are Re-creating their Leaders and Themselves* (Jossey-Bass, New York, 1998).

Dougherty, T.W., Turban, D.B. and Callender, J.C., 'Concerning First Impressions in the Employment Interview: A Field Study of Interviewer Behavior', *Journal of Applied Psychology*, 79(1994): 659–65.

Elliot, J., *Requisite Organisation: A Total System for Effective Managerial Organisation and Managerial Leadership for 21st Century* (Cason Hall, 1996).

Elliot, J. and Clement, S.D., *Executive Leadership: A Practical Guide to Managing Complexity* (Blackwell, London, 1994).

Fitzgerald, C. and Berger, J.G., *Executive Coaching*, (Davies-Black, London, 2002).

Flanagan, J., 'The Critical Incident Technique', *Psychological Bulletin*, 51(1954): 327–58.

Gallwey, T., *The Inner Game of Tennis* (Random House, New York, 1974) (also *The Inner Game of Golf*).

Gardner, H., *Frames of Mind: Theories of Multiple Intelligences* (Basic Books, New York, 1983).

Gattiker, U.E. and Larwood, L., 'Predictors of Career Achievement in Corporate Hierarchy', *Human Relations*, **43**(3) (1990): 703–26.

Gibran, K., *The Prophet* (William Heinemann, London [1926] 1987).

Goffee, R. and Jones, G., (2000) 'Why Should Anyone Be Led By You?', *Harvard Business Review*, Sept–Oct.

Goleman, D., *Emotional Intelligence* (Bloomsbury, London, 1996).

Greenleaf, R.K., *The Power of Servant Leadership* (Berret-Koehler, San Francisco, 1998).

Gyatso, T. (His Holiness the Dalai Lama) *Ancient Wisdom, Modern World* (Little, Brown, London, 1999).

Hersey, P. and Blanchard, K.H., *Management of Organisational Behaviour: Utilising Human Resources*, 5th edn (Prentice-Hall, Englewood Cliffs, NJ, 1998).

Hofstede, G., *Culture's Consequences: International Differences in Work-related Values* (Sage, Newbury Park, CA, 1980).

Hofstede, G., 'Cultural Differences in Teaching and Learning'. *International Journal of Intercultural Relations*, 10(1986): 301–20.

Hofstede, G., *Cultures and Organizations: Software of the Mind* (McGraw-Hill, London, 1991).

Hofstede, G. and Bond, M.H., 'Confucius and Economic Growth: New Trends in Culture's Consequences', *Organizational Dynamics*, **16**(4) (1988): 4–21.

Hudson, F.M., *The Handbook of Coaching* (Jossey-Bass, New York, 1999).

Hunter, D., Bailey, A. and Taylor B., *The Facilitation of Groups* (Gower, Aldershot, 1996).

Kolb, D.A., Rubin, I.M. and McIntyre, J.M., *Organisational Psychology: An Experiential Approach* (Prentice-Hall, Englewood Cliffs, NJ, 1971).

Kotter, J.P., 'Leading Change: Why Transformation Efforts Fail', *Harvard Business Review*, March/April (1995): 59–67.

Kouzes, J. and Posner, B., *Credibility: How Leaders Gain and Lose it, Why People Demand it* (Jossey-Bass, New York, 1995).

Laing, R.D., *The Politics of Experience*, 3rd edn (Penguin, London, 1990).

McCall, M.W. Jr, *High Flyers: Developing the Next Generation of Leaders* (HBS Press, Boston, MA, 1998).

McClelland, D.C., "Testing for Competence Rather than for 'Intelligence'", *American Psychologist*, **28**(1973): 1–40.

McGill, L., *Action Learning* (Kogan Page, London, 1996).

Melamed, T., 'Barriers to Women's Career Success: Human Capital, Career Choices, Structural Determinants or Simply Sex Discrimination', *Applied Psychology: An International Review*, **44**(4) (1995): 295–314.

Melamed, T., 'Career Success: The Moderating Effect of Gender', *Journal of Vocational Behaviour*, 47(1995): 35–60.

Moerk, H., quoted in 'Learning How to Make the Best of Workplace Education', *Financial Times*, p. 9, 19 August 2002.

Morrison, A.M., White, R.P. and Van Velsor, E., *Breaking the Glass Ceiling*, (Addison-Wesley, Reading, MA, 1987).

Moxon, P., *Building a Better Team* (Gower, Aldershot, 1993).

Peters, T.J. and Austin, N.K., *A Passion for Excellence* (Warner Books, New York, 1986).

Peters, T.J. and Waterman R.J. Jr, *In Search of Excellence* (Harper & Row, New York, 1982).

Peterson, D.B and Hicks, M.D. *Leader as Coach* (Personnel Decisions International Corporation, Minneapolis, 1996).

Raven, J.C., *Ravens Advanced Progressive Matrices,* Occupational Edition, (Oxford Psychologists Press Ltd, Oxford, 1995).

Rohnke K., *Silver Bullets* (Project Adventure Inc., 1988).

Sackett P.R., 'Integrity Testing for Personnel Selection: An Update', *Personnel Psychology*, 37(1984): 221–45.

Sacks, J., *Celebrating Life* (HarperCollins, London, 2000).

Schein, E.H., 'Three Cultures of Management: The Key to Organisational Learning', *Harvard Business Review*, **38**(1) (1996).

SHL (Saville & Holdsworth Ltd), *Advanced Managerial Tests*, The Pavillion, Atwell Place, Thames Ditton, Surrey, 1999.

Slim, Field Marshall, *Defeat into Victory* (Cassell, London, 1956).

Smith, M. and Robertson, I., *The Theory and Practice of Systematic Personnel Selection* (Macmillan – now Palgrave Macmillan, Basingstoke, 1993).

Stephenson, P., *Executive Coaching – Lead Develop Retain Motivated Talented People* (Pearson Education, Australia, 2000).

Stroh, L.K., Brett, J.M. and Reilly, A.H., 'All the Right Staff: A Comparison of Female and Male Managers' Career Progression', *Journal of Applied Psychology*, **77**(3) (1992): 251–60.

Sun Tzu, *The Art of War* (trans. Luo Zhiye) (Delacourt Press, Hong Kong, 1994)

Thach, L. and Heinselman, T., 'Executive Coaching Defined', *Training and Development Journal*, March (1999).

Tichy, N.M. and Charan, R., 'The CEO as Coach: An Interview with Lawrence A Bossidy', *Harvard Business Review*, Mar/Apr (1995).

Trompenaars, A., Hampden-Turner, C. and Trompenaars, F., *Riding The Waves of Culture: Understanding Diversity in Global Business* (McGraw-Hill, New York, 1998).

Tuckman, B.W., 'Development Sequence in Small Groups', *Psychological Bulletin*, **63**(1965): 284–499.

Tuson, M., *Outdoor Training for Employee Effectiveness* (Institute of Personnel Management, Harrogate, 1994)

Watson, G. and Glaser, G., *Watson–Glaser Critical Thinking Appraisal* (The Psychological Corporation, Sidcup, Kent, UK, 1990).

West, L. and Milan, M., *The Reflecting Glass* (Palgrave – now Palgrave Macmillan, Basingstoke, 2001).

Whitmore, J., *Coaching for Performance* (Nicholas Brealey, London, 1992).

Witherspoon, R. and White, R.P., *Four Essential Ways that Coaching Can Help Executives* (Center for Creative Leadership, Greensboro, NC, 2001).

Woodcock, M., *Team Development Manual* (Gower, Aldershot, 1994).

INDEX